POSTCARD HISTORY SERIES

Jefferson County

On the Front Cover: In 1928, the west wing and curved stairway were added to the original Jefferson County Courthouse, a building completed in 1869. (Jefferson County History Center.)

On the Back Cover: Section 4 of a four-part set of postcards was taken about 1900 and depicts Brookville, the county seat. (Jefferson County History Center.)

Postcard History Series

Jefferson County

Carole A. Briggs, Eugene E. Deible III,
Shirley J. Sharp, and Fay M. Trentini

ARCADIA
PUBLISHING

ISBN 978-1-4671-2720-2

Published by Arcadia Publishing
Charleston, South Carolina

Printed in the United States of America

Library of Congress Control Number: 2017942409

For all general information contact Arcadia Publishing at:
Telephone 843-853-2070
Fax 843-853-0044
E-mail sales@arcadiapublishing.com
For customer service and orders:
Toll-Free 1-888-313-2665

Visit us on the Internet at www.arcadiapublishing.com

To those who have gone before us and for those who are yet to come

Contents

ACKNOWLEDGMENTS

Hidden in attics and closets, boxes and drawers, and in the minds of our people, our collective history was first recorded when historians like Kate M. Scott, William J. McKnight, and the compilers of *Caldwell's Atlas* put pen to paper. Today, many books describe the communities of Jefferson County, and four historical societies document, collect, and show our past to both county residents and visitors. We acknowledge and thank those folks who have preceded us and the many who support our organizations with their talent, time, and treasure. We especially acknowledge Martha Ann Armstrong, Kenneth Burkett, S. Thomas Curry, the DuBois Area Historical Society, Tom Glover, Patricia Hamblin, Charles Haser, Jane Hetrick, Rob Keith, Linda Morelli, Paula Pompeii, James Sterrett, David L. Taylor, Sylvia Verne, and Christy Weaver for their help with this publication.

Postcards are from the collections of the historical societies in Brockway (Brockway Area Historical Society, abbreviated BAHS), Brookville (Jefferson County History Center, abbreviated JCHC), Punxsutawney (Punxsutawney Area Historical and Genealogical Society, abbreviated PAHGS), and Reynoldsville (Reynoldsville Historical Society, abbreviated RHS).

INTRODUCTION

Divided back? Undivided? One-cent stamp or two? Made in Germany? Date stamp? For most history organizations, postcards are important for documenting our communities. They provide us with pictures of our past and with comments from people now gone. They help us date places and show us what folks deemed important about the places in which they lived.

Postcards were a predominate way to communicate in the 20th century, and today flea markets and antique shops offer old ones for sale. Heirs sorting estates find boxes of postcards in attics and bureau drawers. Fortunately, many of them end up in local historical societies.

Although not incorporated until 1970, the Brockway Area Historical Society (BAHS) began in 1953 when a small group of interested people met in the *Brockway Record* newspaper office to discuss how best to gather and preserve information and artifacts from the area's past. As the society accumulated more and more material, it became apparent that it needed a permanent place for storing and exhibiting these items. Vernon F. Taylor, who grew up in Brockway and became a very successful businessman, offered to provide property on which to locate a museum and additionally to provide the initial funding needed for the construction of such a building. The society broke ground in April 1972, dedicated the building that September, and opened the Taylor Memorial Museum to the public in the spring of 1973.

The Brockway Glass Annex was added in 1991 to house and display company archival material and the varieties of glass produced in the area. In 2004, the society added a second story to provide both a work area and storage. The *Saga*, a semiannual publication, was first issued in the spring of 1994 and is sent to all society members. There are now over 250 members, including 112 life members.

One of the most interesting postcards from the Brockway Area Historical Society's collection is from 1908—a postcard that pictures both the building and the workers at the Brockway Machine Bottle Company. From this modest start, it would become a precursor of the Brockway Glass Company, one of the world's largest glass container manufacturers.

The Jefferson County Historical Society began in 1967. The very first postcard accessioned is a colored print of Brookville's Main Street with many automobiles and a pesky streetlight at the courthouse intersection. The white border tells us it was made between 1915 and 1930. The second postcard is a humorous one sent from Gladys in South Bend, Indiana, to John Shively, who spent his summers in Brookville. Shively's father was a US senator from Indiana who married a Brookville woman. The postcard was sent 1909; John was 13, and Gladys missed him. The third is a photograph of Brookville-born New York City vaudeville manager Sam Scribner and his friends on a beach, wearing swimsuits that date the postcard to some time in the 1930s.

Today, the Jefferson County Historical Society owns three buildings—the Jefferson County History Center (JCHC), where research facilities, exhibits, offices, and a gift shop are available; Brady Craig House, where photographs, objects, and documents are processed; and the Margaret Johnson Archives, where materials are stored. The society has documented nearly 20,000 books, documents, objects, and photographs, including more than 550 postcards.

In the fall of 1975, the seeds of a historical society were planted in Punxsutawney when a group prepared an application for that town to become a US Bicentennial Community in 1976. A society formally organized the following year. In 1982, the Bennis House, 401 West Mahoning Street, was donated and became headquarters for the Punxsutawney Area Historical and Genealogical Society (PAHGS), an all-volunteer organization.

The PAHGS operates five facilities in the Punxsutawney area—Bennis House, the Snyder Hill School House, the Lattimer House, the Punxsutawney Area Coal Memorial, and an archive building—and marked its 40th anniversary of preserving Punxsutawney-area history in 2017. Its postcard collection provides a visual history of the commercial, industrial, and cultural development of the Punxsutawney area. One records the state constabulary arriving. Two others highlight Punxsutawney's famous groundhog.

Jefferson County's youngest historical society began in 1998, when a group met with Gene Deible III. Over time, he had gathered a large assortment of Reynoldsville photographs, documents, and objects, including bound copies of the *Star*, an uninterrupted edition from 1892 to 1946. That virtue of completeness attracted the attention of the National Endowment for the Humanities and its venture to document Pennsylvania's newspapers through the Pennsylvania Newspaper Project. One requirement, and a prerequisite for converting the *Star* to microfilm, was an application from an organized historical society, hence the meeting in 1998. The Reynoldsville Historical Society (RHS) was granted 501(c)(3) status, making the organization official on March 21, 2005.

After a decadelong but unsuccessful attempt to secure the Buffalo, Rochester & Pittsburgh Railroad ticket office, the RHS board of directors gave unanimous approval in 2013 to purchase the former Delaney Brothers Pennzoil station on Reynoldsville's Main Street. That December, papers were signed, and the Reynoldsville Historical Society at last had a permanent home. Restoration began immediately, creating a space that is now the Archive Room. Improvements continue.

Though young, the society has a collection of nearly 300 postcards that show 20th-century life in that community. One image in particular, of a small boy dressed in coal-mining attire, changed Deible's perception of the importance of postcards. He said, "While many were designed only to be sold, there was also the practice of local photographers printing the postcard format onto the backs of family portraits or unique subjects. These personal images are the jewels that give us a true glimpse of everyday life."

Prior to 1901, the federal government permitted private postcards with advertising or an image on one side and the address on the other, along with an authorization line. The government dropped the authorization line in 1901, but cards still had no line on the back and until 1907 did not permit writing on the address side. The Divided-Back or Golden Age era of postcards lasted from 1907 to 1915. White borders signified the Early Modern era from 1915 to 1930. The Linen Card era began in 1930, and the Modern Photochrome era began in 1939.

The postcards in this volume represent all five eras of postcard production, and they have been important sources of documentation for all of our organizations. We are pleased to share some of them with you.

One

Welcome to Jefferson County

Archeological evidence of Native American settlements exists throughout the county and confirms that they hunted and traveled here. However, very few remained after the "last purchase" in 1784, when settlers of European backgrounds began to arrive.

Land speculators purchased warrants in this large expanse of land named Northumberland County, engaged surveyors to identify the best lands near the confluence of streams, and patented the property. Northumberland was divided first into Allegheny and Lycoming Counties, and in 1804, Lycoming gave birth to Clearfield, Jefferson, McKean, Potter, and Tioga Counties. Jefferson County included land that later became Elk and Forest Counties.

By virtue of its location at the confluence of the North Fork and Sandy Lick and its centrality in the more than 1,000 square miles that comprised the original county, commissioners named Brookville the county seat in 1830.

Through dense forests, the early settlers, predominantly Scots Irish, followed Native American paths barely wide enough for a horse to pass. The Waterford and Susquehanna Turnpike, begun in 1812, made travel easier.

Streams became public highways, people of German backgrounds arrived to farm, and by 1860, the population had grown to 18,270 people—people who timbered, farmed, and built churches, schools, shops, and small businesses.

Soldiers returned from the Civil War with new ideas. The exploitation of mineral and energy resources and multiple railroad lines in the 1870s attracted more people. Entrepreneurs built expansive Victorian homes during these prosperous times.

Coal mining replaced the dwindling timber industry, and Eastern and Southern Europeans arrived to mine and live in company towns. Belgians worked in the new glass industry. The population peaked in 1910, then diminished as people moved away during two world wars and two depressions.

The population aged, and the last quarter of the 20th century saw an influx of medical personnel from countries around the world and the development of Pennsylvania's tourism industry.

Though low, today's population of 44,073 (in 2016) is primarily white yet more diverse than at any time in its history—a population that enjoys and appreciates what small towns and rural communities offer.

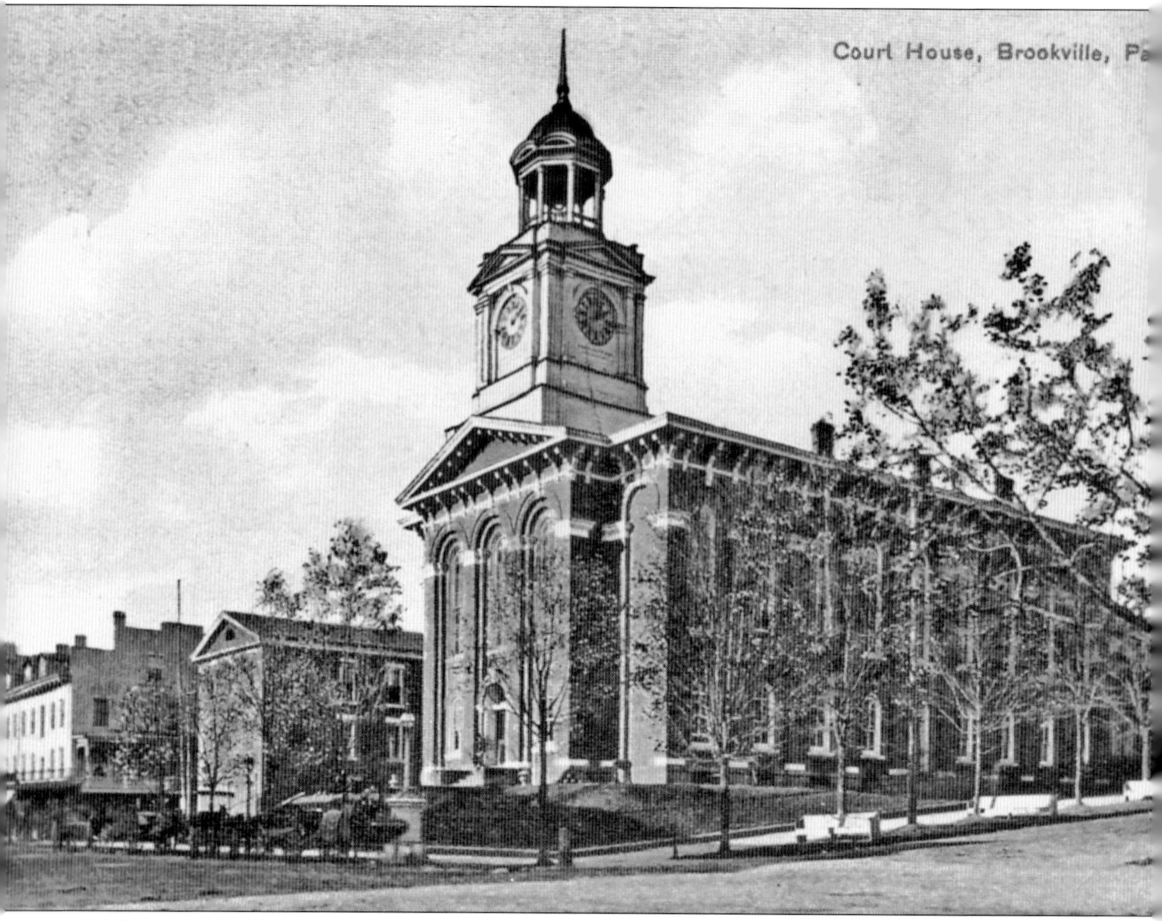

When Brookville became the county seat in 1830, builders first erected a jail and then a courthouse on the corner of Main and Pickering Streets. They completed a second jail (the smaller building to the left of the courthouse) in 1856. Historian Kate M. Scott describes the second courthouse (shown), dedicated in 1869, as "a very handsome one. The second story courtroom with commodious jury-rooms in the rear is a large, handsome room, well-lighted through beautiful stained-glass windows." The first floor contained offices for the prothonotary, treasurer, sheriff, commissioners, and the county superintendent of common schools. The Village Improvement Society raised funds and dedicated a fountain in 1903. Historian William J. McKnight christened it "Harriet-Amelia" in honor of the two women who led the endeavor. It was lit, and an interior gas jet prevented it from freezing, so man and beast could drink any time day or night throughout the year. On a cold night in 1907, a fellow found the water frozen, opened the door, saw the gas jet had gone out, lit a match, and Harriet-Amelia met its demise. (JCHC.)

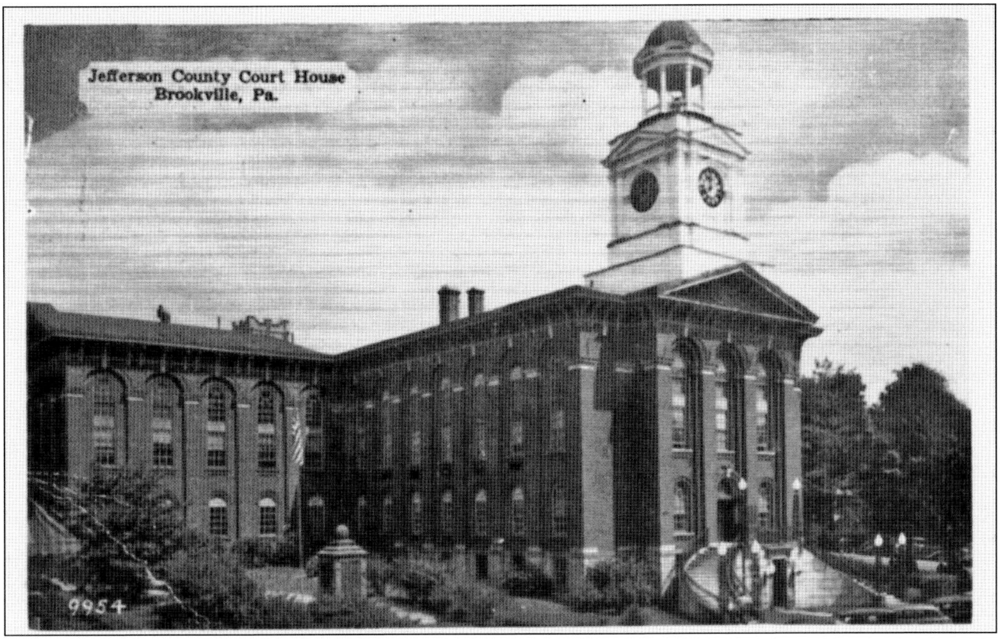

The second courthouse cost $78,742 ($1.41 million in 2017). By the mid-1920s, county business had increased substantially, so county offices moved to the vacant Brookville Auditorium Building, or "White Elephant," and commissioners oversaw the addition of the west wing and the replacement of the original straight entrance stairway (above). This renovation cost $270,509 ($3 million today). County business continued to increase, and for several years, some county business was conducted from the old county home. This was deemed illegal because the building was in Pinecreek Township and not in the county seat, so the commissioners acquired additional space in 1995 at Jefferson Place, located half a block east of the courthouse. A $5 million renovation project completed in 2009 earned a Pennsylvania Initiative Award from the Pennsylvania Historical and Museum Commission. Today, some deem it the most beautiful courthouse (below) in the commonwealth. (Both, JCHC.)

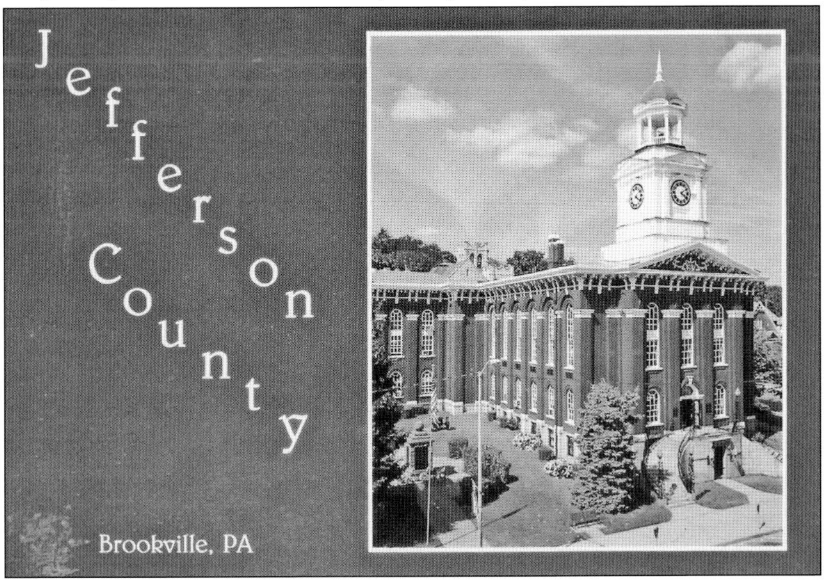

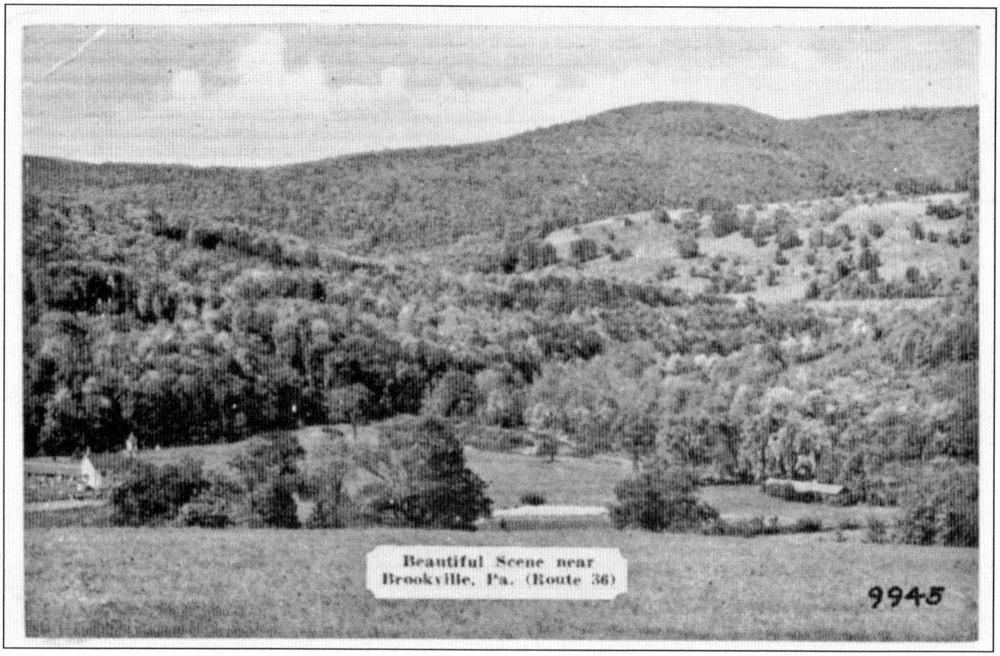

The Allegheny Plateau, characterized by rolling hills and steep valleys, covers two-thirds of Pennsylvania, including Jefferson County (above). Settlers came to timber and farm. According to historian Scott, they found a great variety of trees: white and yellow pine; hemlock; white, red, and black oak; chestnut; sugar maple; beech; hickory; elm; cherry; ash; and birch. Rivers include the Clarion River in the north; the North Fork and Sandy Lick Creeks, which join in Brookville to form Red Bank Creek; and Mahoning Creek in the south. All flow west into the Allegheny River system. Below the surface lie oil, natural gas, clay, limestone, and the largest field of bituminous coal in the entire country—natural resources that gave rise to 19th-century industries and towns like Anita (below), built in 1889 by the Berwind-White Coal Company. (Above, JCHC; below, PAHGS.)

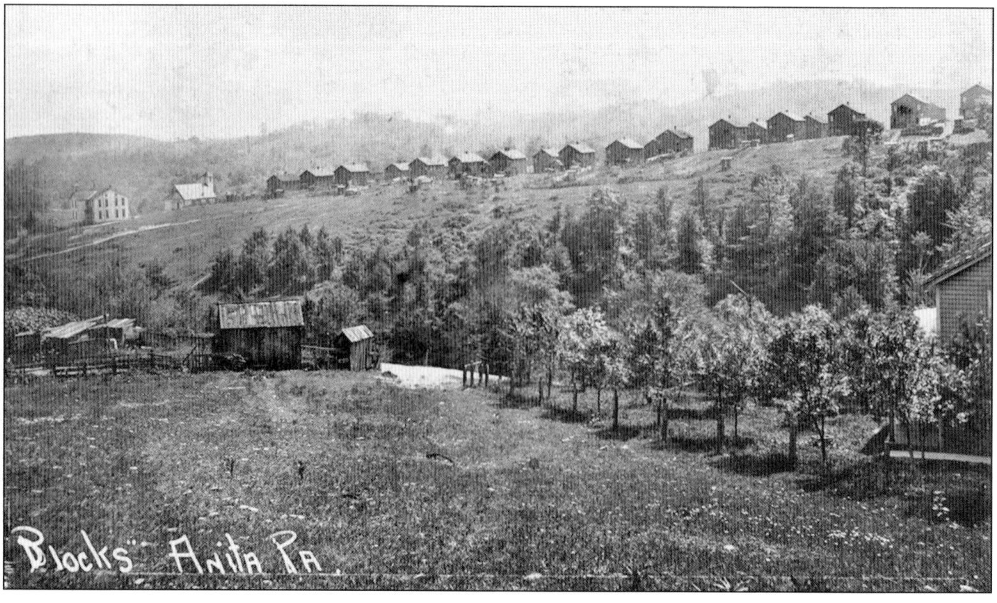

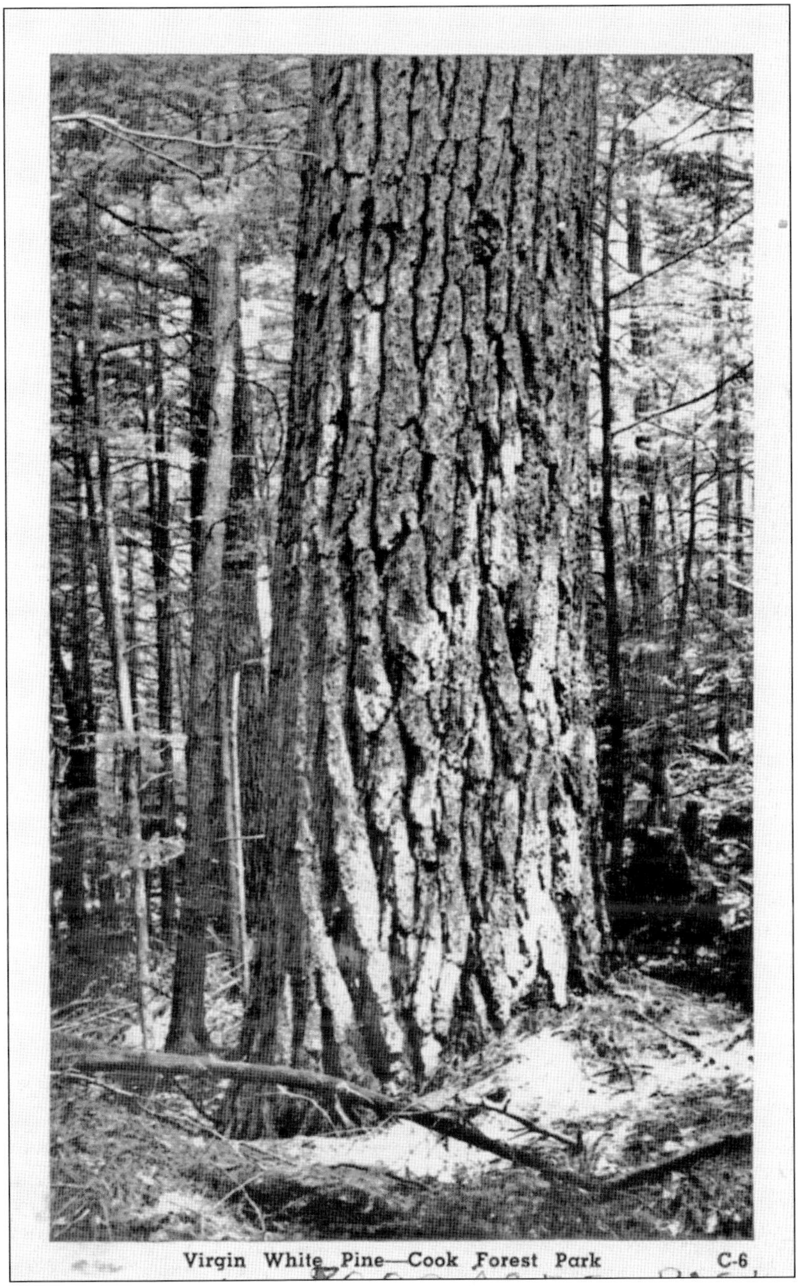

John Cook settled in the Clarion River area about 1826. For a century, he and his heirs timbered but were careful to preserve a large stand of virgin pine. The Cook Forest Association formed in the 1920s to save this area, so typical of the forests the first settlers had found—hemlock that reached great heights, mountain laurel, and rhododendron. The association, endorsed by national natural resource groups and Gov. Gifford Pinchot, raised $200,000 to help the commonwealth purchase 6,055 acres from A. Cook Sons Company in 1927 for $640,000; it became the first Pennsylvania state park acquired to preserve a natural landmark. An impressive area known as the "cathedral forest" includes massive white pines that reach heights of 200 feet. Although the forest is located in Forest County, Brookville is known as the "Gateway to Cook Forest." (JCHC.)

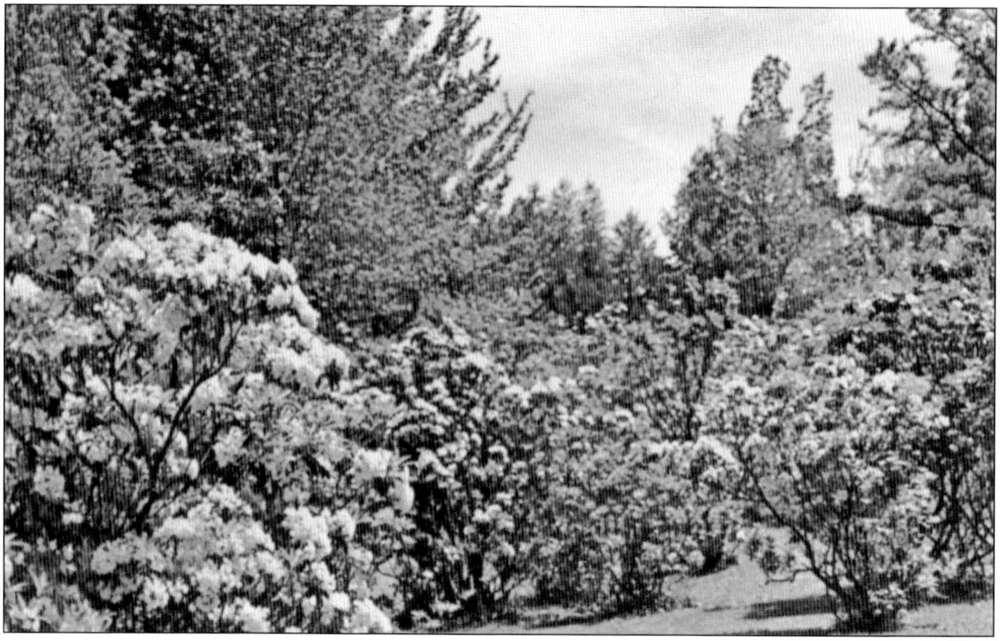

The hardy pioneers found the county wooded and lush, with a profusion of flowers and shrubs, especially the mountain laurels and rhododendrons that flourish from southern Maine to northern Florida. In 1888, historian Scott wrote, "In the fields are found magnificent lilies, while the pride of the woods is the brilliant laurel, and the lovely rhododendron, which in season are nowhere found in greater profusion or more rich in coloring." Elk, deer, black bear, wolf, fox, beaver, panther, wildcat, otter, mink, martin, lynx, muskrat, raccoon, skunk, and small game roamed the woods. Streams held an abundance of speckled trout and pike, and birds, including eagles and wild passenger pigeons, flew among the trees. Today, the mountain laurel is celebrated each June and hunters tramp in the woods for turkey, deer, bear, and small game. (Both, JCHC.)

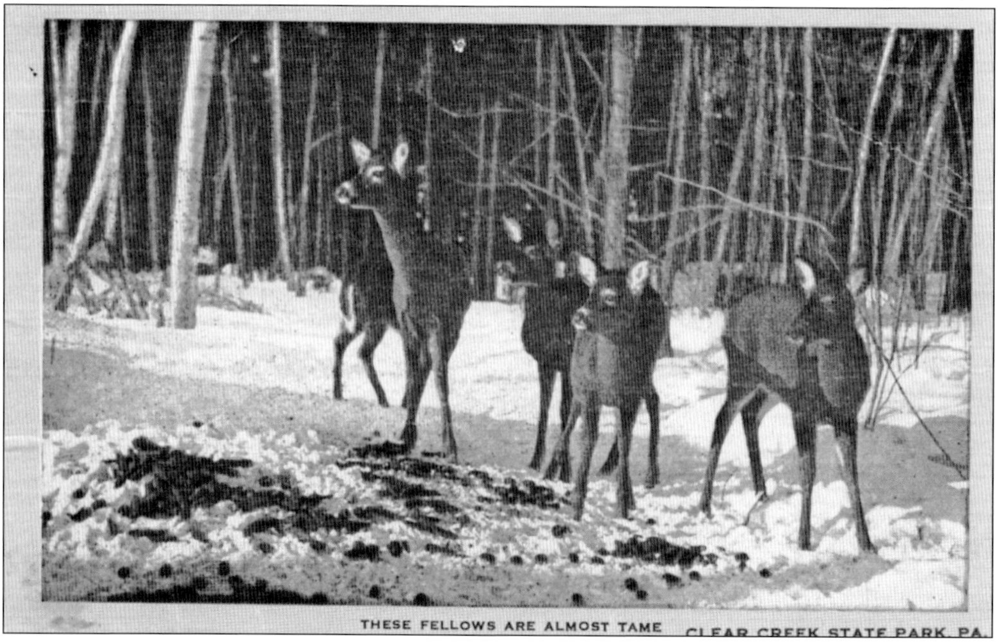

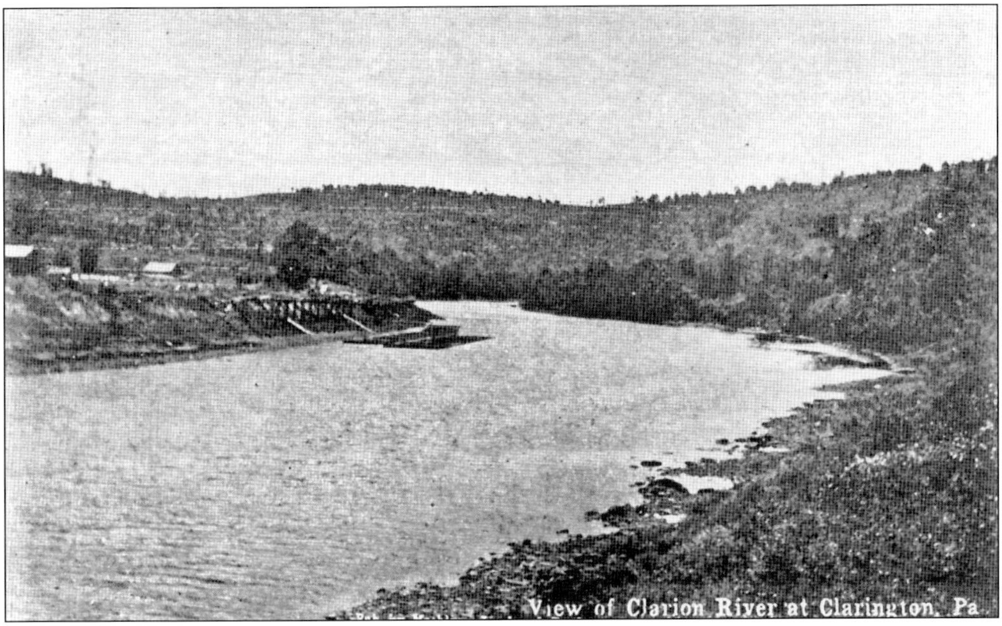

With headwaters in Johnsonburg, the Clarion River separates Jefferson from Forest County in the north and flows 110 miles to the Allegheny River. Archaeologists have documented evidence of Delaware, Seneca, and Iroquois Indians in the area. The river was once the site of logging, major sawmills, raft-building, leather tanning, and wood-chemical plants. Kayakers have replaced the timber rafts of the past (above), and camps and homes line the Clarion's banks. Cook Forest and Clear Creek State Parks border the river, and hikers and drivers alike enjoy the scenic views found between Clarington (above) and Cooksburg (below). The Clarion is part of the National Wild and Scenic River Program and was the Pennsylvania Department of Conservation and Natural Resources pick for River of the Year in 1996. (Both, JCHC.)

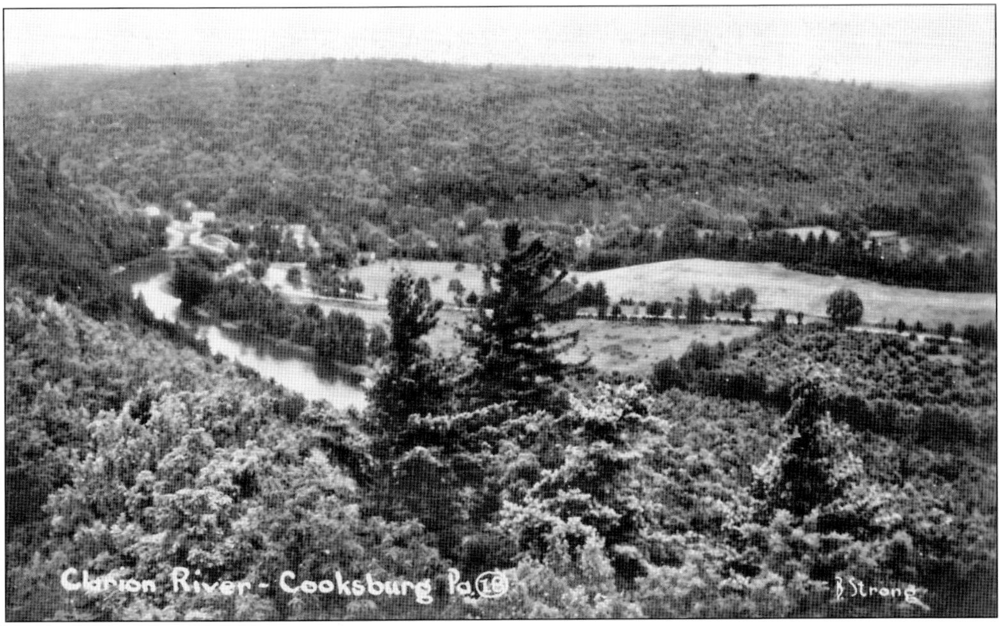

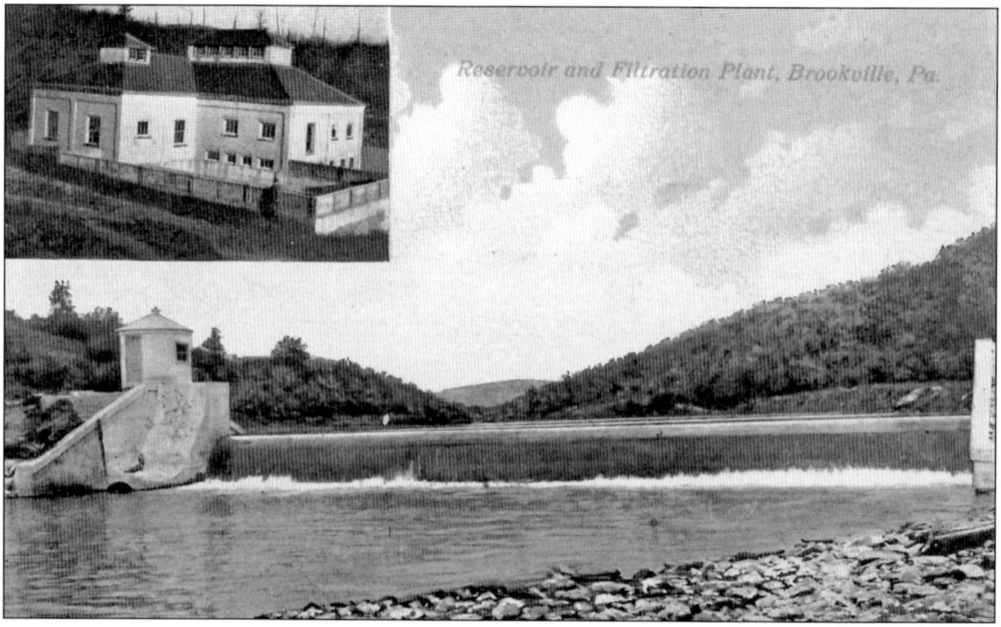

North Fork Creek flows through the county's northeast corner, and prior to the railroad's completion in 1874, it provided river transportation for timber. The creek also supplies water to Brookville. A private company operated the Brookville Water Works between 1883 and 1911. A second opened in 1911, providing high-quality water for more than a century. Brookville's municipal authority opened a modern facility north of the previous plant in 2012 at a cost of more than $10 million. When the Sandy Lick enters the county, it flows through Reynoldsville. Builders constructed the first of five wooden bridges in 1822; the last was destroyed by the 1889 flood. Two iron bridges (below) followed, and on October 30, 1913, the present concrete arch bridge opened. Anyone who crosses this overpass has an appreciative understanding of its nickname, "The Tickle-Belly Bridge." (Above, JCHC; below, RHS.)

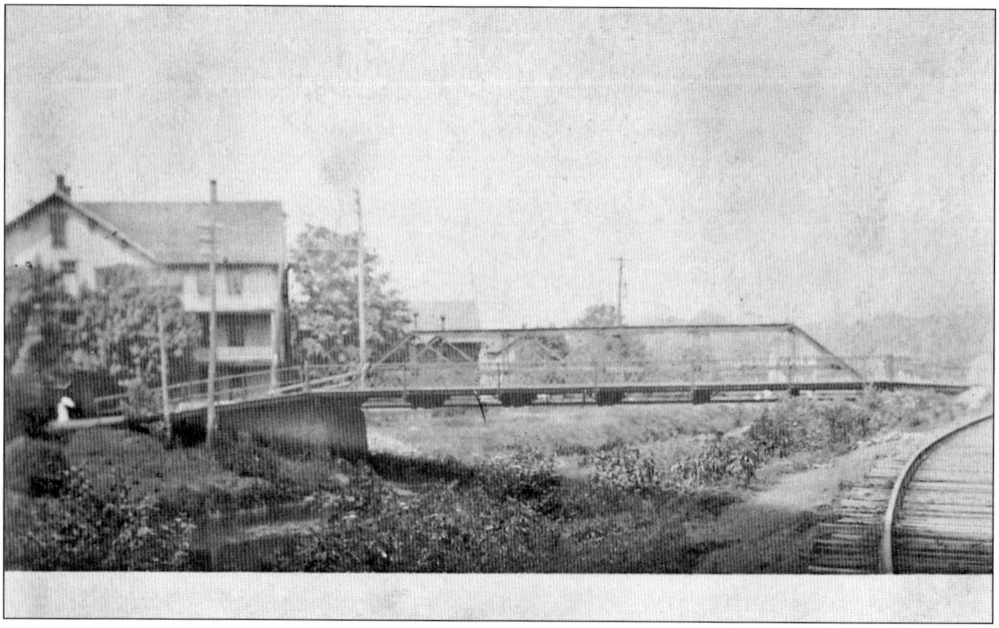

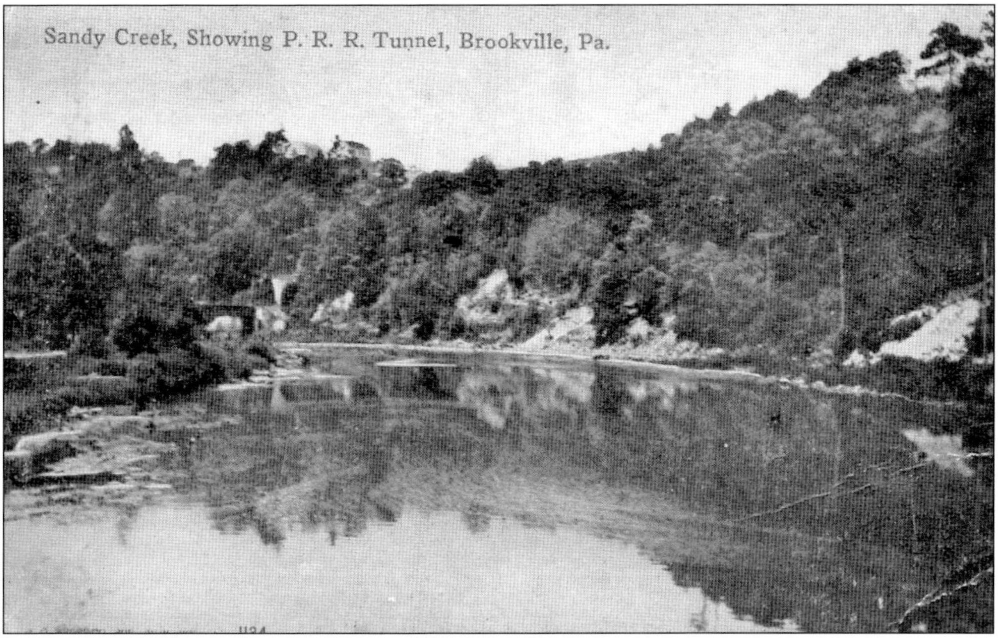

Sandy Lick Creek (above) has its origins in Clearfield County and winds its way west through rolling hills and steep valleys, terrain that requires bridges and tunnels. A tunnel and double truss iron bridge made rail traffic through the hill possible around the turn of the century. The Sandy Lick merges with the North Fork in Brookville to form Red Bank Creek, which flows west, emptying into the Allegheny River at Red Bank. This made possible the rafting of timber from the woods to markets in Pittsburgh. Historian McKnight wrote, "The pioneer county bridge was . . . a curious pile of wood and stones." Eventually, it was covered, but it was weakened by a flood in 1905. The town fathers replaced it with a succession of metal bridges (below) before building the present concrete structure in 1986. (Both, JCHC.)

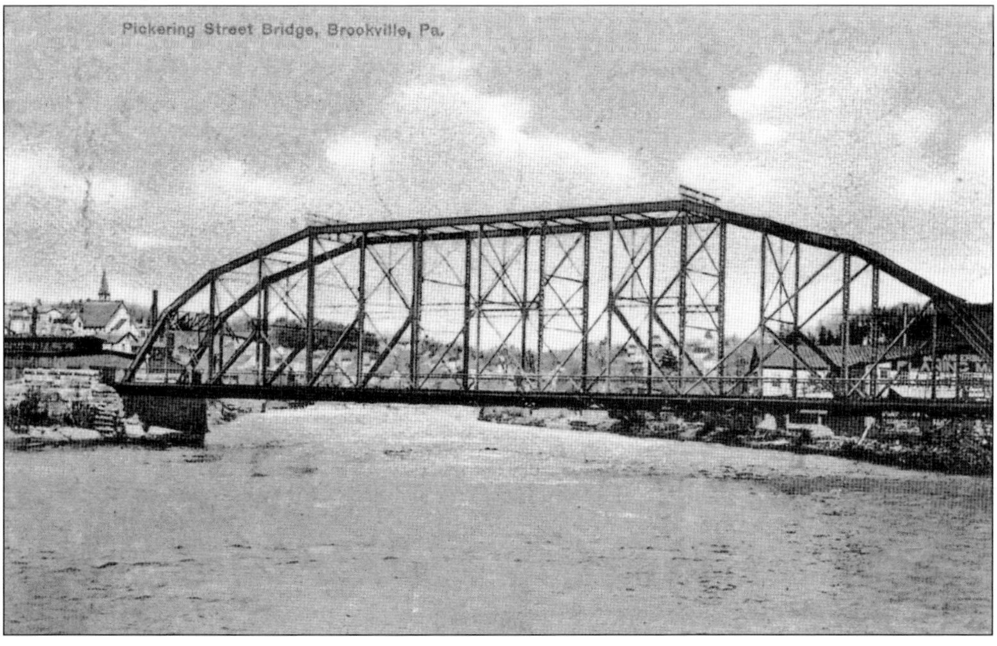

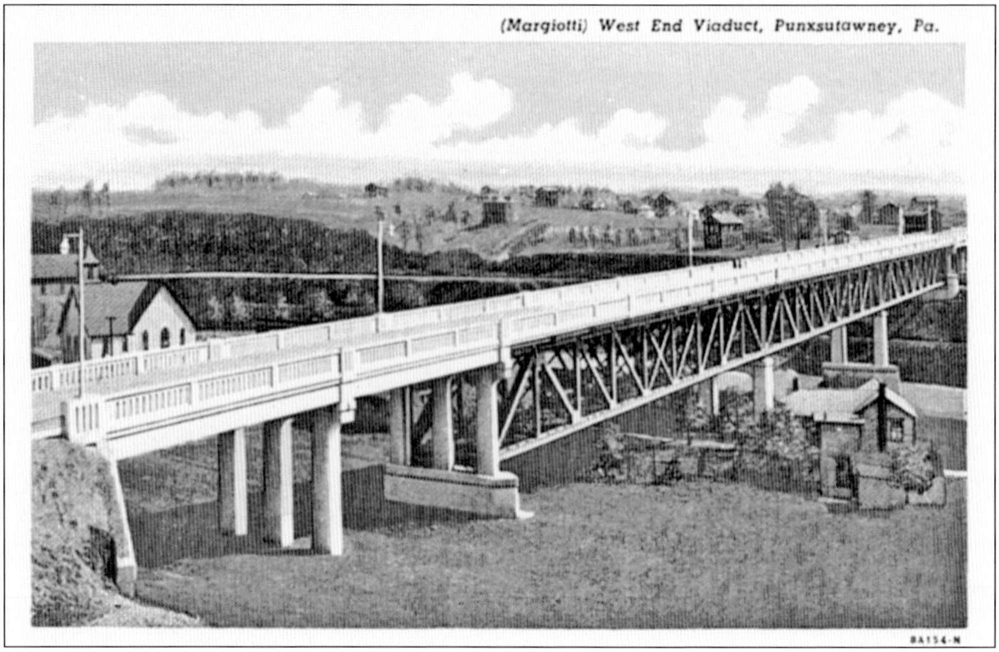

Beginning in 1937, the deck truss bridge 70 feet above Mahoning Creek on Pennsylvania Route 436 facilitated traffic flow from the west end of Punxsutawney to the south side. Originally named the West End Viaduct, it is locally referred to as Margiotti Bridge, for Charles J. Margiotti, who achieved national prominence and was appointed state attorney general under Govs. George Earle (a Democrat) and James Duff (a Republican). Work began in 2016 to replace this last truss bridge in Jefferson County with a two-lane, four-span girder bridge. (PAHGS.)

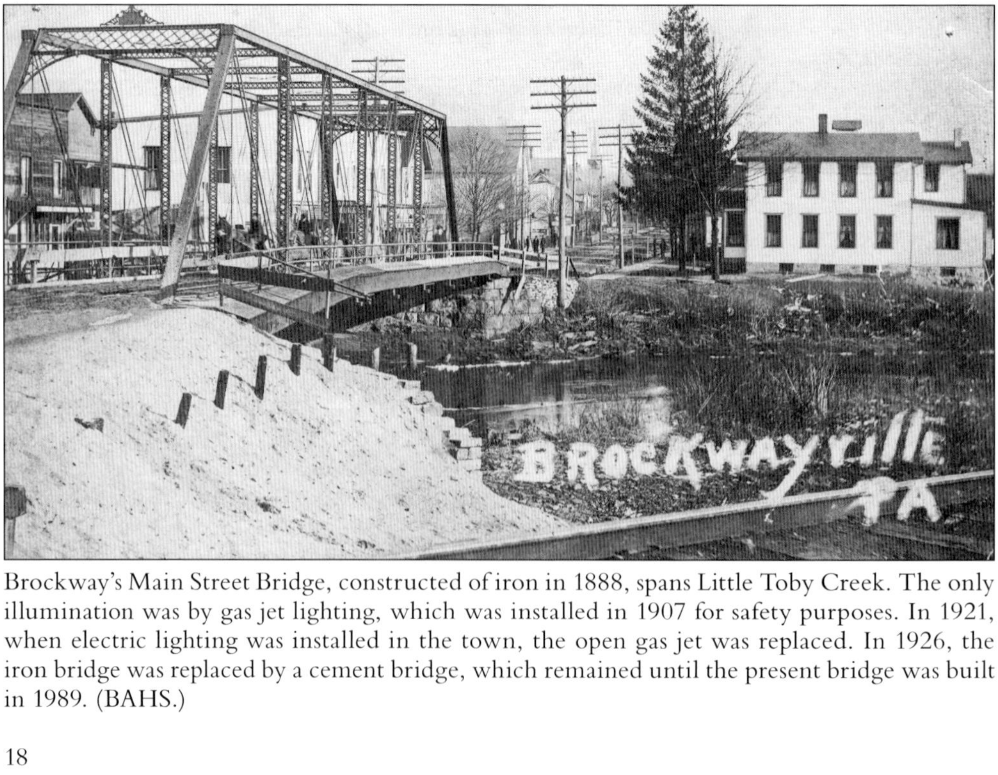

Brockway's Main Street Bridge, constructed of iron in 1888, spans Little Toby Creek. The only illumination was by gas jet lighting, which was installed in 1907 for safety purposes. In 1921, when electric lighting was installed in the town, the open gas jet was replaced. In 1926, the iron bridge was replaced by a cement bridge, which remained until the present bridge was built in 1989. (BAHS.)

Two

Towns

There is a similarity to main streets across America, and this is certainly true of the main streets of Jefferson County. Native American trails that once crisscrossed the land that eventually became Jefferson County had become the main streets of many towns and villages by the beginning of the 20th century. Planks replaced dirt and were in turn replaced by brick, which gave way to the more expensive macadam and concrete.

The county's 11 municipalities, incorporated between 1830 and 1922, today range in population between 66 people living in Worthville and 5,814 people living in Punxsutawney. Others choose to live in the 23 townships.

Once, peddlers sold water to housewives in Brookville, who were not satisfied with their well water. Then entrepreneurs formed companies, laid pipe, and sold water to households. Companies strung wire and sold telephone service and electricity. Municipalities bought out private companies and formed authorities that provided water and sewage services.

Major fires in the towns' business districts saw the earlier wooden structures replaced with fire-resistant brick. Volunteer fire companies organized.

The years from 1875 to 1920 brought wealth to Jefferson County. Local lumber, floated downstream, built cities, including Pittsburgh and Cincinnati. Railroads reached the county in 1874, sparking an expansion of the economy. Industrial mining enriched landowners who sold their coal rights. The population increased dramatically as mine workers and railroaders joined the workforce. Farmers shipped their products to city markets. Jefferson County coal fueled ocean steamers sailing out of New York and smelted iron in Buffalo. Those made wealthy by this economic boom built handsome homes, invested in factories, and sustained the progress.

With the coming of the automobile, new neighborhoods rose at a distance from commercial areas and people drove to town to shop or see a movie. Small shops became modest department stores. Parking meters appeared. Grocery chains like A&P introduced the supermarket. Banks merged and changed their names. The completion of Interstate 80 brought fast-food chains that offered pizza and hamburgers and easy access to shopping malls miles away.

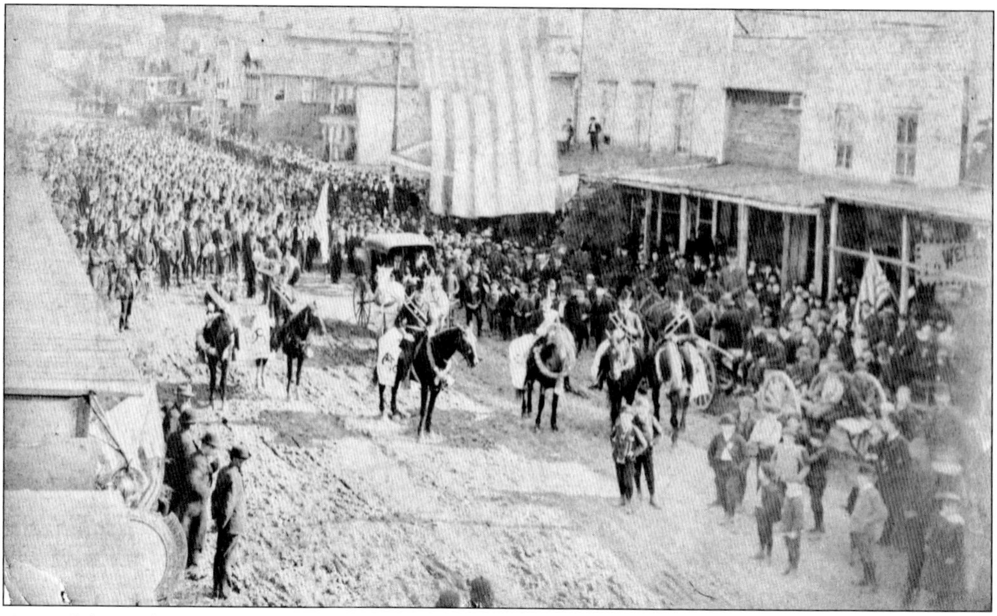

One of the earliest photographs of Reynoldsville (above), taken before any of the brick and stone structures were erected, typifies county communities prior to 1875—wooden buildings with porches covering wooden sidewalks and ankle-deep mud in the dirt streets. The fire of 1875 burned most of the business district and cleared the way for new, more permanent buildings. Town fathers incorporated Punxsutawney (below) in 1849. A 1906 bird's-eye view of the residential and business section highlights the growth and urbanization of the town in the first decade of the 20th century. Seen from across Mahoning Creek, the pedestrian bridge in the foreground leads from the Punxsutawney Brewery and Punxsutawney Beef & Provision Company on the south side to South Gilpin Street. The seven-story Spirit Publishing Company building is in the background at center left. (Above, RHS; below, PAHGS.)

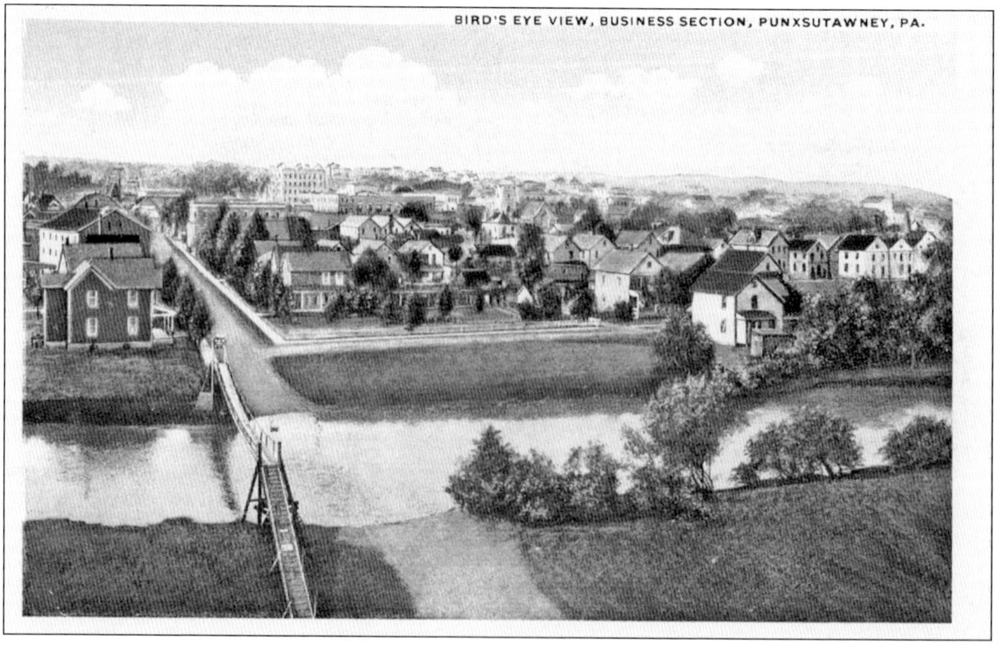

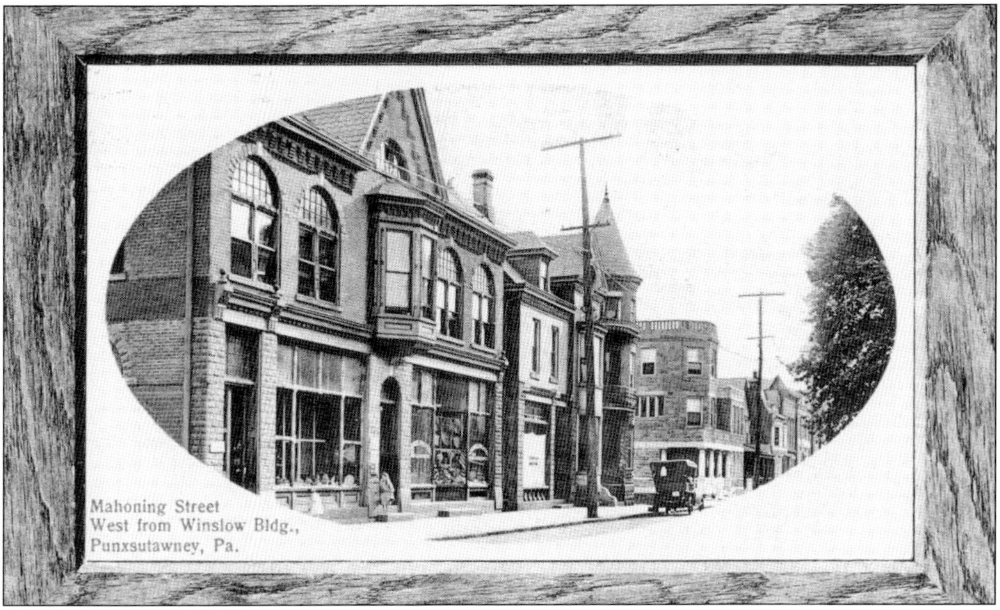

A postcard pair produced some time between 1892 and 1907 shows the Winslow Building (above), built by attorney Reuben C. Winslow on the southwest corner of Punxsutawney's Mahoning and Gilpin Streets. It contained five store spaces on the first floor and several elegant office spaces on the second. The Mahoning Hardware and Implement Company purchased it in 1920. The Murray family operated the company from 1937 until 2003, and a national chain drugstore occupies the site in 2017. Punxsutawney's business district expanded westward along Mahoning Street. Along the south side (below) was Eberhart's store, which housed the G.C. Murphy 5&10 Store and is currently occupied by Indiana University of Pennsylvania's Culinary Arts Academy; the Snyder Building, which housed the McCrory 5&10 Store and Arcade; and the Fink Building, later J.C. Penney, Wolf Furniture, and now Miller Brothers Furniture Store. (Both, PAHGS.)

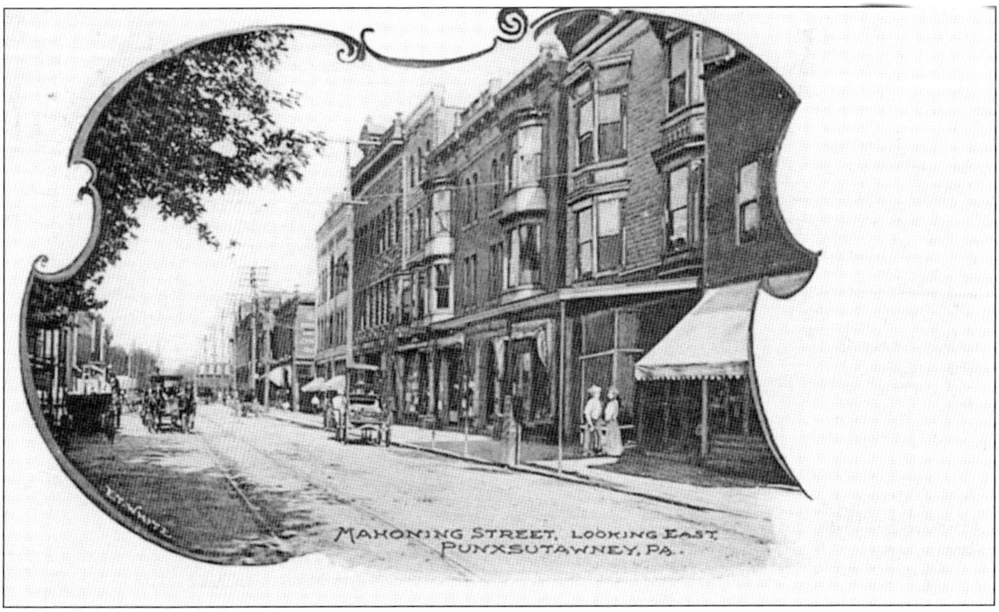

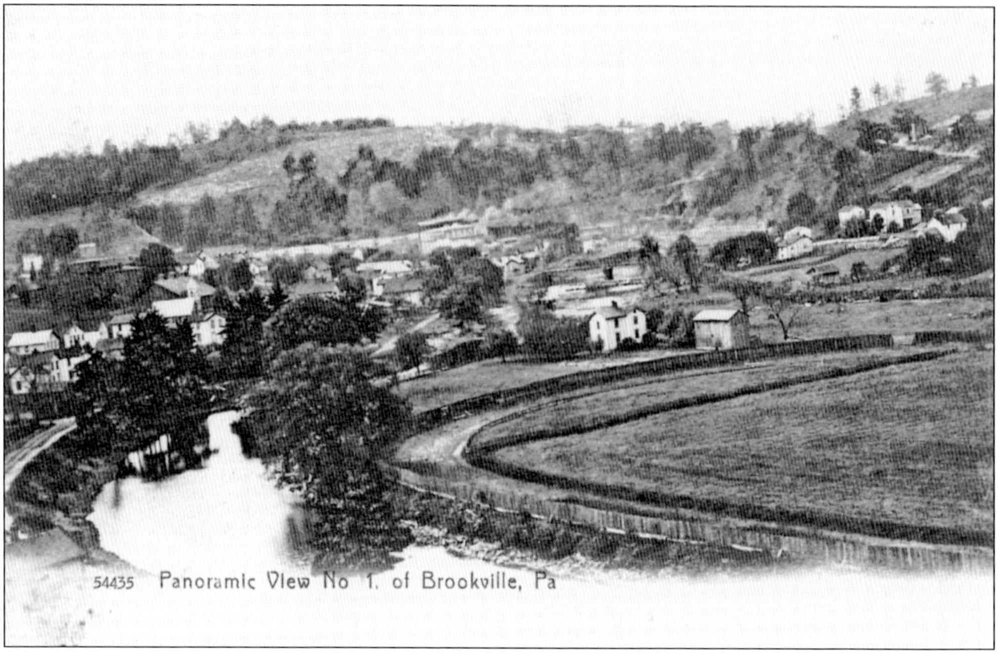

By 1900, Brookville's neighborhoods had spread in all directions, and the population had grown to 2,472. The Jefferson County Fairgrounds and the quarter-mile racetrack occupy the land between the rivers in this panoramic view 1of Brookville. The courthouse cupola is apparent in view four, as is the Central School building high on "Knowledge Knob." Church steeples are easily identified: view 2 shows Immaculate Conception Roman Catholic and the Evangelical church (which existed on Pickering Street at that time); view 3, the spire of the Old Presbyterian Church across from McCracken Hall with a cupola; and view 4, the Evangelical Methodist, Baptist, and Grace Lutheran churches. Retail shops, manufacturing plants, and many homes are evidence of the bustling community of people who walked to and from their businesses, their daily shopping, their schools, and their churches. (Both, JCHC.)

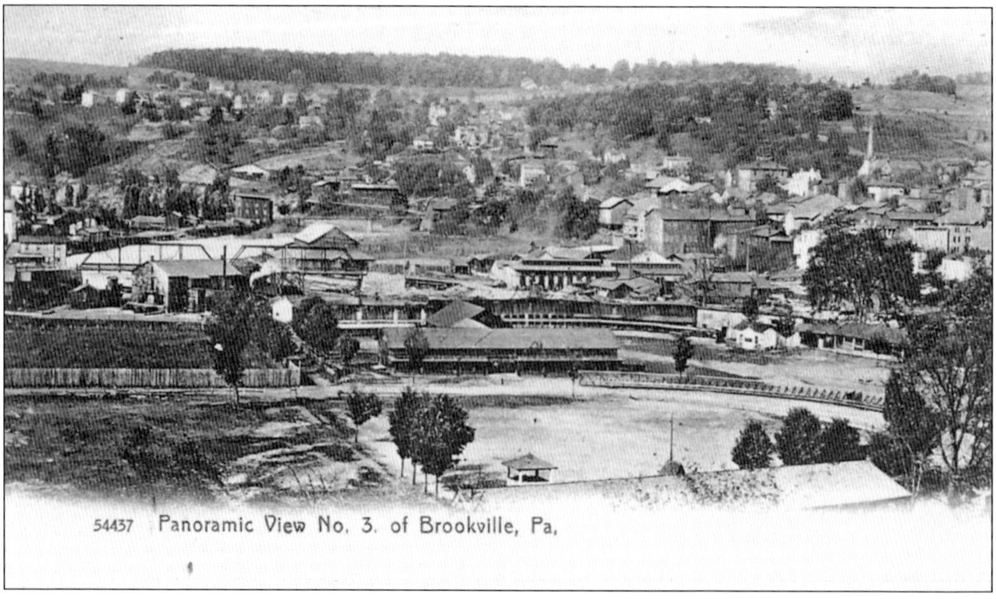

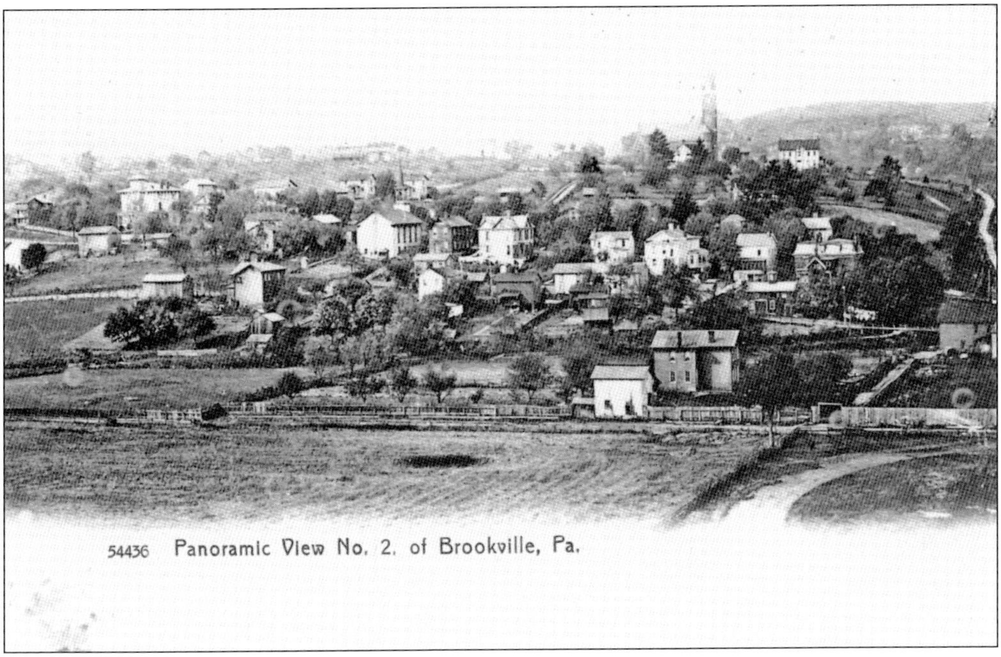

Dating images like this wonderful four-part panoramic view and a similar large 10-foot-long panorama that hangs in the Jefferson County History Center requires some sleuthing. It is known that Presbyterians bid goodbye to their old spired building on March 6, 1904, which dates this panoramic view as prior to 1904. The panorama in the History Center shows an orchard growing within the racetrack. Several postcard panoramas are dated 1911, information that helps date the panorama at the History Center as taken sometime prior to 1911 but several years after 1904. (Both, JCHC.)

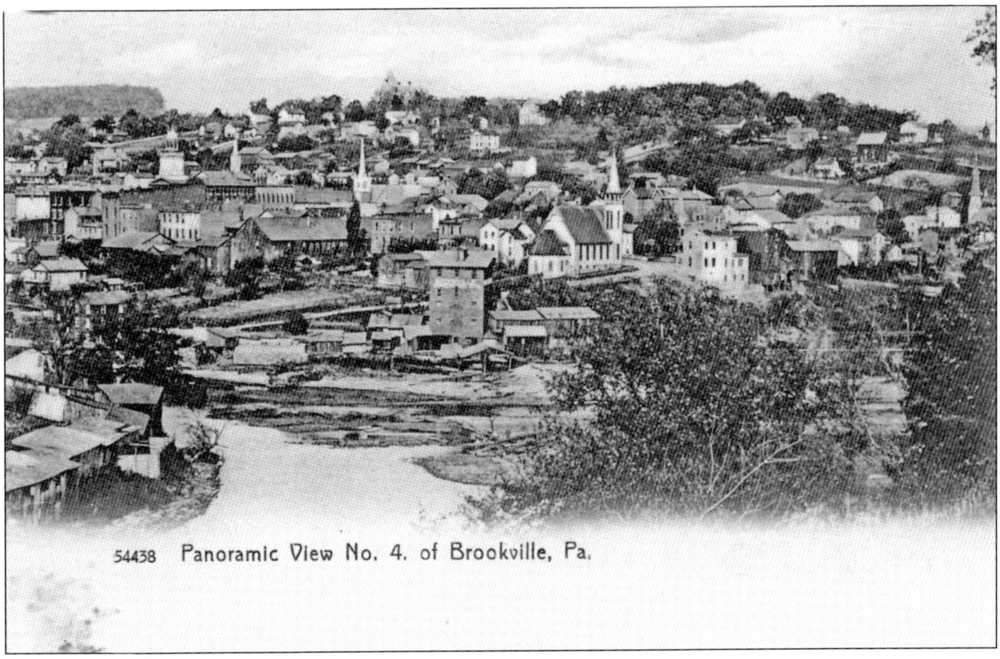

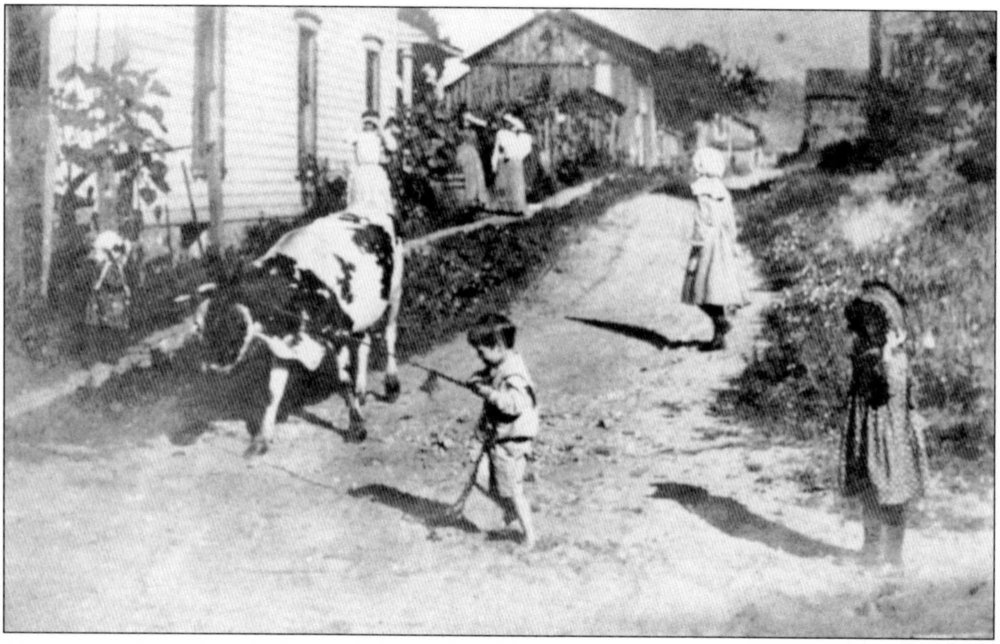

There was a time when the homes in Reynoldsville more closely resembled farms than residences. Before the city council passed ordinances regulating keeping livestock within the borough limits, it was not uncommon to see chickens, goats, horses, pigs, and even the occasional cow in the streets and alleys (above). The Arnold Block (below) was named for the privately owned Arnold & Seeley Bank, pictured on the left side of the postcard. Established in 1883, the bank was nationalized in 1905 under the name Peoples Bank. The Bing & Stokes Hardware Building is shown on the right. Telephone poles and a lamppost indicate that telephone service and electricity had come to Reynoldsville, dating this postcard as some time after 1901. (Both, RHS.)

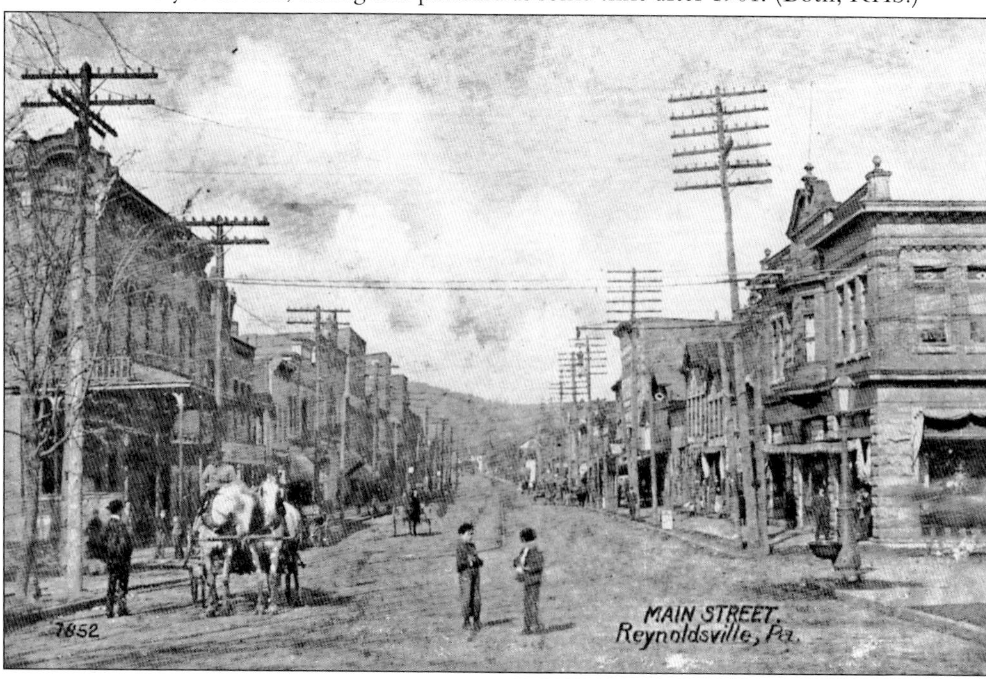

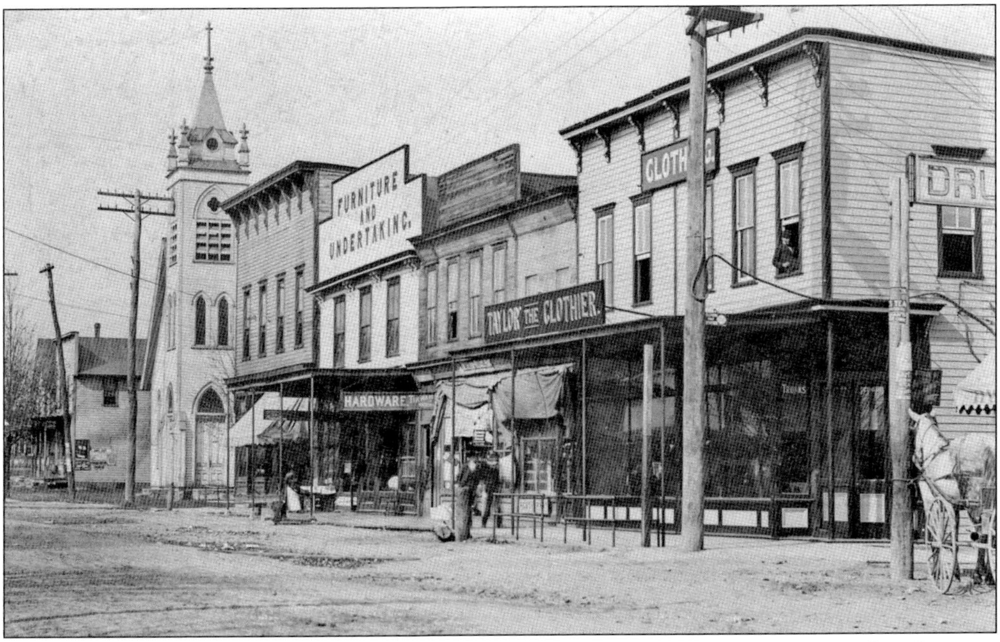

Alonzo and James Brockway arrived in 1822. The area was known as Brockwayville when Dr. A.M. Clarke arrived in 1835, and he laid out the town the following year. Incorporated in 1883, it was known as the Borough of Brockway by 1925. The dirt streets were paved with Shawmut bricks in 1914 (above). The image below shows the south side of Main Street intersecting Fifth Avenue in the early 1900s and includes the Logan Hotel, presently the Brockway Sportsman's Club. The traffic light at the intersection has been removed. On the corner is the First National Bank building, which later became the post office until 1962. Note the produce on the sidewalk of the American Stores Co. building. The entire corner was demolished to make way for the Savings & Trust Company in the early 1970s. In 2016, about 2,024 people lived in Brockway. (Both, BAHS.)

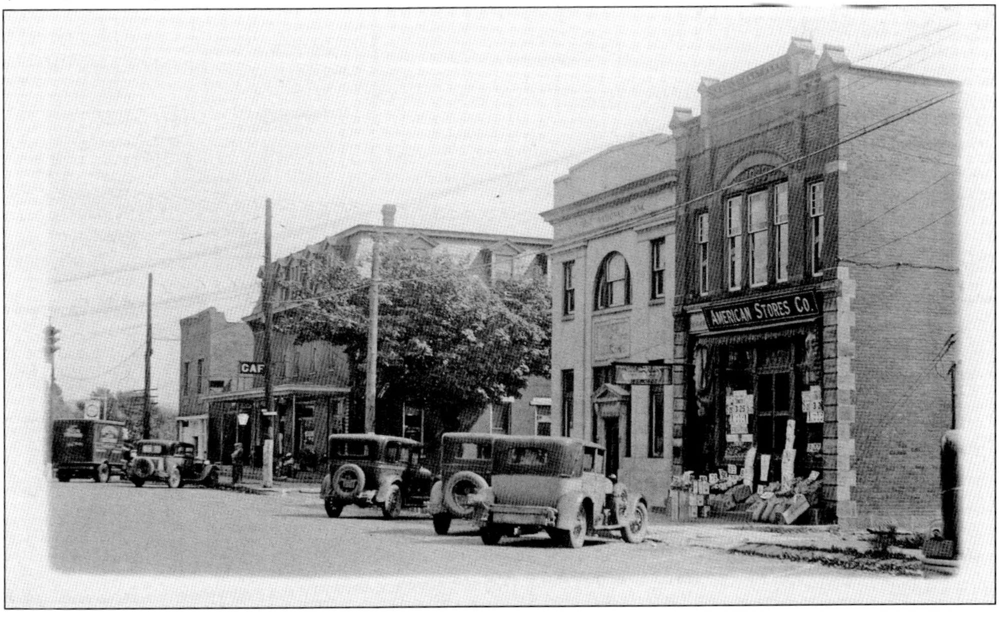

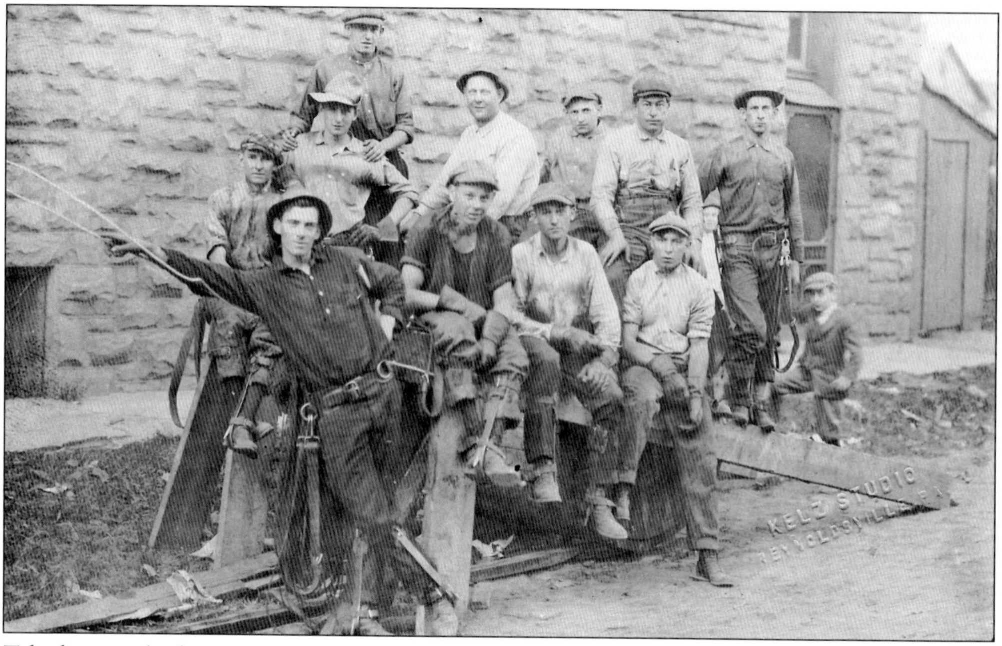

Telephone poles began appearing in the 1880s and 1890s. In August 1891, the Central District Printing & Telegraph Company of Pittsburgh, part of the Bell Telephone System, erected a telephone line that extended from Indiana to Punxsutawney and through Reynoldsville to Clarion. Later, the DuBois District, which included Jefferson County and part of Clearfield County, was established. These linemen are taking a break from stretching telephone cable along Fifth Street in Reynoldsville. (RHS.)

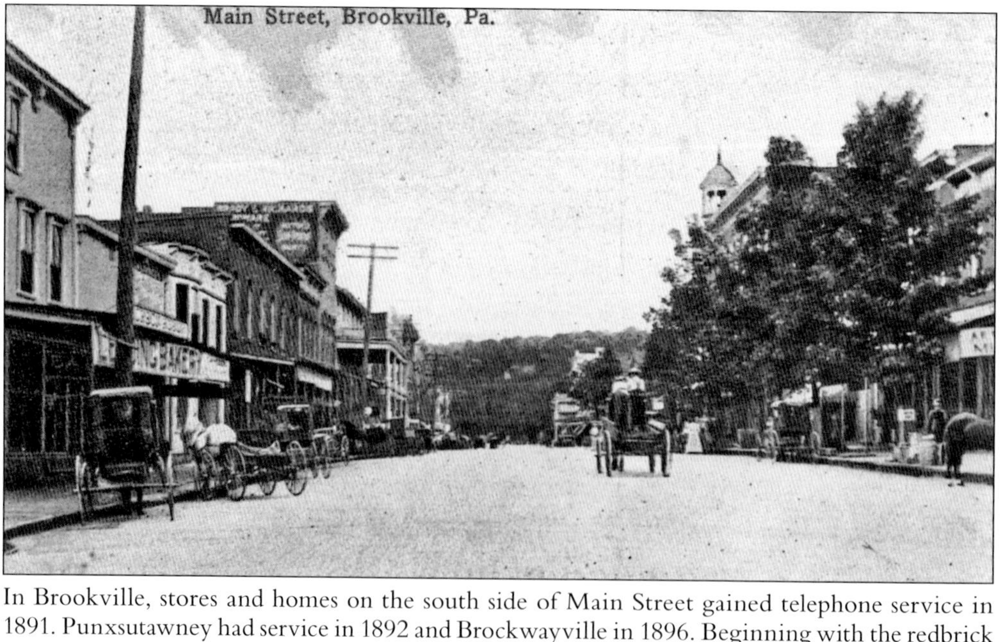

In Brookville, stores and homes on the south side of Main Street gained telephone service in 1891. Punxsutawney had service in 1892 and Brockwayville in 1896. Beginning with the redbrick building are four that still stand today—former *Jeffersonian Democrat* offices, now C&A Toys and Angelo's; Sandt Drug Store, now Fusion Atelier; Brookville Hardware, now the Christian Bookstore; and the Central Hotel, now home to several businesses. (JCHC.)

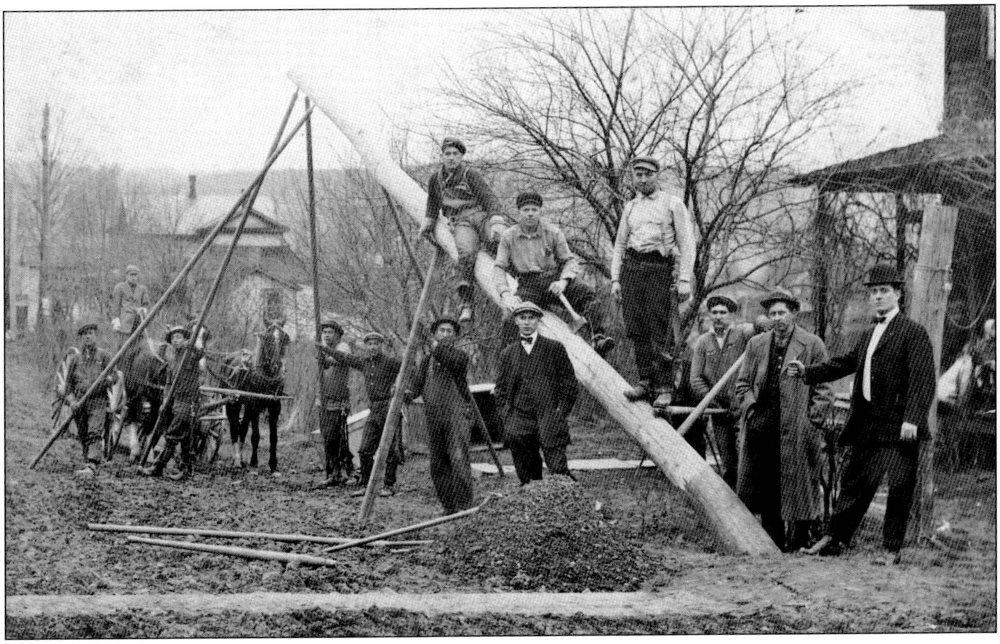

As communities increased in size, private companies offered telephone service. In 1896, Brockwayville cut off telephone service from a Williamsport company and began service with the Central District Printing & Telegraph Company of Pittsburgh. Lines needed to be installed from Falls Creek to complete the improved service with a "string" of its own, including a central office and exchange. The crew above is erecting a telephone pole on Maple Street. One can assume that the gentleman on the far right is a telephone company official. The c. 1907 view below is of the north side of Main Street east of Fifth Avenue. The large building on the far left is the Excelsior Building, now the location of a True Value hardware store. The poles are telephone poles. (Both, BAHS.)

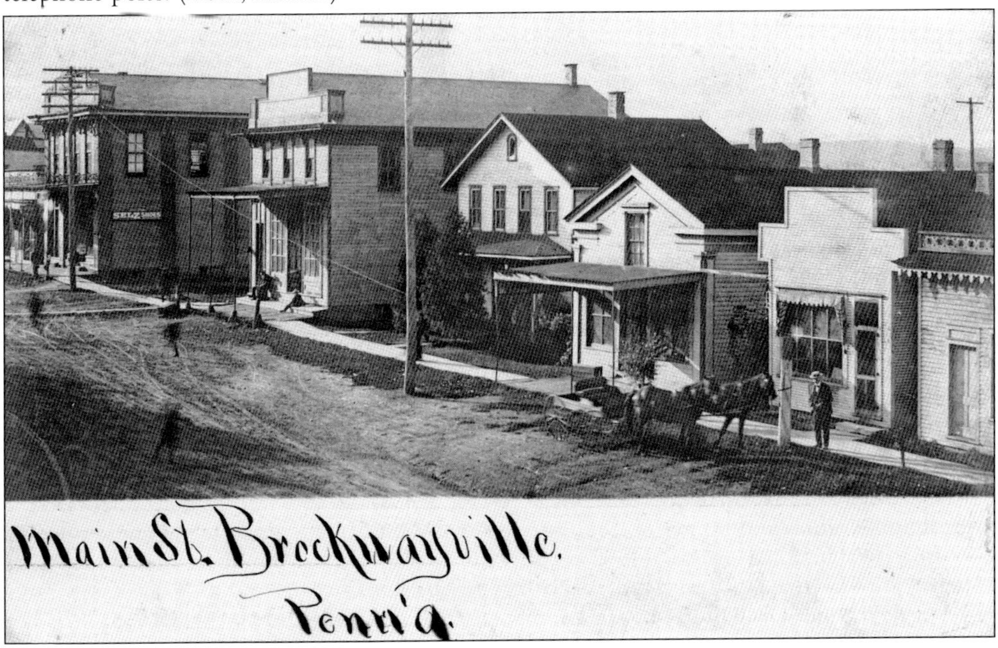

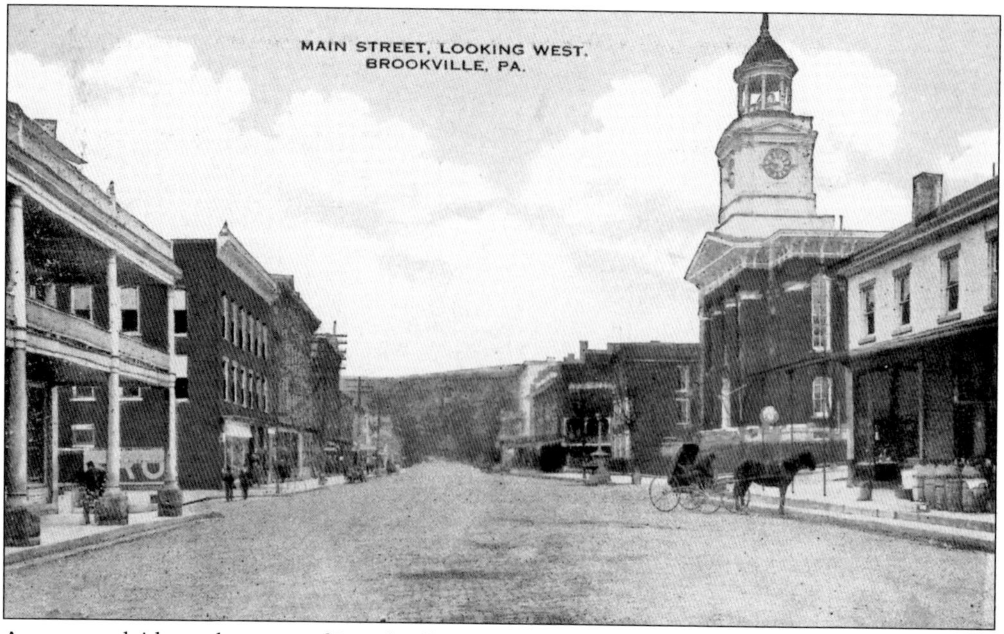

A surveyor laid out the town of Brookville in 1830. Main Street (above) was an extraordinarily wide packed-dirt thoroughfare and part of the Susquehanna & Waterford Turnpike. A series of four big fires between 1854 and 1874 leveled blocks on Main Street, giving rise to many of the late Victorian–style buildings that remain today. In this view looking west on the south side of Main Street are the porches of the Central Hotel (1875), Uriah Matson Building (1878), McKnight Building (1871), and Marlin Opera House (1883–1884), and on the north side are the New Commercial Hotel (1872), American Hotel (1857), jail, courthouse (1869), and Harrison Matson Building (1845). In a view looking east (below) are two buildings that existed in 1910: the New Commercial Hotel and the American Hotel. The courthouse and, on the right, the Marlin Opera House still stand. (Both, JCHC.)

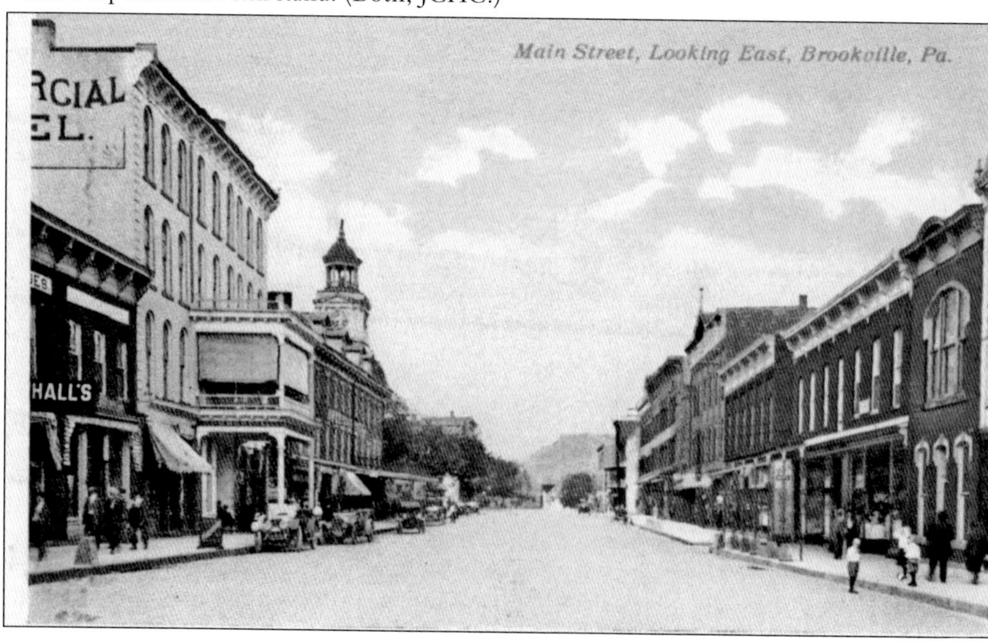

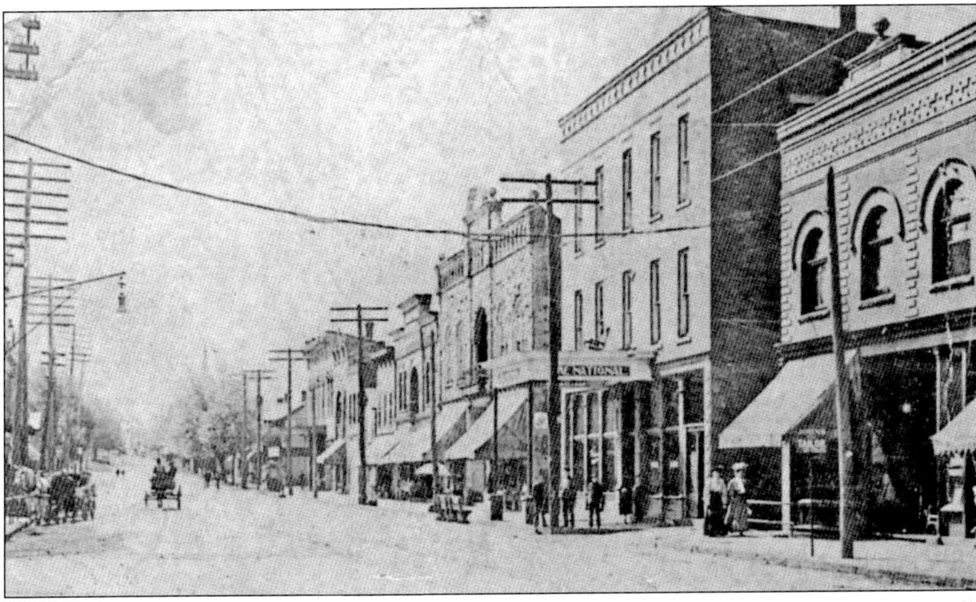

The National Hotel, with its porch roof covering the sidewalk, was the last holdout in Reynoldsville for this common Main Street practice. In 1893, the borough council appropriated money to plank Main Street from the iron bridge to Seventh Street. The road surface consisted of wooden planks laid edgewise and spiked together. Bricks replace the planking in 1904–1905. In 2016, 2,688 people lived in Reynoldsville. (RHS.)

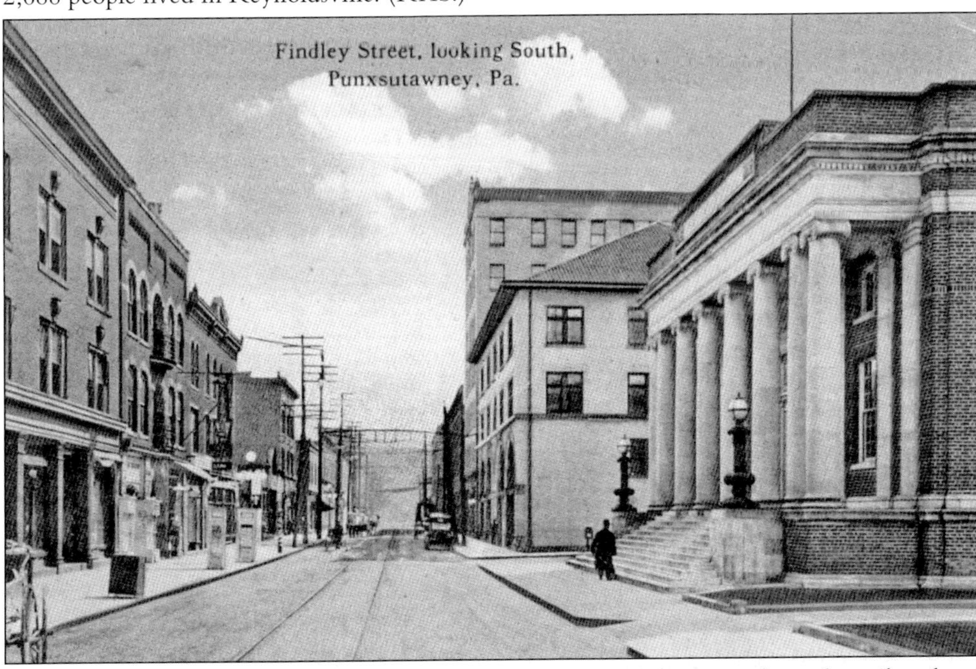

In 1918, Punxsutawney's North Findley Street, the downtown access from the railroad and trolley stations, had elegance—along with trolley tracks down the middle. On the right are the federal building and post office, currently the Weather Discovery Center; the YMCA; and the Spirit Building, Punxsutawney's first "skyscraper." The Area Transportation Authority building, a sports bar, and a fast-food restaurant have replaced the buildings on the left. (PAHGS.)

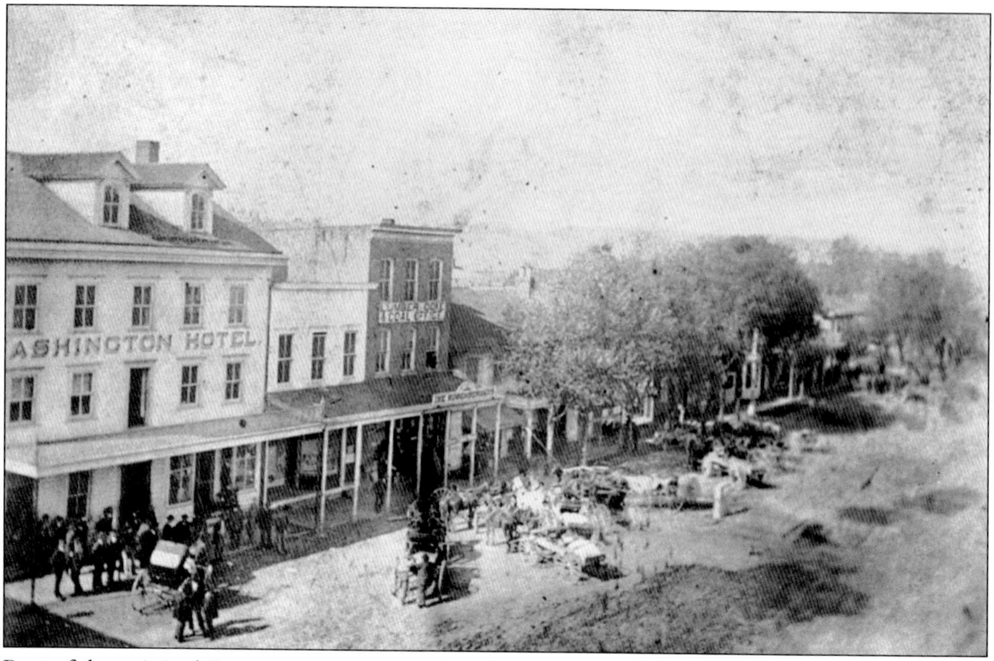

Part of the original Punxsutawney town plan, the plaza (above), a strip of land opposite Barclay Square along Mahoning Street between North Jefferson and North Penn Streets, served as a marketplace for farmers and became the central business district, with hotels and business buildings. When the circus came to town, it set up tents and displays on the plaza. Grandstands were set up there for parades. Gov. Edwin S. Stuart watched the first Old Home Week parade from such a grandstand in 1909. Most of the buildings (below) in this section of Punxsutawney were razed when urban renewal took place in the 1970s. The buildings in the distance near the East End Bridge have been replaced by Mahoning Towers, a senior living facility. (Both, PAHGS.)

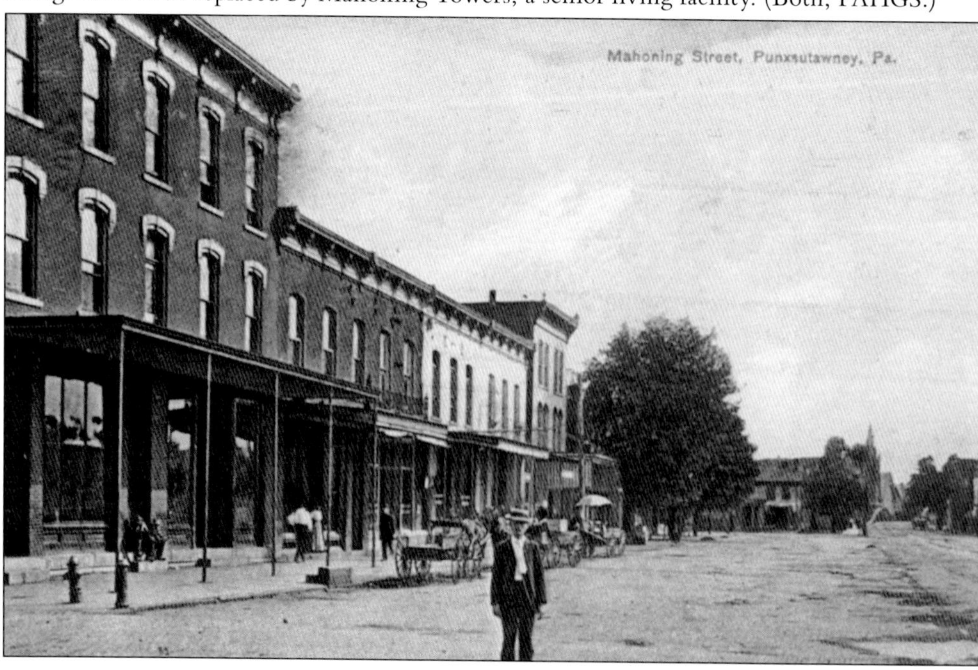

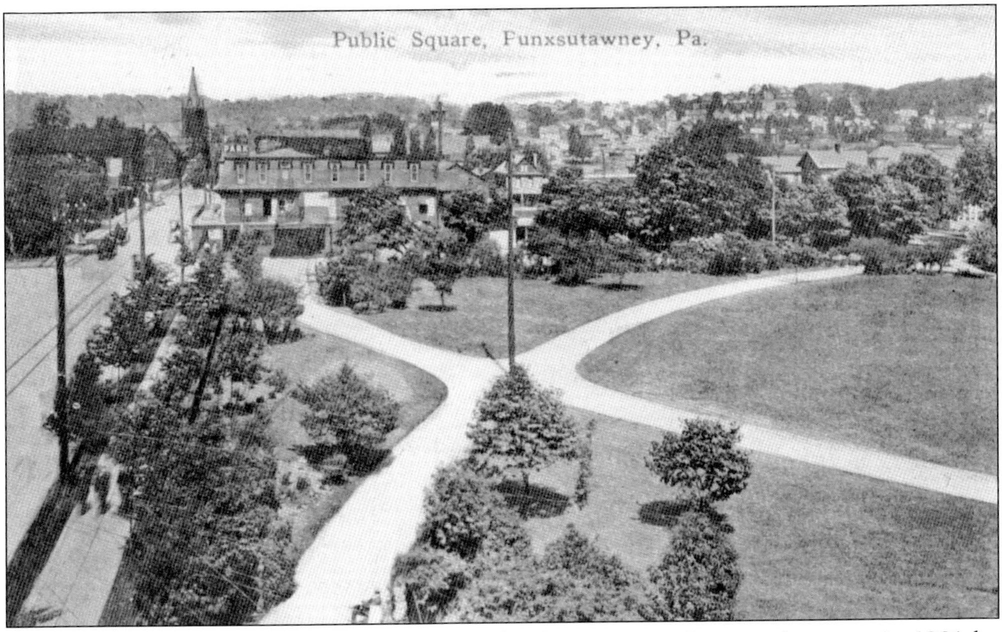

Located in the heart of Punxsutawney, Barclay Square was given to the town in 1821 by Rev. David Barclay, who included it on his town map. In 1901, William H. Rogers of the Punxsutawney Iron Company hired landscape architect Shelby Noyes, whose "oasis" plan included curving walkways that remain as significant design elements. Pictured about 1910, to the east (above) are the commercial buildings beyond the park and the developing residential area of Punxsutawney's East End. To the west (below) is the town's main business district, with the historic Pantall Hotel and the towering Spirit Building. Prior to 1902, political gatherings, circuses, sporting events, and other community activities were held in the park, where many of the town's livestock also roamed. The park continues to be a place for townspeople to gather for events. (Both, PAHCS.)

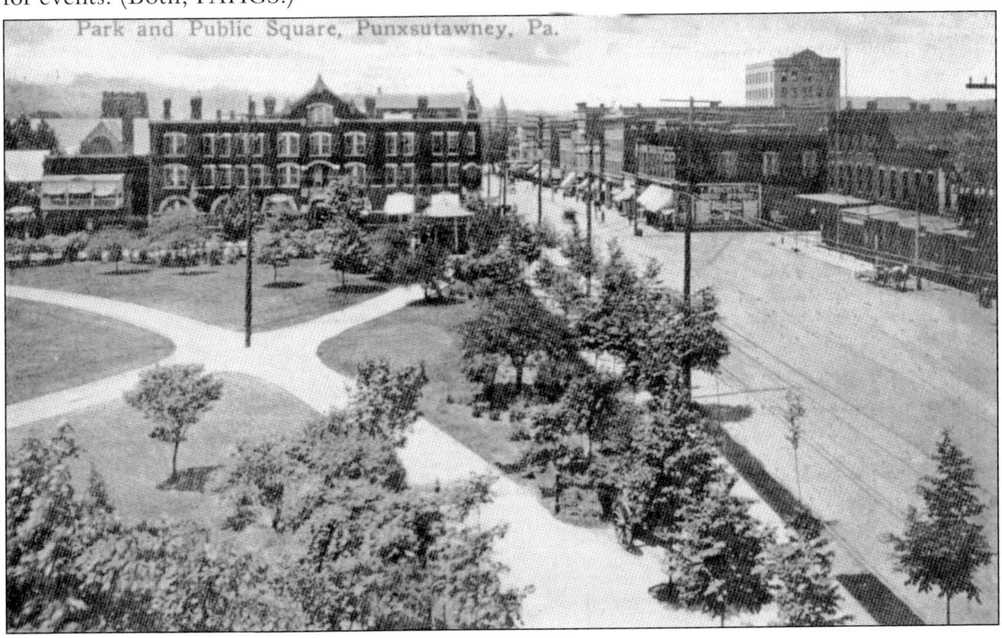

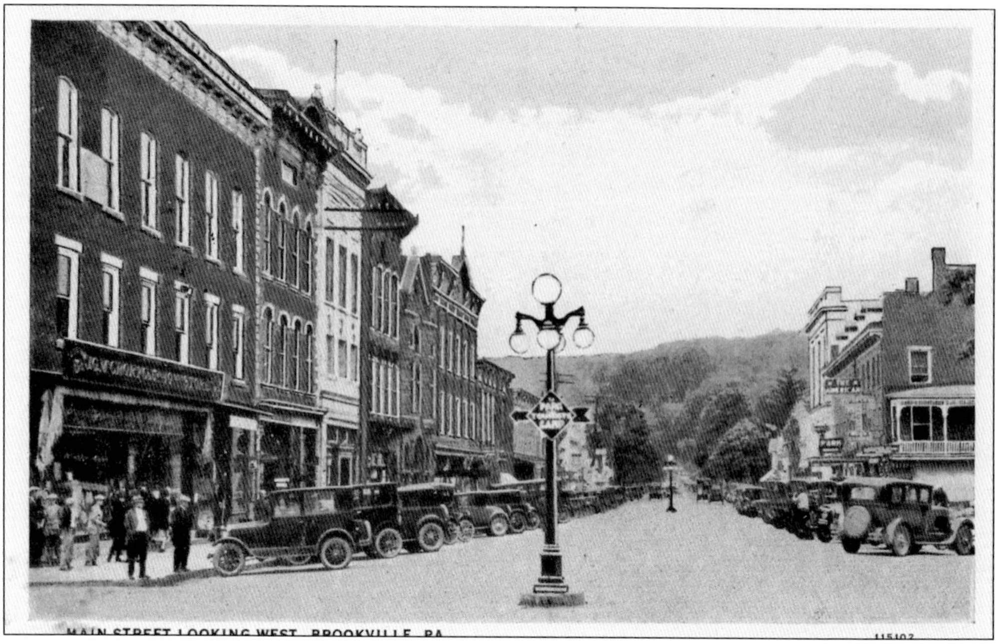

Electricity and automobiles arrived around the turn of the century. By 1904, the first automobiles were traveling Brookville's Main Street, a practice that led to the installation of light poles, but not traffic lights, in the middle of several intersections. Accidents caused their eventual removal, and today, modern traffic lights control traffic in town. (JCHC.)

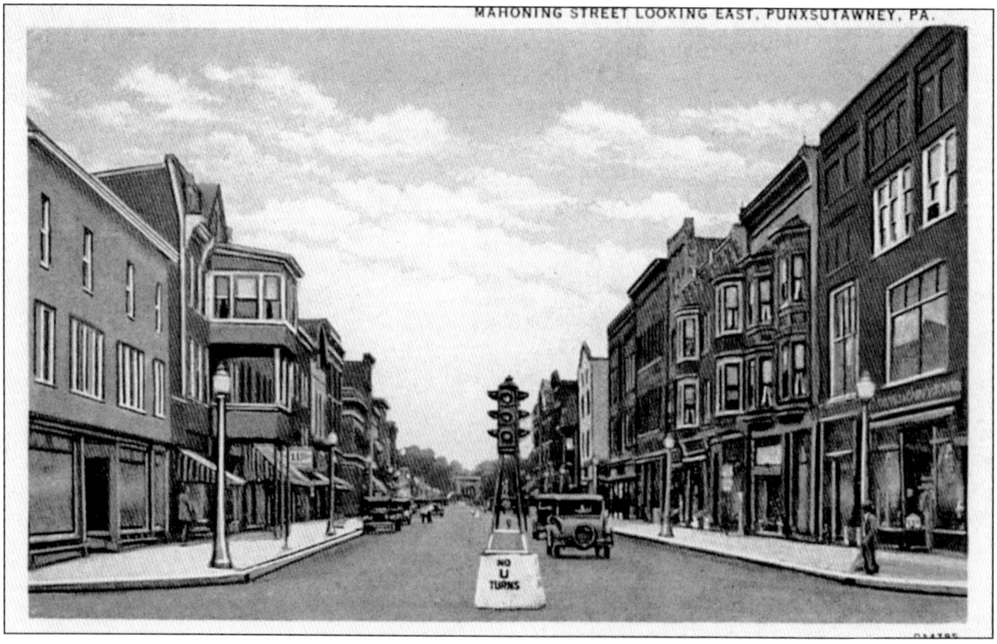

A pedestal traffic light installed in 1930 at the intersection of West Mahoning and Gilpin Streets in Punxsutawney controlled the increased movement of automobile traffic through the town. The electrically operated traffic signal replaced a policeman. This view is facing east from Gilpin Street. More visible signal lights, suspended overhead, replaced the pedestal traffic lights by 1940. (PAHGS.)

In 1921, the Brockway Light, Heat & Power Company constructed a building at the east corner of Evergreen and James Streets and began generating electricity. Initially, it used steam boilers and generators from Ridgway to produce electric power, but later, it converted to the use of diesel engines and generators. The company eventually was sold to the Pennsylvania Electric Company, and the building was razed in 1964. (BAHS.)

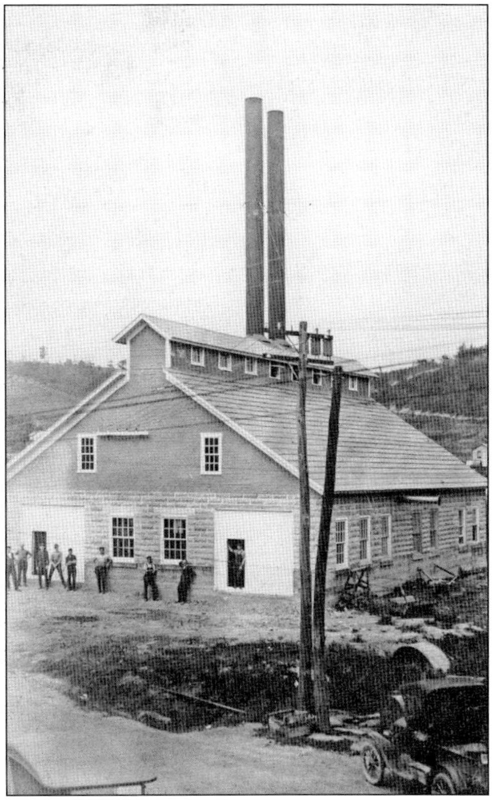

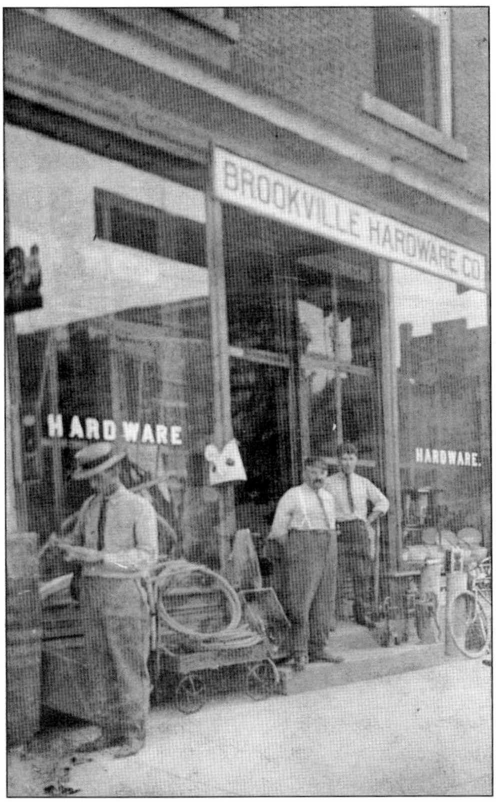

The general stores of the 19th century gradually gave way to stores like the one George Pearsall built on Brookville's Main Street in 1878. He sold hardware, as did his successors, W. Evans and his son, who operated the Brookville Hardware Company. Today, local hardware stores have given way to national chains like Ace and True Value, and this building is now the Christian Bookstore. (JCHC.)

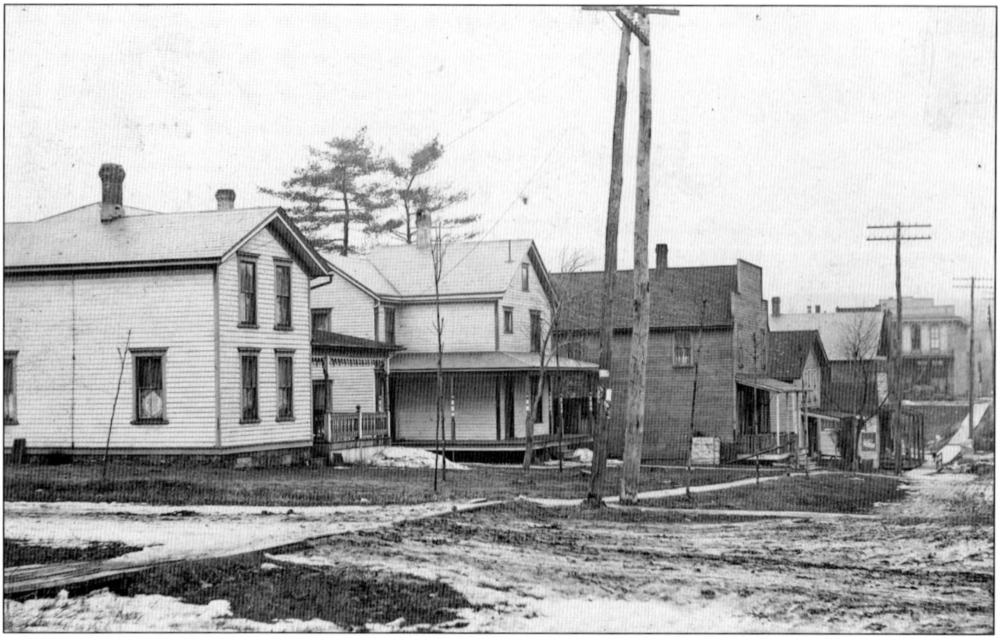

Few buildings that stood when electricity arrived in 1921 remain in Brockway. Seen in this view looking toward Main Street from the intersection of Broad Street and Fifth Avenue (above), a brick house replaced the first building on the left, but the second house still stands. Much of the rest has been razed or totally renovated. The Brockway Hose Company building is now a restaurant. A late-1940s view (below) of the north side of Main Street shows Humphrey's Furniture with the Odd Fellows lodge on an upper floor. The Beadle Building at the end of the block is now True Value Hardware, and the Borough Building has replaced the Citizens Bank. (Both, BAHS.)

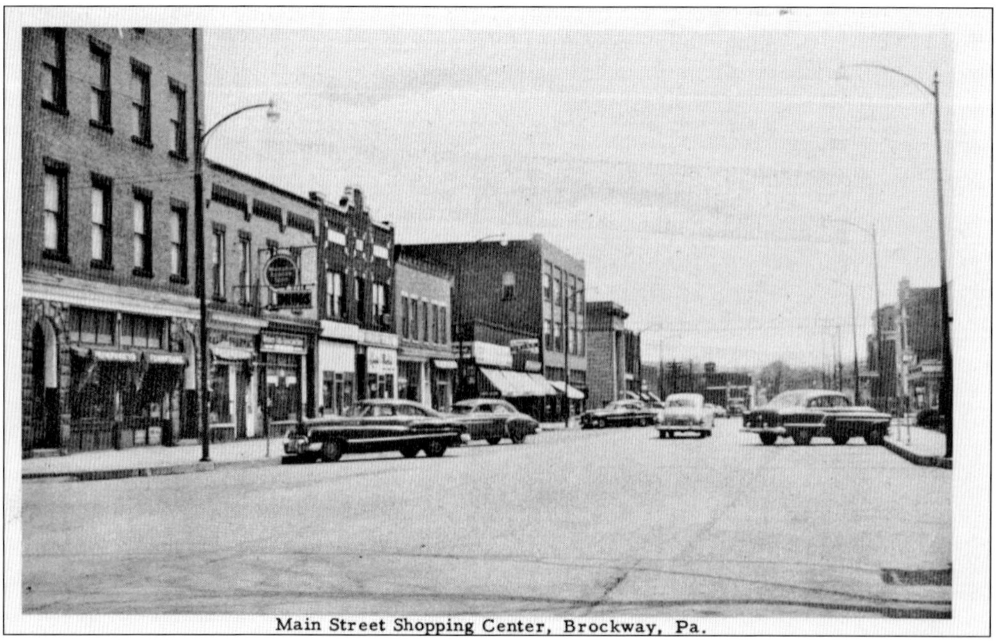

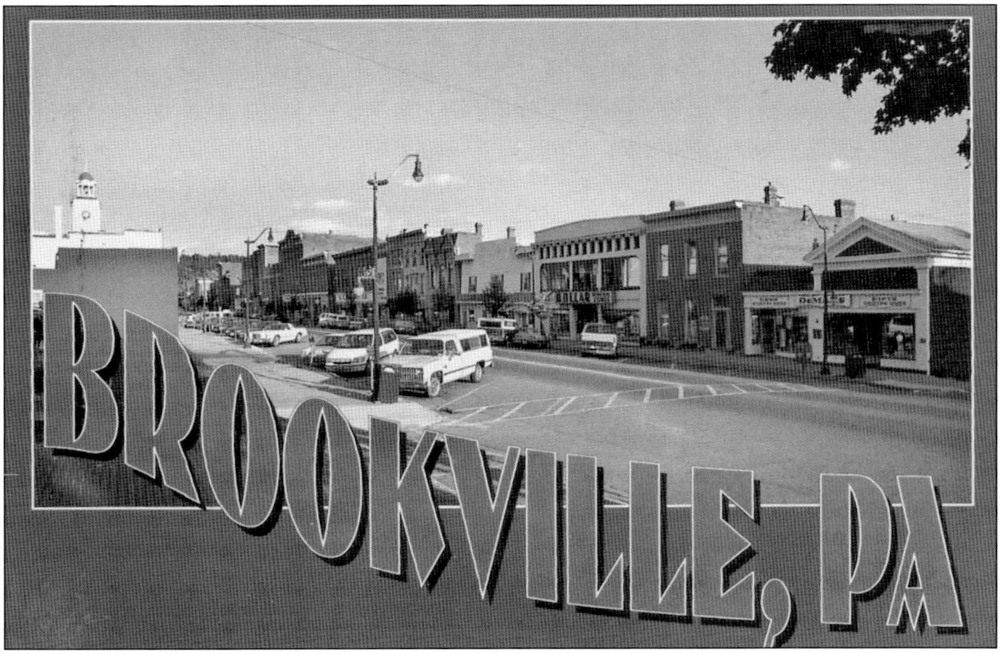

The Brookville National Historic District (registered in 1983) includes 90 acres in and around Main Street and 263 contributing buildings, including, from left to right above, the Jefferson County Courthouse (with its cupola, 1869); the Marlin Opera House (the tallest building, 1883–1884); the Rodgers-Canning Building (1878), now Goodwill; Gordon-Corbet Law Office, now Farmer's Bank; Siegel Building, now Loafin' Bakery; Balmer Building (1902), now Dittman's; Richard Arthurs's home (1893), now McKinley CPA; DeMotte Building (1995); the cream Baker Buick Building (1919), now vacant; Judge Joseph Henderson's home (1865), now Dennison Law; and Henderson's Tin Shop (with a triangular pediment, 1860), now DeMan's. Buildings on the north side of Main Street, below from left to right, include the S&T Bank; Town Square (2016); Jefferson County Courthouse; Harrison Matson Building (1845), now Tonell's; Parker P. Blood Building (1875), now Area Office on Aging; and a corner of the Edelblute Building (1875), now the Jefferson County History Center. (Both, JCHC.)

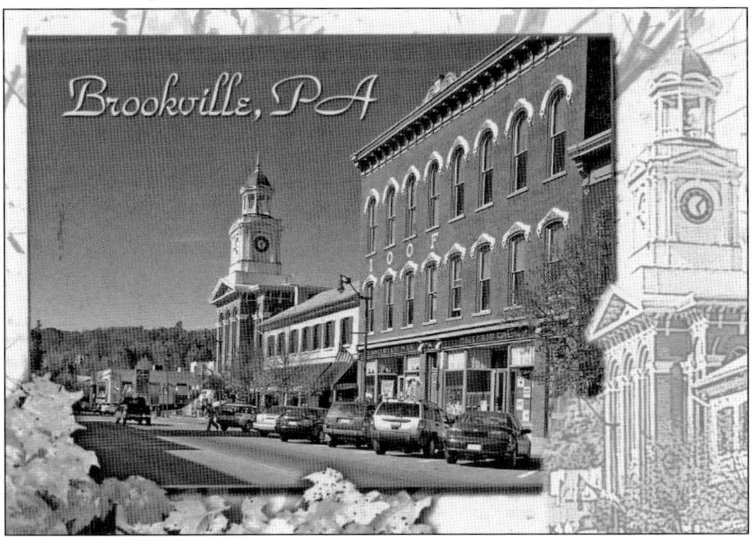

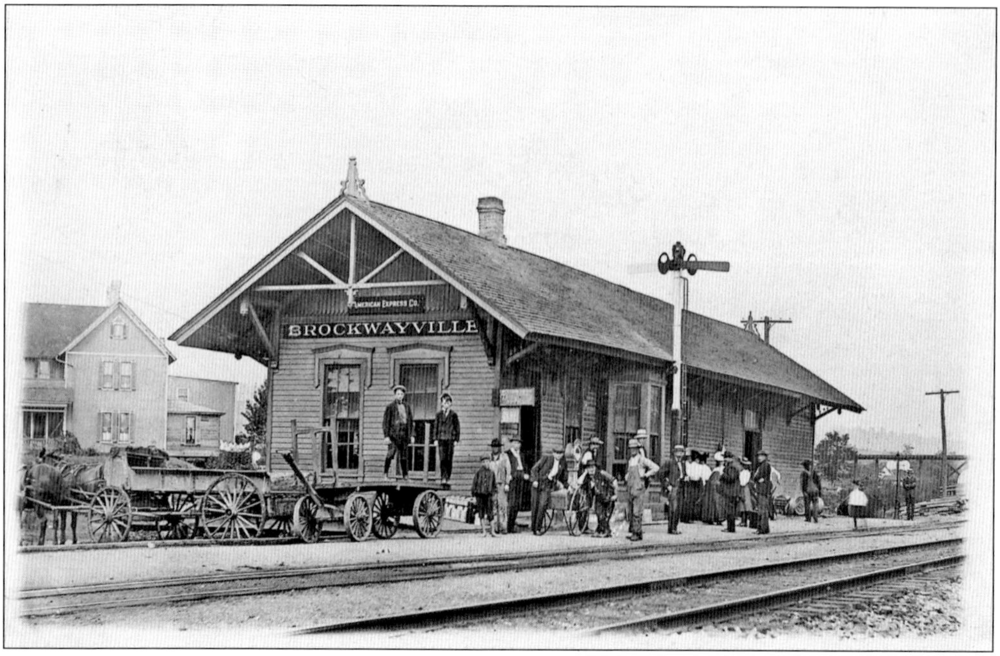

The importance of railroads to rural areas cannot be overestimated. Brockwayville's citizens must have been quite overjoyed when news came that three railroads had their eyes on the area's coal. The Rochester & Pittsburgh (R&P) Railroad won the race and completed its line and depot in 1883, with its "golden spike" driven right in Brockwayville. The R&P would be consolidated into the Buffalo, Rochester & Pittsburgh (BR&P) in 1887. (BAHS.)

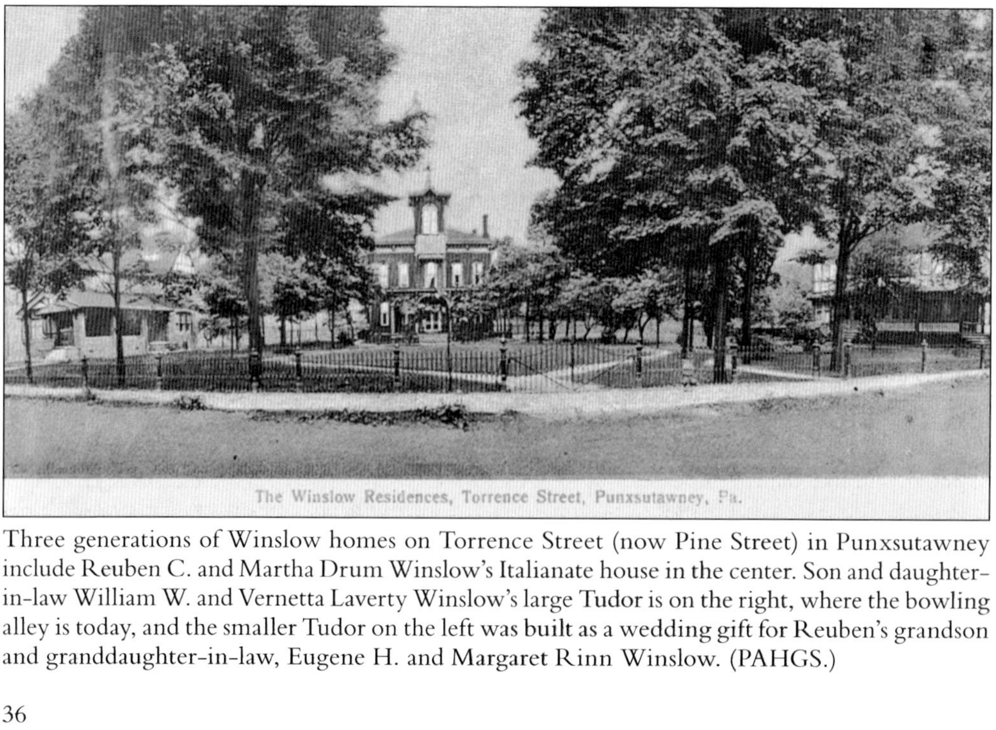

Three generations of Winslow homes on Torrence Street (now Pine Street) in Punxsutawney include Reuben C. and Martha Drum Winslow's Italianate house in the center. Son and daughter-in-law William W. and Vernetta Laverty Winslow's large Tudor is on the right, where the bowling alley is today, and the smaller Tudor on the left was built as a wedding gift for Reuben's grandson and granddaughter-in-law, Eugene H. and Margaret Rinn Winslow. (PAHGS.)

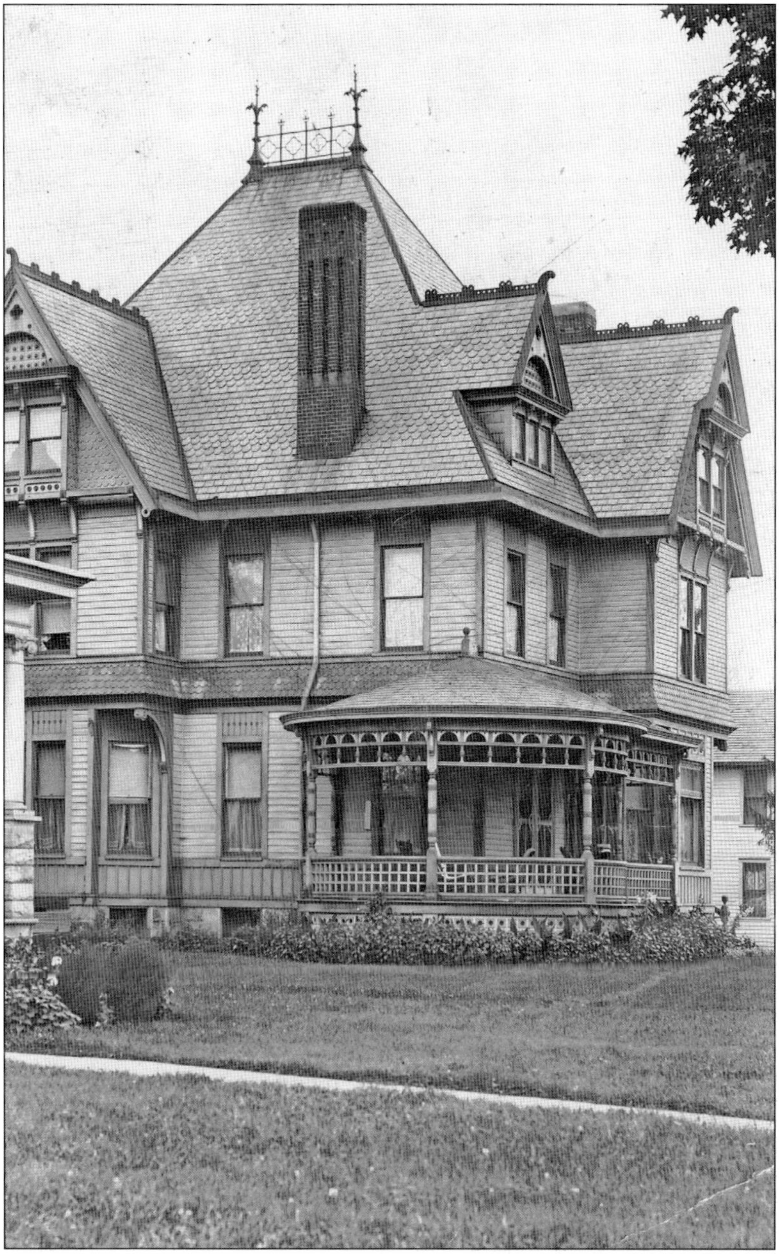

Housing at the turn of the century included modest homes built by coal companies and grand Victorian structures like the Queen Anne built by Brockway lumberman William G. McCain in 1890 at the corner of Main Street and Tenth Avenue. By 1902, the timber of the county was depleted, and like many timbermen of his time, McCain moved to pursue lumber interests in Tennessee. Alton R. Chapin, who operated a general store and later a furniture and undertaking business, purchased the home. In 1910, he became the cashier at the First National Bank. In 1926, H.E. Kilgus, founder of the Brockway Clay Company, bought the home. The popular, asymmetrical Queen Anne–style houses were built between 1876 and 1915 and are identified by their gabled roofs; wraparound porches; spindlework; single-paned, double-hung windows; and often a tower or turret. (BAHS.)

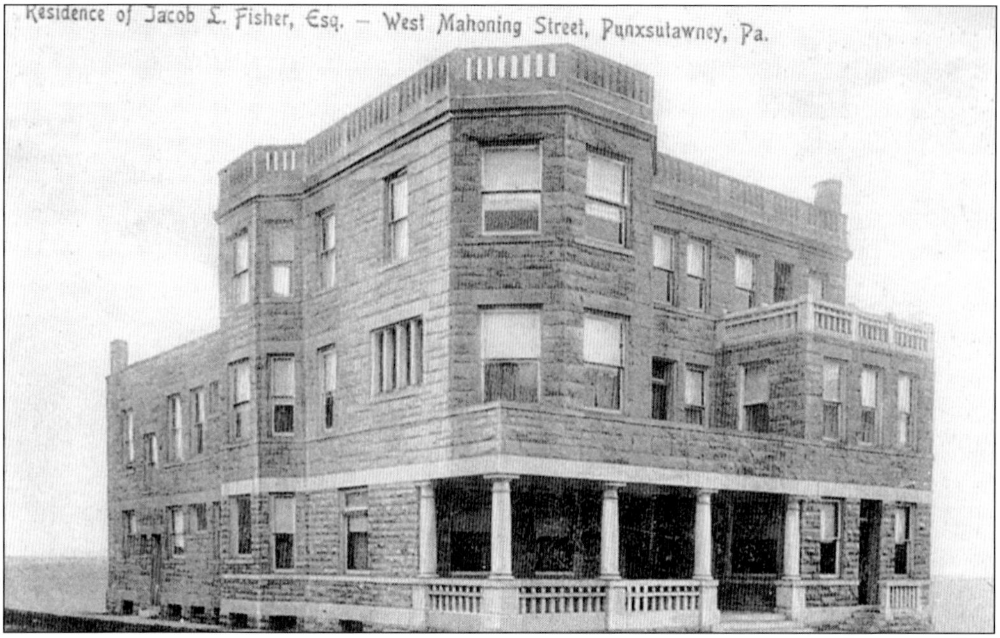

The 1908 residence (above) of Jacob L. Fisher, Esq., with three floors and 27 opulently furnished rooms, was located on "Millionaires' Row" in Punxsutawney. Fisher hosted Pres. William Howard Taft there in 1919. The John Jacob Fisher Post of the American Legion purchased and donated it to the borough in 1944 for the town's public library. The library occupied the building until it moved to the civic center building. David Brown's stone house (below), built in 1915–1916 in the East End, is an architectural treasure among Punxsutawney's heritage of older homes. Located on East Mahoning Street at Dinsmore Avenue, the house was built following the Mission style of architecture. For the exterior, the oilman, lumberman, and businessman used various stones and objects collected from friends and on his travels around the world. (Both, PAHGS.)

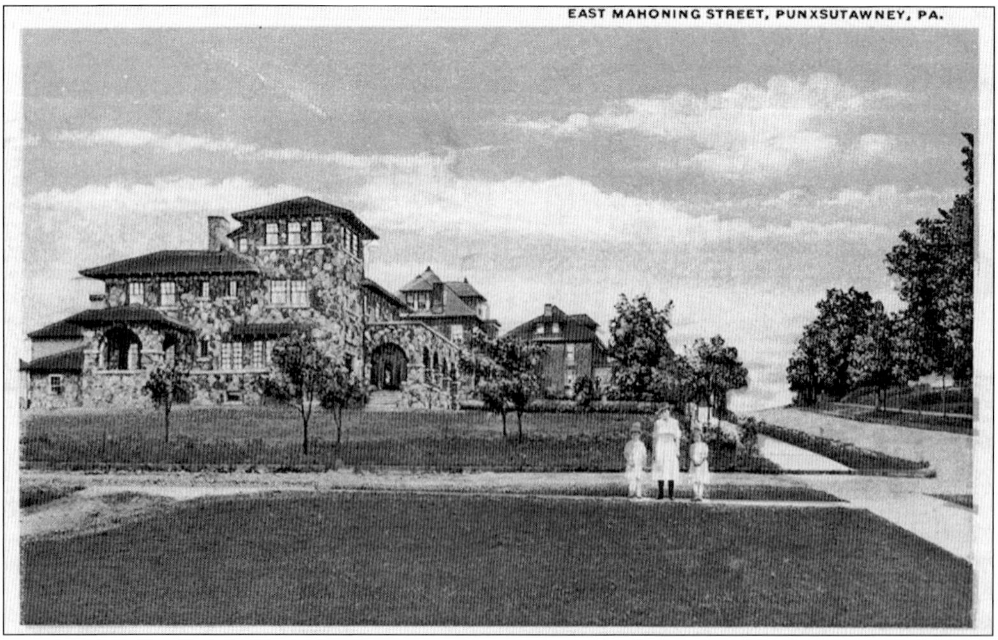

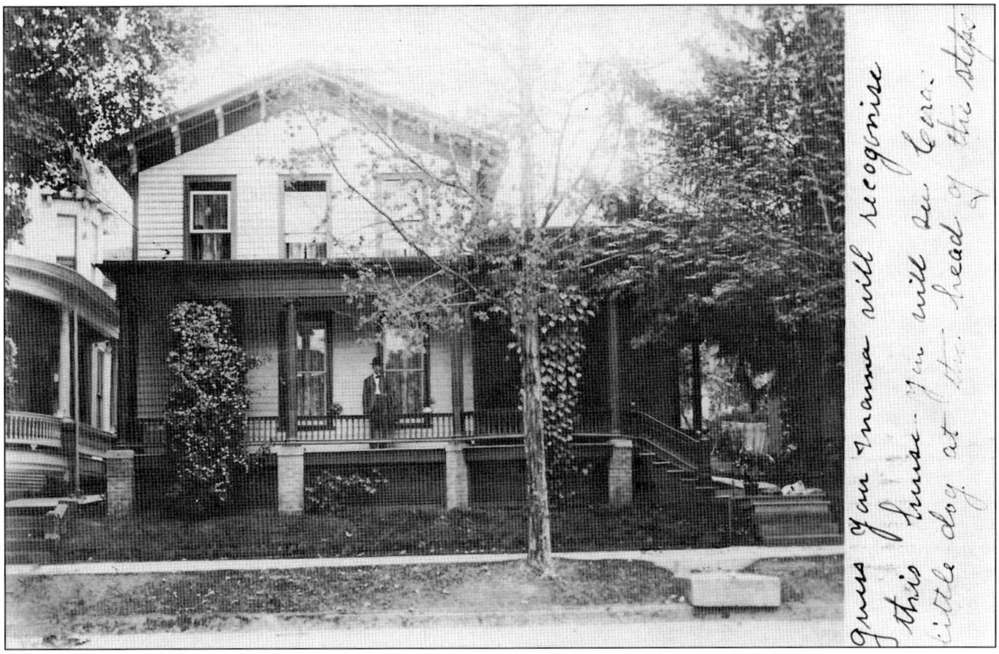

Brookville's historic district and other areas include homes and buildings representing most periods of Victorian architecture: Steamboat Gothic, Italianate, Folk Victorian, Stick-Eastlake, Second Empire, Richardsonian Romanesque, and Queen Anne. Grocer James M. Canning and his wife raised a daughter and son in his vernacular Greek Revival home on Main Street (above). His son, James S., was an accomplished musician who wrote several musicals performed in Brookville. Associate judge Henry Truman built his Queen Anne–style home (below) on the corner of Main Street and Franklin Avenue in 1880. A merchant and lumberman, he was also president of the National Bank of Brookville. Of particular interest is the striking two-story oriel window on the east side. The original brick pavement still exists. Brookville's 2016 population was 3,836. (Both, JCHC.)

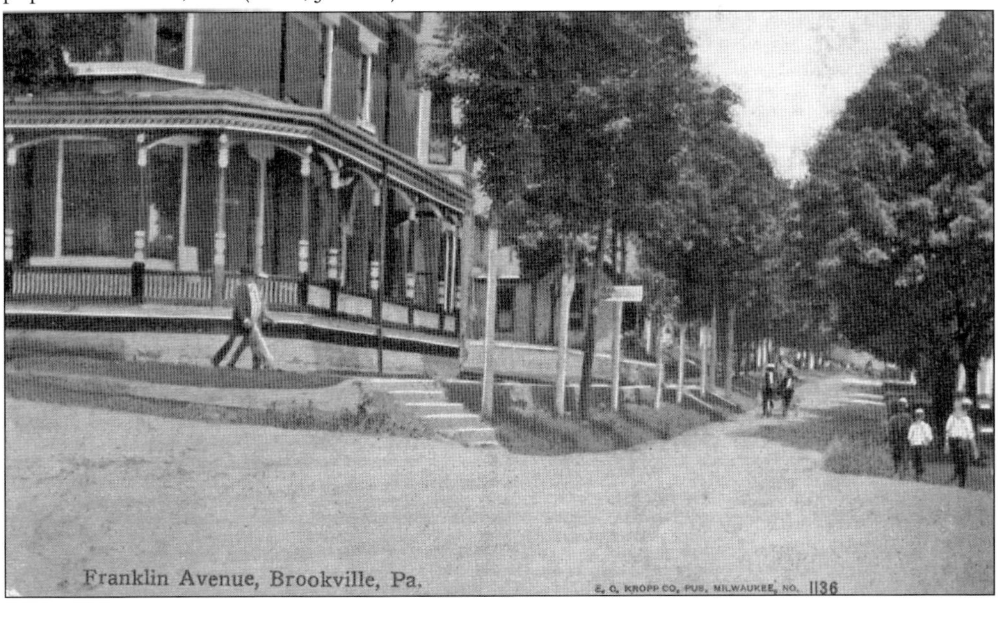

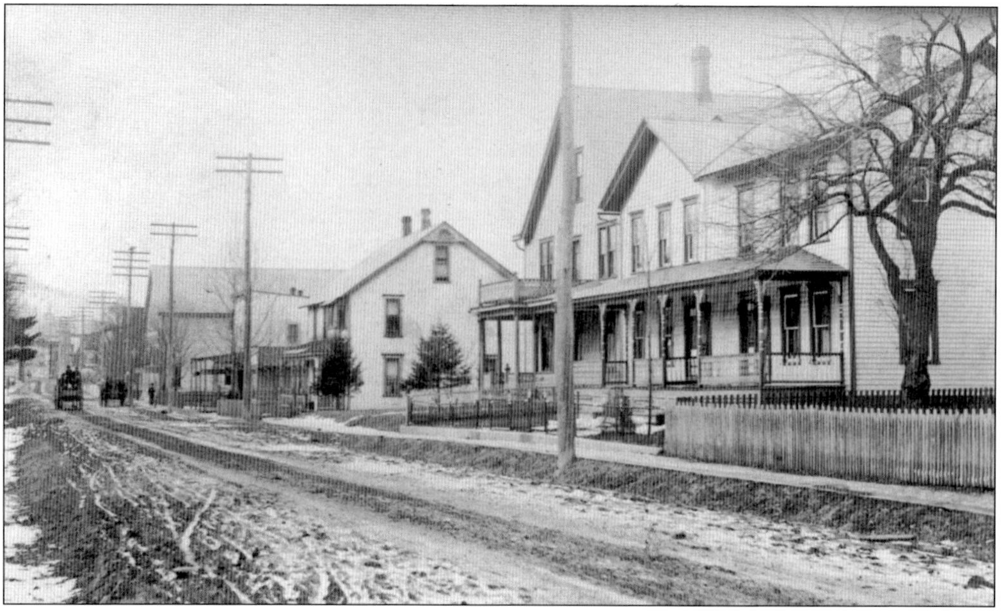

Paved with Shawmut bricks and cleared of snow, Brockway's Main Street (above) is lined with electric poles, dating the photograph to 1921 or some time later. In a view looking west from the south side of the intersection of Main Street and Eighth Avenue, the opera house, now Keith Brothers, is in the distance. The first of three houses was the site of Kester's Photographic Studio. Robert L. Warren built the white house (below) on the north side of Main Street in the early 1920s. The first president when Brockway Glass Company formed in 1933, Warren became board chairman in 1949. Wendell M. August lived in the brick house. He established a forge for making wrought iron and later became a pioneer in the decorative use of aluminum. He moved to Grove City in 1931 and founded the widely known Wendell August Forge. (Both, BAHS.)

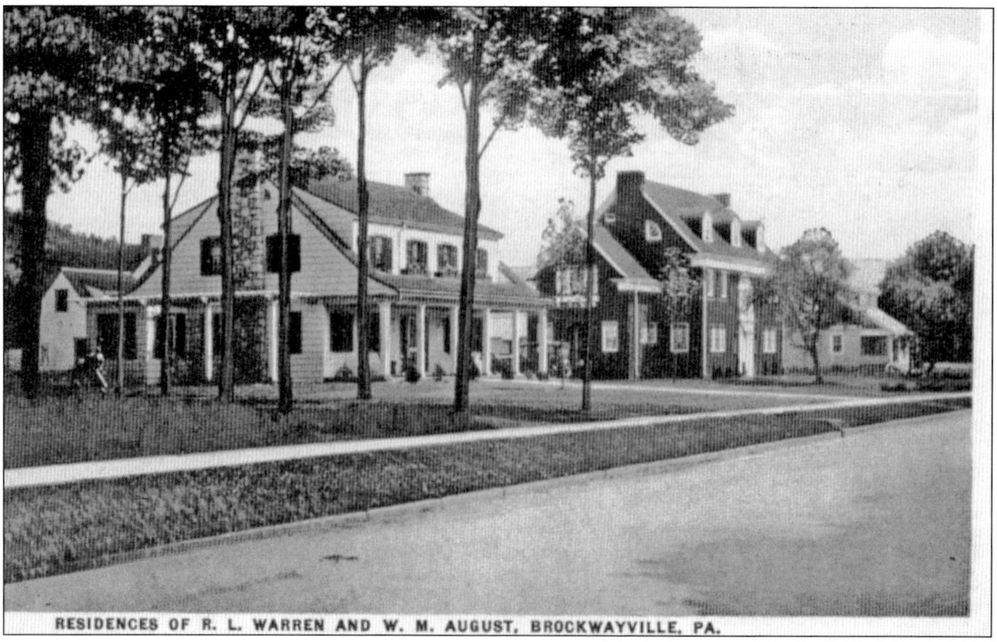

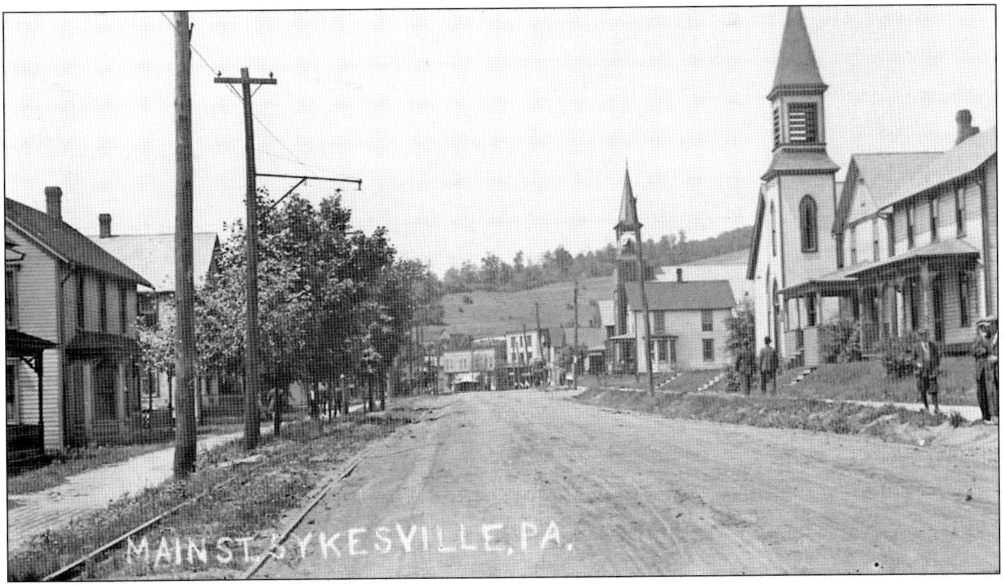

Jefferson County is home to smaller communities like Sykesville (incorporated 1907, population 1,127 in 2016), and Falls Creek (incorporated 1900, population 1,012 in 2016). Sykesville (above) was originally known as Shaffer Town, named for its first resident, Henry Shaffer. The first town council included Burgess J.E. Rishell, Pres. C.C. Gadd, and secretary A.L. Zimmerman, as well as Abraham Fye, Earl Long, I.Z. Swanson, and James Shaffer. The steeples above are of the Methodist (center) and Baptist (right) churches. The Smith Hotel, at the end of the street, has been demolished to make way for a new town square. Between 1914 and the early 1970s, the Gocella Stone and Sand Quarry (below) and the Jackson China Company in Falls Creek employed many people. Today, Jackson china is a sought-after collectible. (Above, RHS; below, JCHC.)

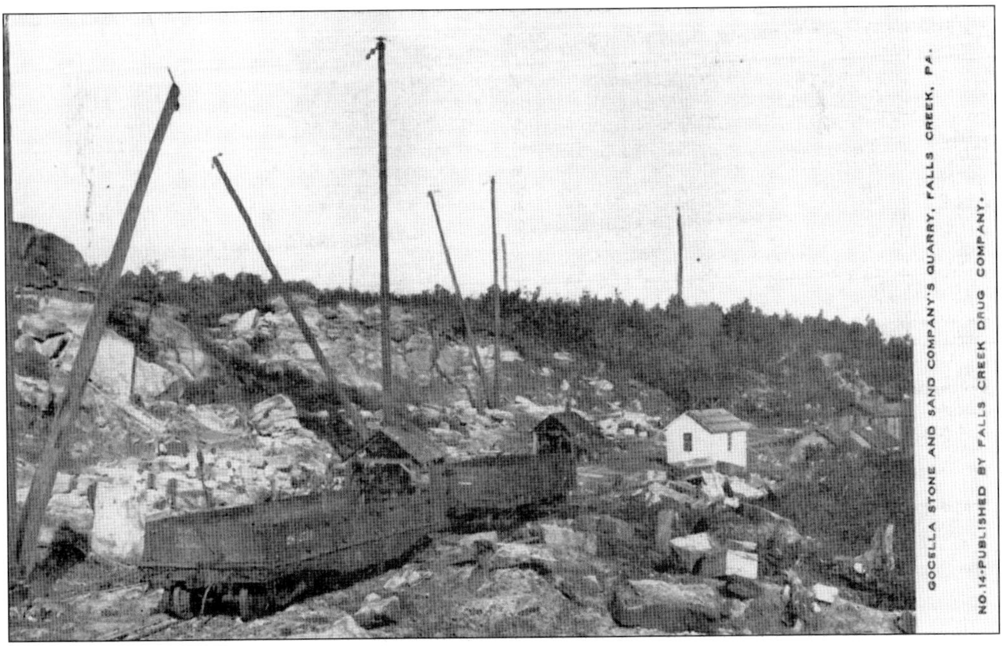

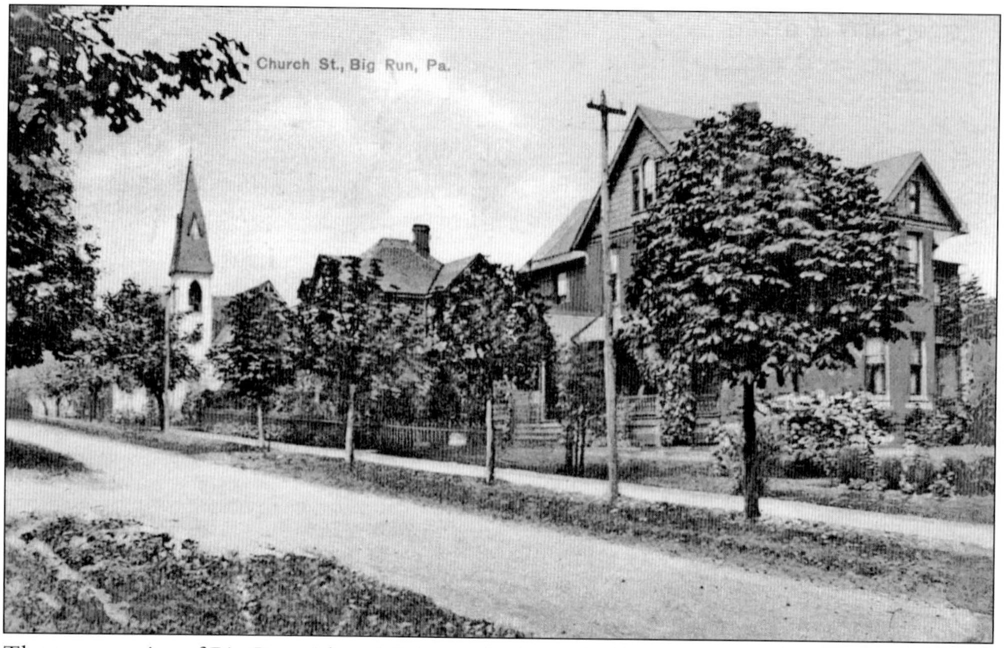

The community of Big Run (above) is located where Big Run enters Mahoning Creek in the south of the county. Incorporated in 1867, it was home to 608 people in 2016. The stately houses along this street were built for the families of William Irvin of the Big Run Tannery. The church is the Christian Church of Big Run. A greenhouse is located between the first two houses. Summerville (below), once known as Troy, was incorporated in 1887 and had a population of 514 in 2016. Purchased by the Glen-Gery Company in 1986, Summerville's Hanley Brick Company manufactured products that are featured in the Worldwide Plaza, Chrysler Building, and Mount Sinai Hospital in New York City and Washington Harbor in the nation's capital. (Above, PAHGS; below, JCHC.)

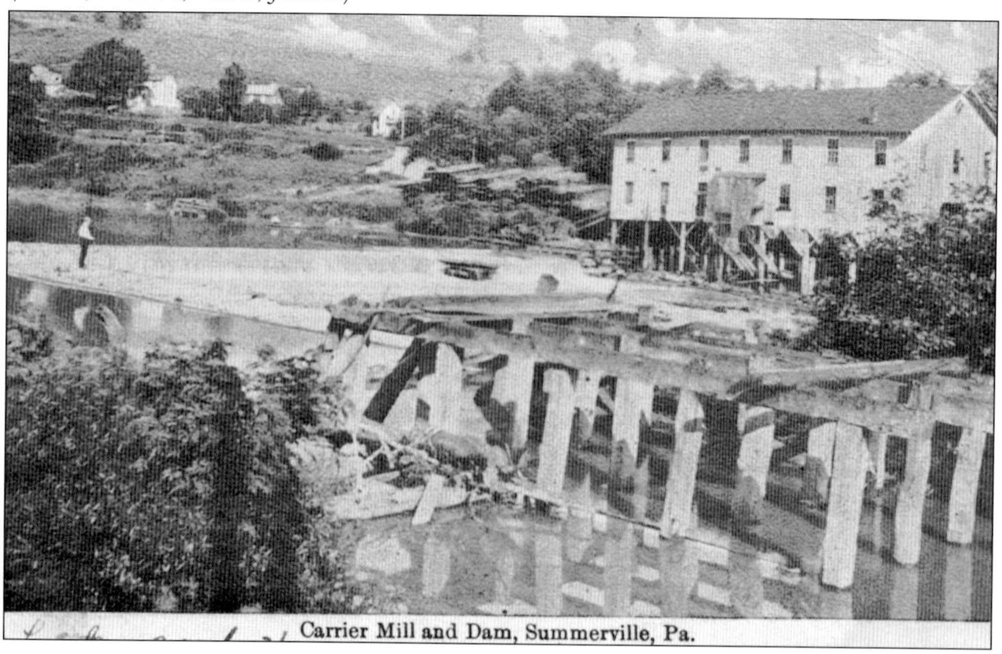

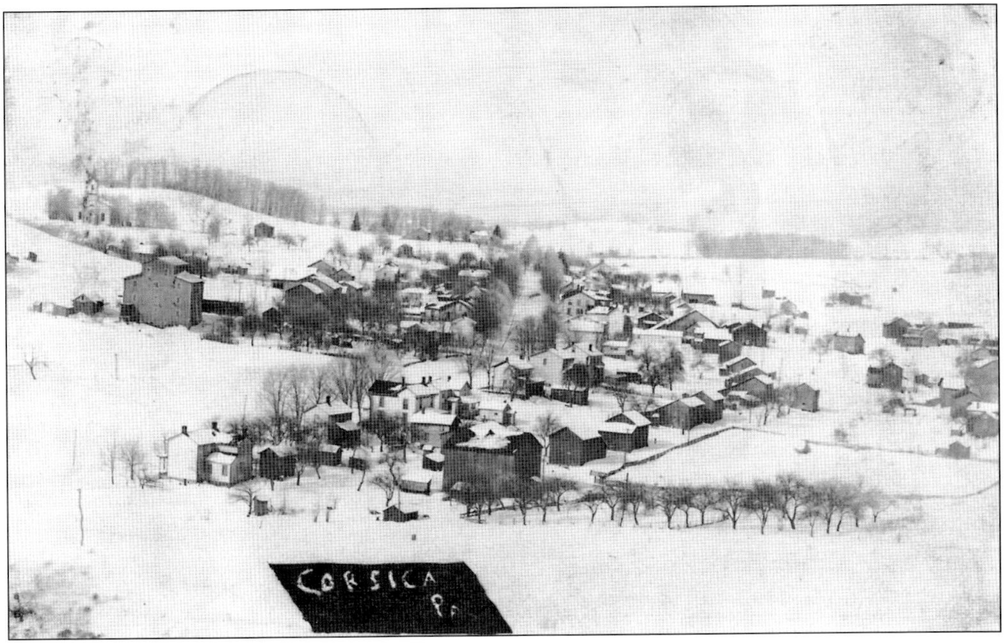

The town of Corsica (incorporated 1860, population 349 in 2016) lies seven miles west of Brookville along US 322. The steeple of the original Pisgah Presbyterian Church is to the left in the early-1900s postcard above. The building burned to the ground in 2003, and a new structure took its place. Today, the large building serves a congregation of about 150. Timblin (incorporated in 1922, population 153 in 2016) and Worthville (incorporated 1878, population 66 in 2016) are the two smallest municipalities in the county. Many of the unincorporated villages that exist within the 23 townships were once coal company towns, like Ramsaytown (below), pictured in 1912, when the population was more than 2,000. (Both, JCHC.)

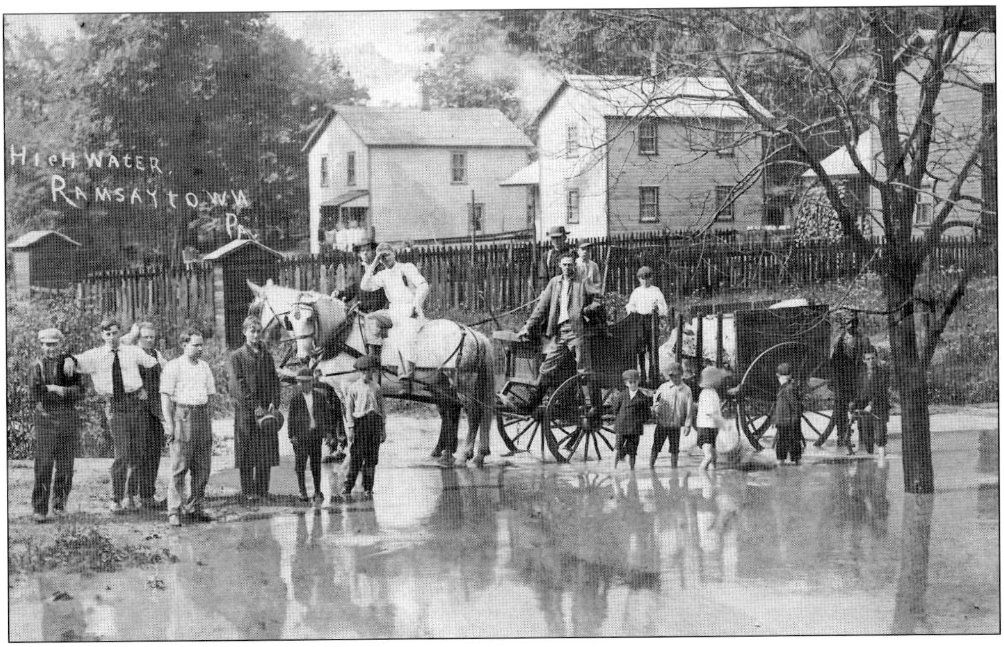

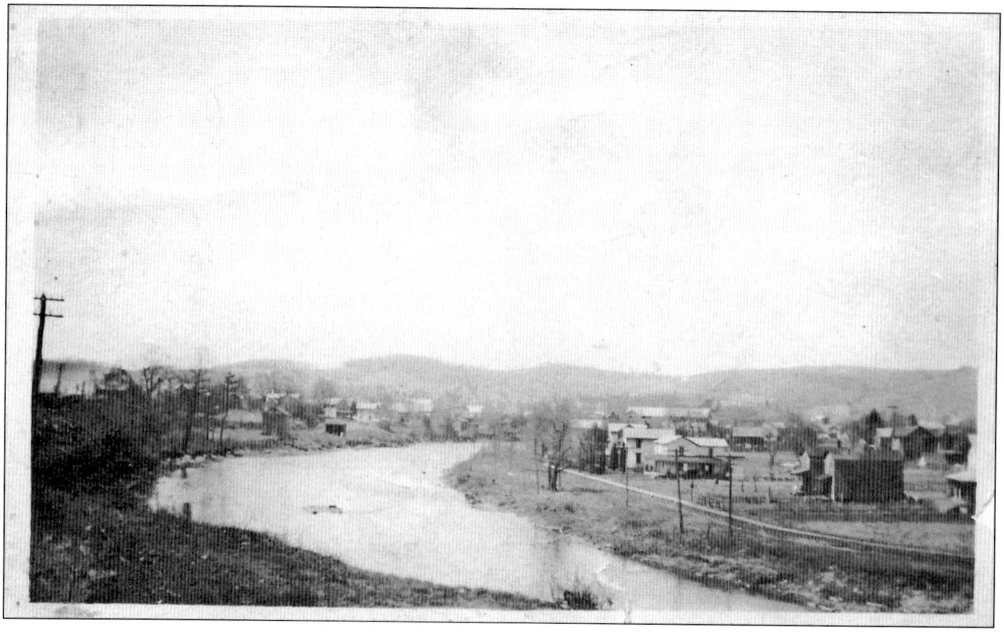

Baxter (above) is typical of many of the unincorporated villages of the county. Located on Red Bank Creek between Brookville and Summerville, Baxter was the site of logging and farming during the 19th century. The railroad replaced river traffic in 1874, and State Route 28, from Pittsburgh to Brockway, replaced the dirt road that wound beside the water, but nothing replaced timbering and farming. Like Baxter itself, the general store and railroad station (below) are typical of a bygone era. (Both, JCHC.)

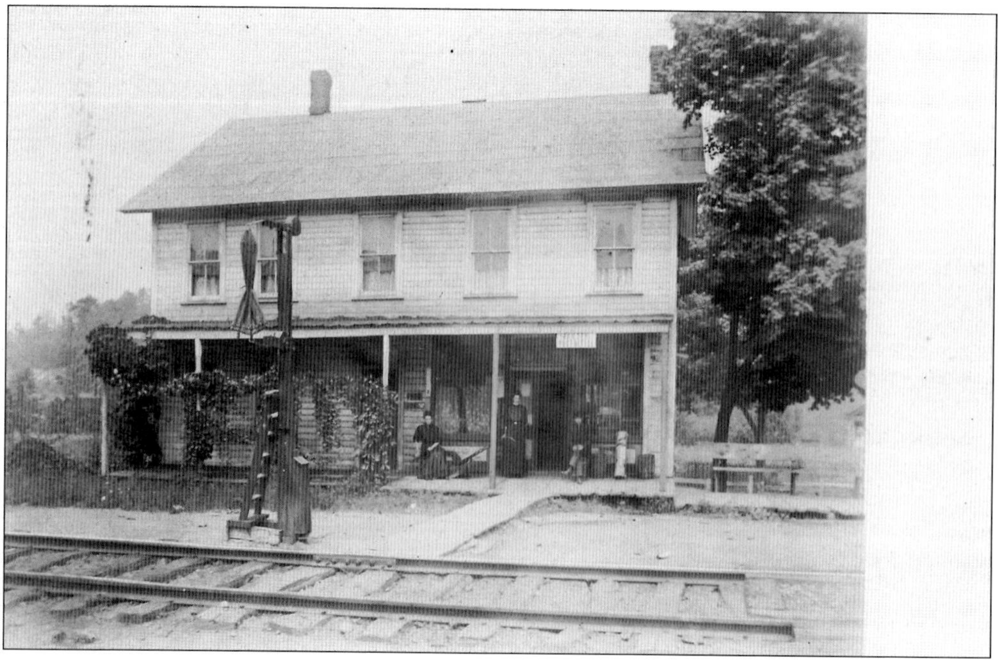

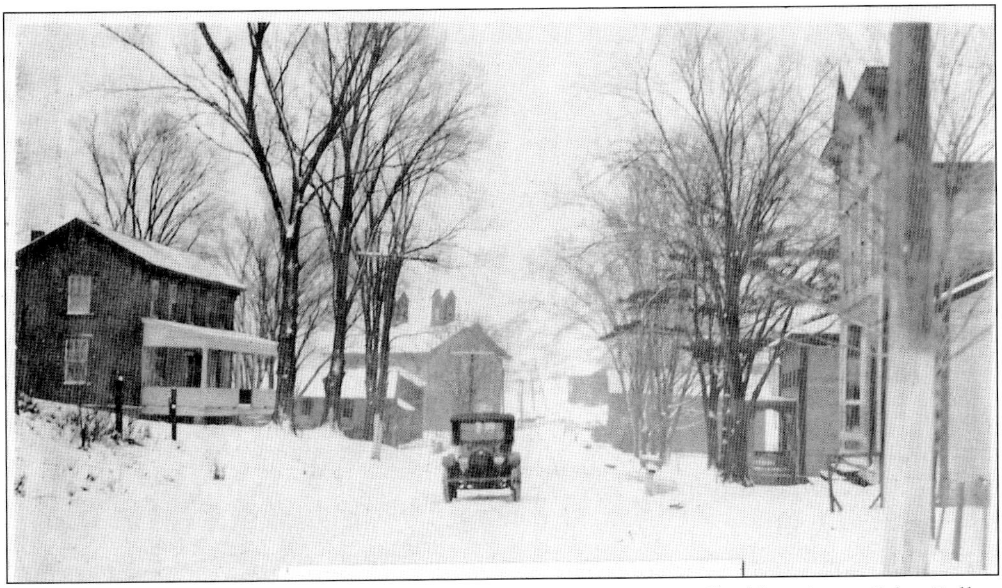

The first settler to clear the wilderness in what is now Prescottville (above) was John Fuller. He and his family arrived in 1824 and built a log cabin east of the Susquehanna & Waterford Turnpike. In 1857, Charles H. Prescott, of Maine, settled in what would become Prescottville, just outside of Reynoldsville. While difficult to imagine today, from 1860 to 1870, this area was the hub of industry and business activity. For many years, lumbering and the gristmill were the primary industries. The M.H. Stiles Grocery Store in Prescottville supplied local residents with all of their necessities. General stores of the time sold everything from groceries to plumbing supplies and were essential to the daily lives of rural citizens. J. Hiles (below) operated the store in later years. (Both, RHS.)

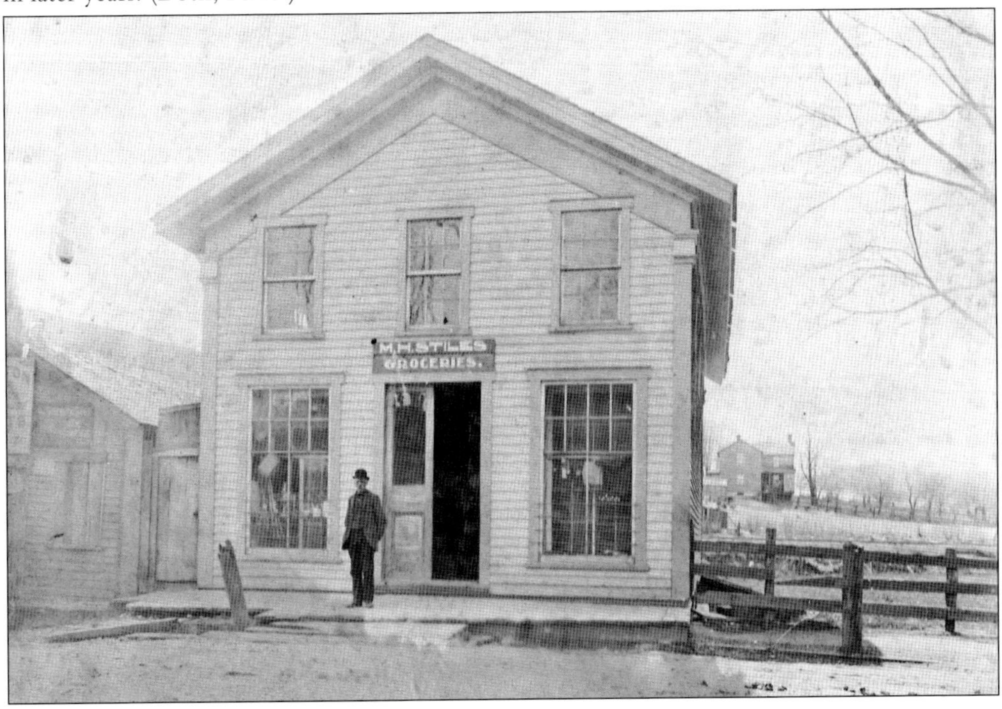

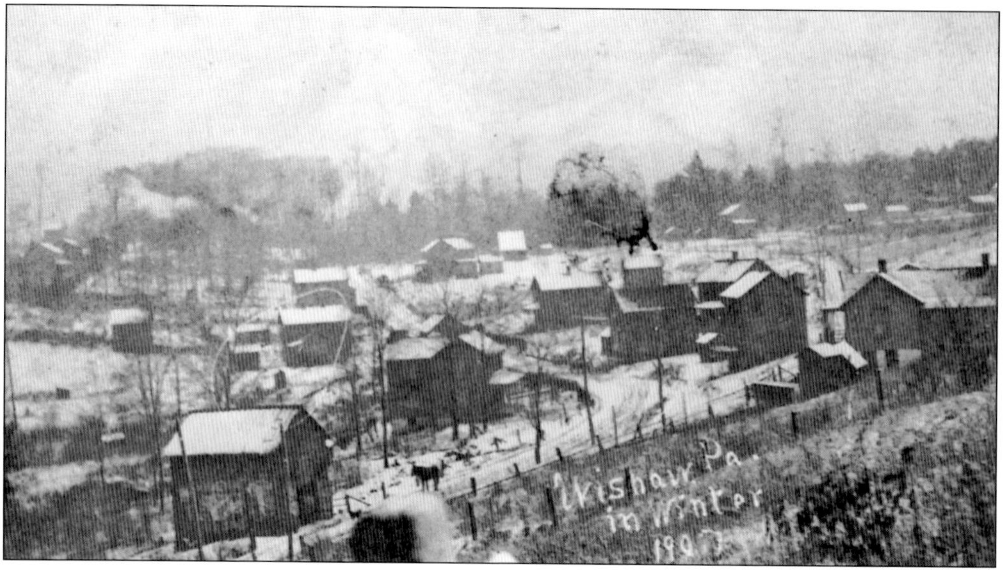

Adrian Iselin named Wishaw (above), known first as Trout Run, after employee W.I. Shaw when the Rochester & Pittsburgh Coal Company opened the first of seven mines there in 1901. When the mines opened, a second wave of immigrants from Italy joined the Scots Irish who had emigrated from Lanarkshire, Scotland. "The Blocks" (below) referred to the Italian section of the community, where families lived in four rows of double houses and shared a common water source. During the 1918 influenza pandemic, the close living quarters enabled the disease to spread rapidly. All but 10 of the 400 people living there contracted the disease, and 78 people died, nearly 10 percent of Wishaw's population. The Wishaw mine was one of the two largest bituminous coal mines in Pennsylvania. It closed about 1926. (Both, RHS.)

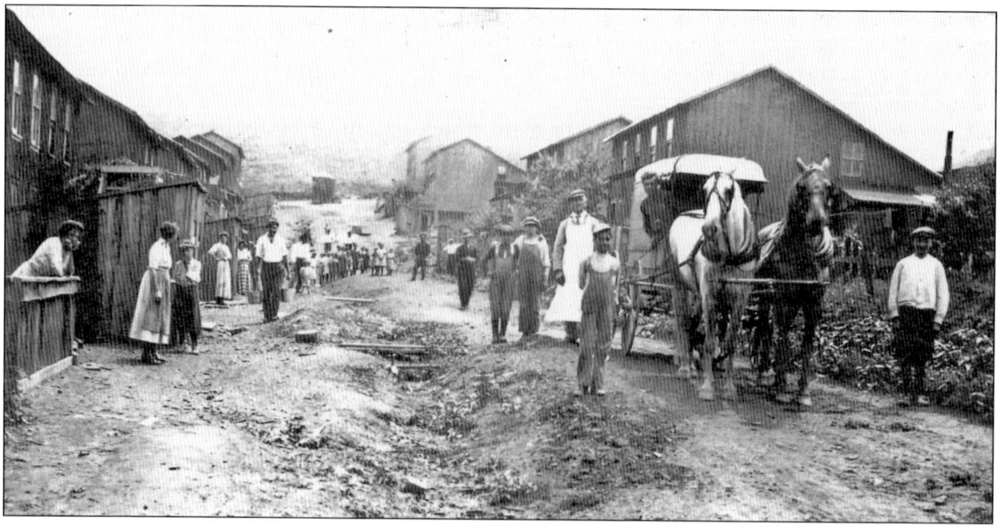

Three

Hotels and Shops

Travelers need food and rest, and so when Joseph Barnett and his family moved to Jefferson County in 1797, he kept an inn, built with Native American help. The appointed commissioners met there to determine the location of the new county seat, and many folks stayed there. To the south, in Punxsutawney, Dr. John W. Jenks built a home in 1818, and historian Kate M. Scott notes that "travelers from far and near made his house their stopping place."

In Brookville, even before 1830, when the first lots were surveyed, Joseph Eason had built a hotel named the Red Lion, where surveyors stayed while laying out the town. That same year, William Clark built a hotel on Jefferson Street. A third man arrived in 1830 and built a hotel on the corner of Main Street and Spring Alley. He named it the Globe, but as with many 19th-century hotels, ownership changed often, as did the name. It was the Jefferson House in 1904 when the owner razed the building and built a new Jefferson House.

At first, peddlers traveled through the county, but it did not take long for settlers named John Smith and Benjamin McCreight to set up general merchandising stores in Brookville. Other settlers did the same: Charles Barclay in Punxsutawney, Thomas Reynolds in Reynoldsville, and Robert Moorhead in Brockwayville. Stagecoaches and wagon trains delivered the goods needed and desired by the people.

Once stopping places for stagecoach travelers, hotels became even more important with the completion of the railroad in 1874. Around 1900, there were eight hotels in Brookville, nine in Punxsutawney, fourteen in Brockwayville, and at least six in Reynoldsville, all offering rooms to traveling salesmen, loggers who came for the weekend, and permanent residents.

As rail travel diminished and I-80 opened, hotels closed, and motels and bed-and-breakfasts began to appear. Retail stores closed, and people traveled to malls in Clarion, DuBois, and Indiana, Pennsylvania. Internet service arrived, and so did door-to-door delivery by UPS, FedEx, and the US Postal Service.

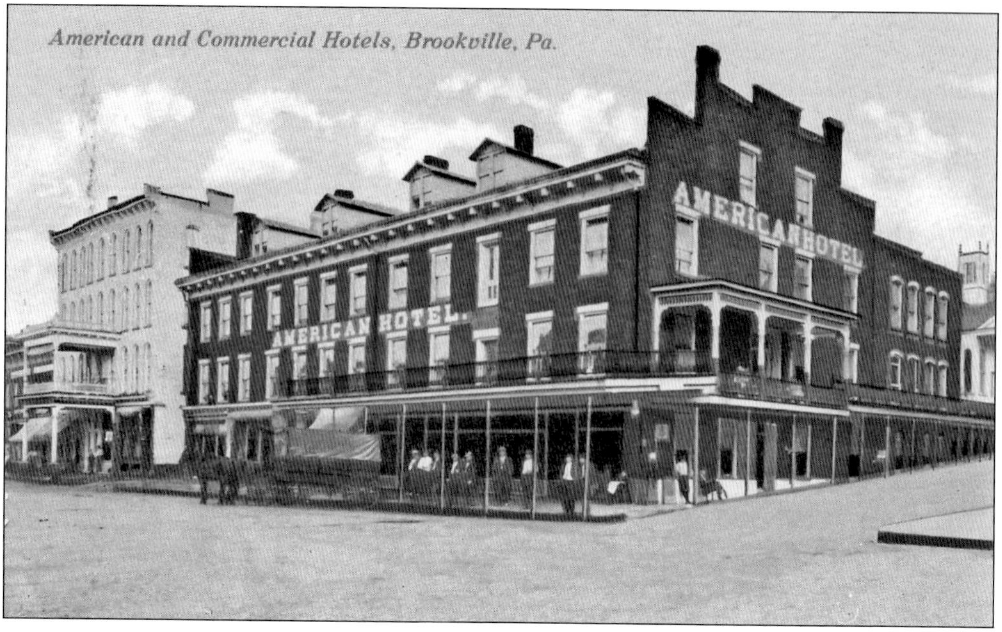

Located immediately west of the courthouse, the large American Hotel dominated Brookville's Main Street for more than a century. In 1856, fire destroyed the original hotel, built by Elijah Heath, and it was replaced by a large brick building (pictured above in 1910). This was demolished in the 1960s, and a service station occupied the lot until it was replaced by Brookville's Town Square, a project of Historic Brookville, Inc. Robert Clements replaced the earlier Royal Exchange Hotel with the Clements House in 1871 on property almost adjacent to the American Hotel. When new owners took possession in 1883, they renamed it the New Commercial Hotel (below), pictured after a 1911 snowstorm. Renovated as Brookville Title & Trust in 1921, it is now the S&T Bank. (Both, JCHC.)

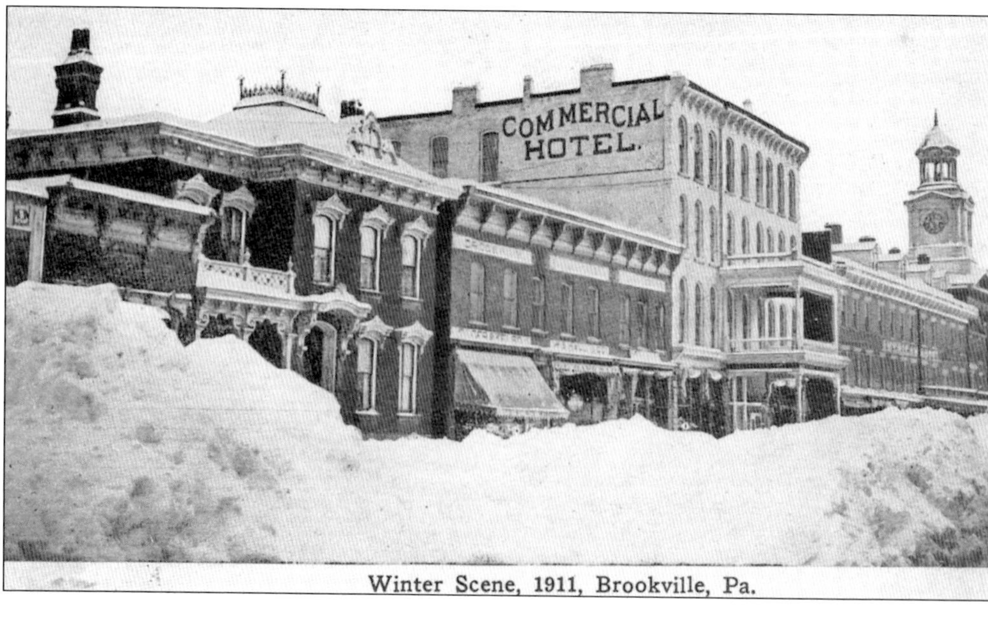

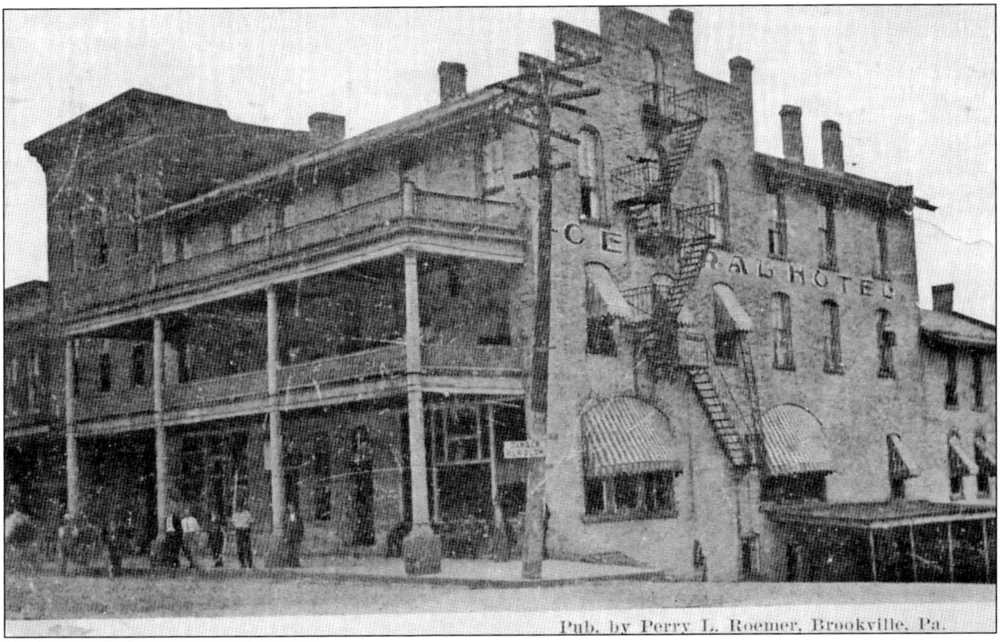

In Brookville, the Franklin House stood diagonally across from the courthouse from 1832 until destroyed in the big fire of 1874. Richard Arthurs bought the land and built the large Central Hotel (above), a four-story building that still stands. Andrew Logan moved to Brockwayville in 1885 and purchased the Railroad House. In September 1889, the *Brockwayville Record* reported that a fine new hotel was planned to accommodate the hotel traffic that came to town. In 1890, the original structure on the site was moved to the rear to make way for the new construction of the Logan House. Later, the original structure was demolished. Logan and his wife Rosanna Smith built, owned, and managed the Logan House for 26 years. The Logan House was known as the Penn-Way in 1935, when it was purchased by the Brockway Sportsman's Club. The top floors were removed in 1980. (Above, JCHC; below, BAHS.)

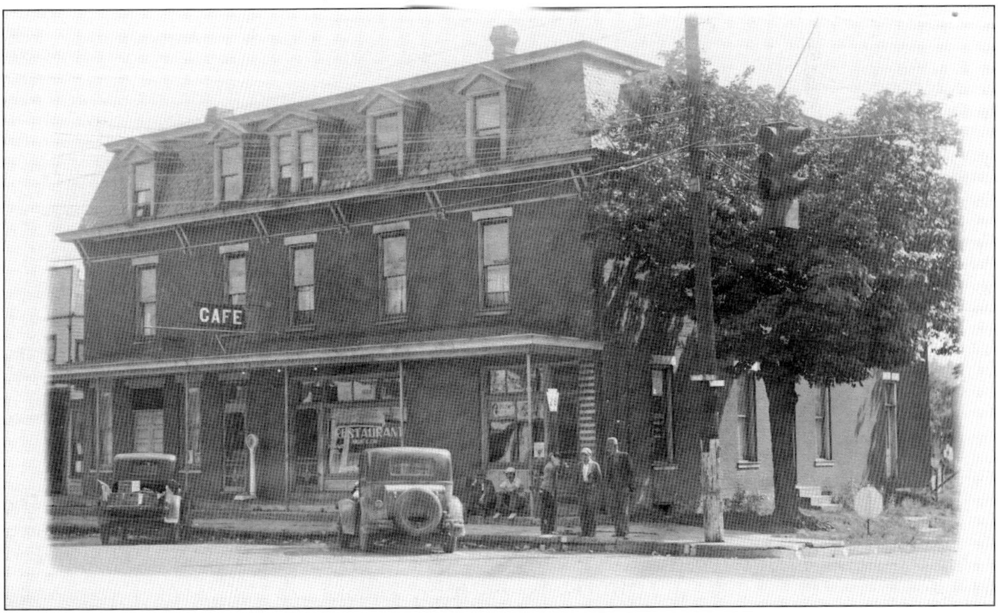

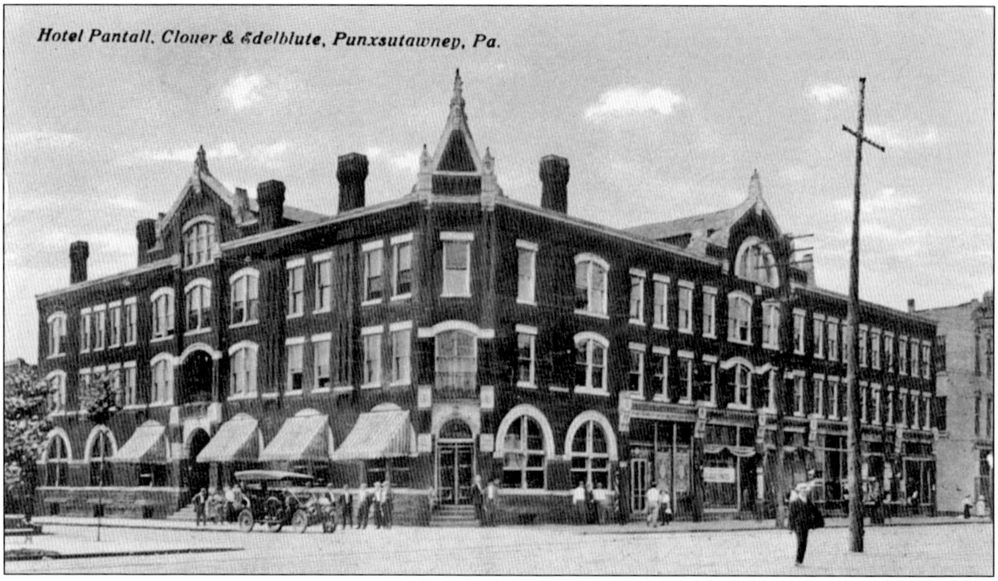

As Punxsutawney became commercially important, the town became a destination for business and industry executives from major cities in the eastern United States. Theophilus Pantall's magnificent hotel, opened in January 1889, contained over 100 rooms, four shops, dining and meeting facilities, and all modern conveniences. The 150-by-125-foot building (above), with cornices and windowsills of iron and stone, was deemed nearly fireproof for its time and felt to be the finest building in this part of Pennsylvania. The Hotel Belnap (below) was a premier destination in Reynoldsville for travelers and businessmen. Located at the corner of Fourth and Main Streets, it offered first-class accommodations as well as a billiard hall, restaurant and bar, and transportation to and from the train and trolley stations. In 1902, a room was $1 per day. (Above, PAHGS; below, RHS.)

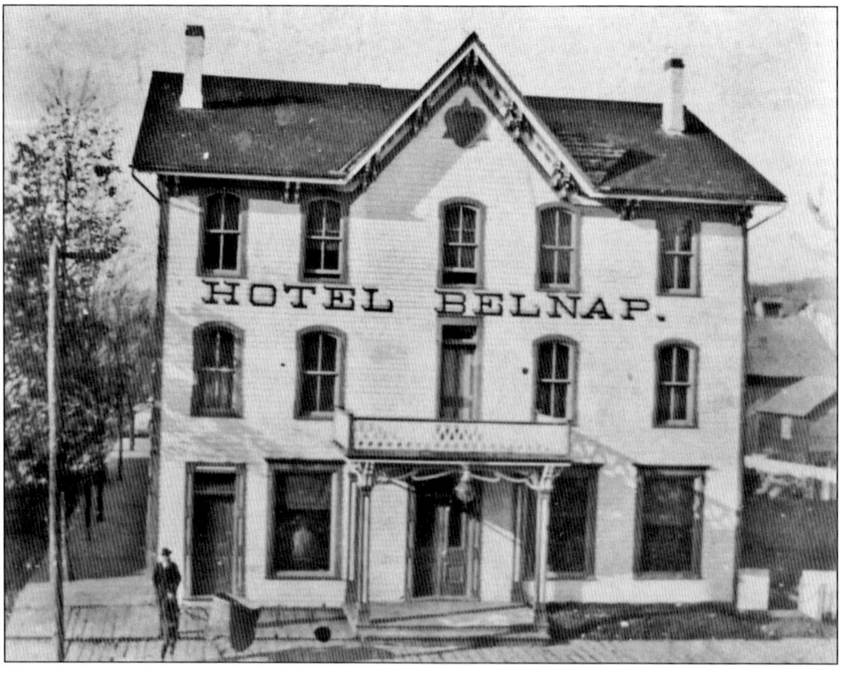

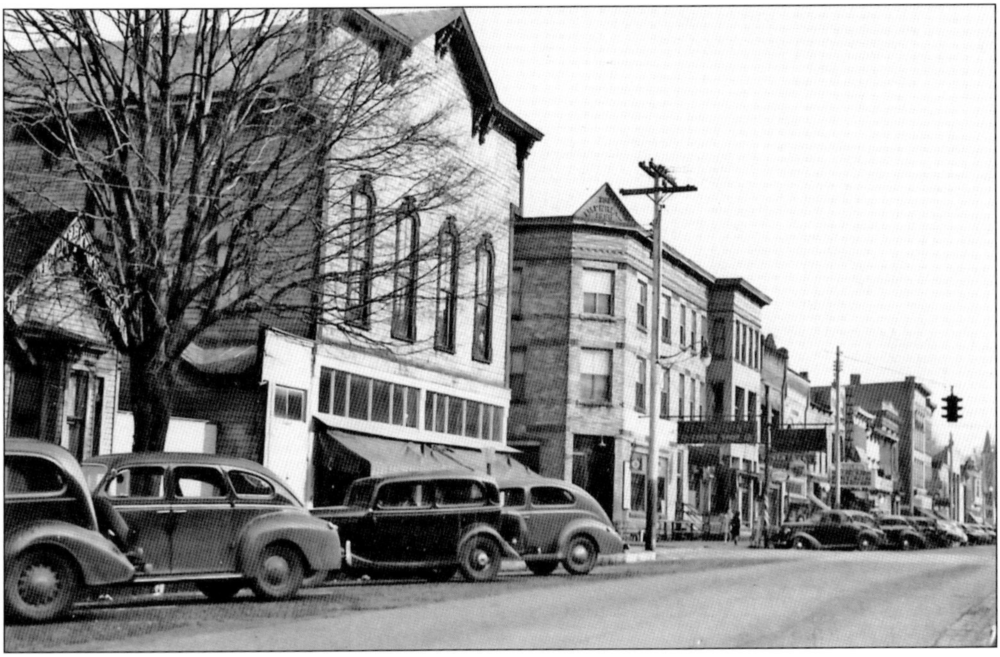

The 1876 Centennial Building (above, left) occupied the corner of Fourth and Main Streets in Reynoldsville, across from the Imperial Hotel. In 1901, the second-floor auditorium became the center of political turmoil when union leader Thomas Haggerty, Mary Harris "Mother" Jones, and striking Enterprise Silk Mill workers struggled for equal rights and equal pay. An early-1900s view of Brockway's Main Street (below) includes McLaughlin and Brothers blacksmith shop on the left and tracks leading to the West Clarion mines up the valley to the right. Cement replaced the board sidewalk, and the post office and Mengle Memorial Library replaced R.K. Morey's feed stable on the far right. Today, the busy intersection teems with buses heading to the Brockway Area District schools on North Street. (Above, RHS; below, BAHS.)

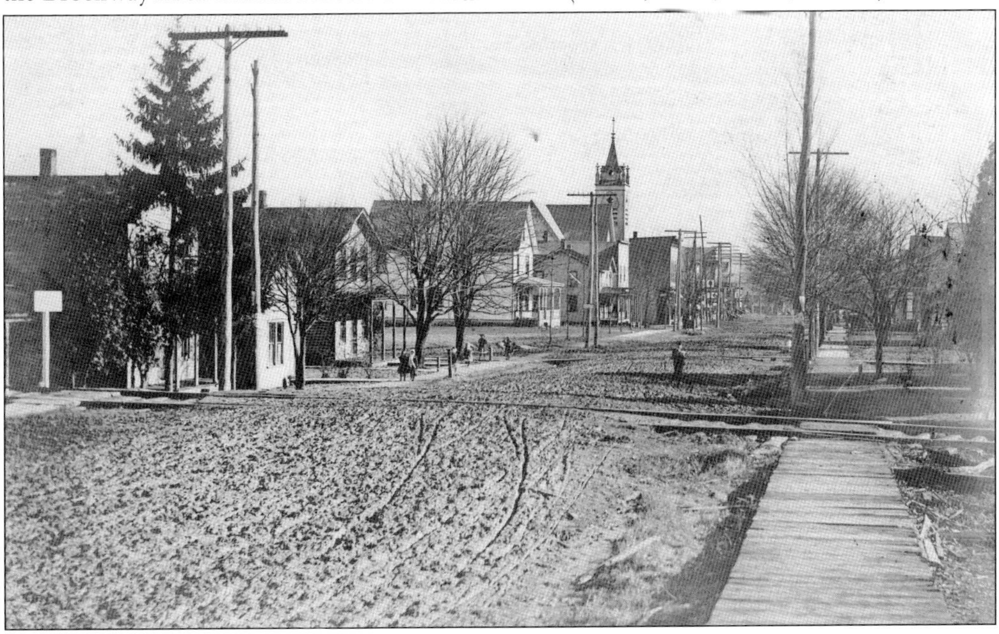

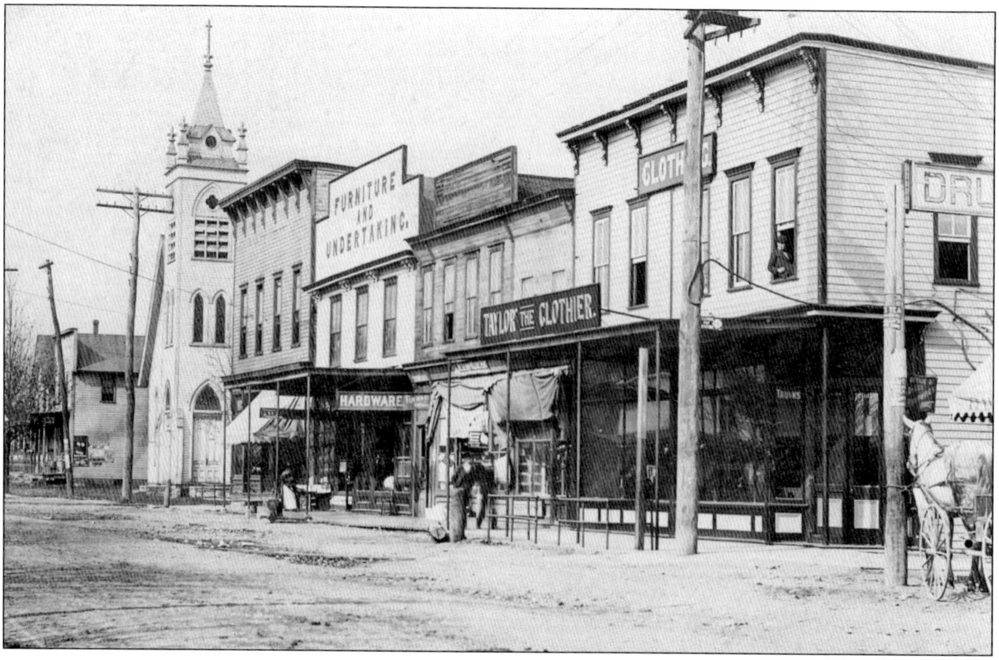

Pictured prior to the fire of March 24–25, 1910, the north side of Brockway's Main Street between Fourth and Fifth Avenues (above) included the Moorhead Methodist Church (which did not burn) and five structures that housed the Odd Fellows Hall, the *Brockwayville Record* office, Sayer's Barbershop and Bowling Alley, the People's Restaurant, a furniture and undertaking establishment, a hardware and tin shop, and Taylor, the Clothier, on the corner. A 1930s view (below) of the same block includes the Citizens Bank with its distinctive Ionic columns and the Beadle Building across Fifth Avenue. The Beadle Company was a small department store on the first floor. Professional offices and apartments were on the second and third floors. The extensive use of awnings reduced the sun's heat in buildings facing south. (Both, BAHS.)

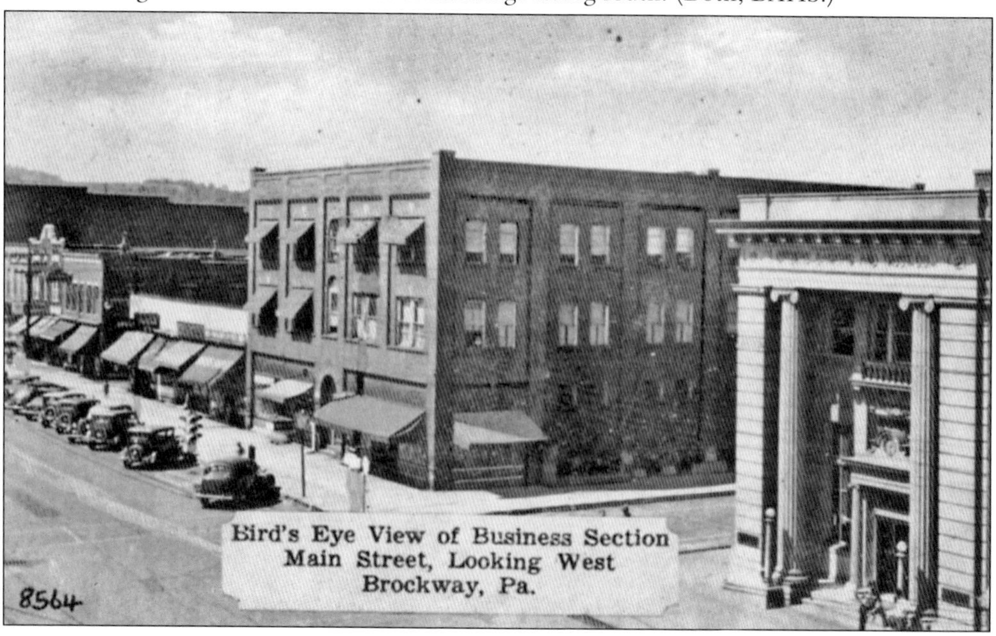

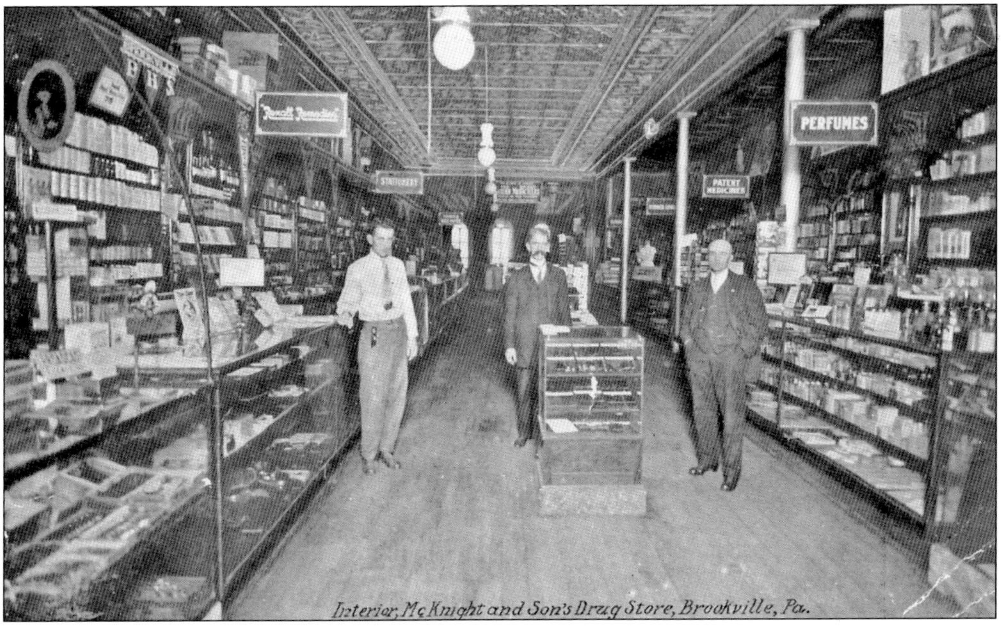

Physician, historian, coal investor, state senator, and entrepreneur describe just a few of the endeavors of Dr. William J. McKnight. He and his brother opened a drugstore in 1863 that unfortunately burned more than once. In 1871, they built the brick building (above) that today houses the Courthouse Café and Grill. Dr. McKnight died in 1917, after completing a two-volume history of the county. Amelia Melchoir married John Wilson Henderson in 1868, and she went into the millinery business. They eventually bought and lived in the building (below) that is now the Pennsylvania State Store on Brookville's Main Street. In 1920, W.L. McCracken wrote that she had "the distinction of having the oldest business concern now trading in town." (Both, JCHC.)

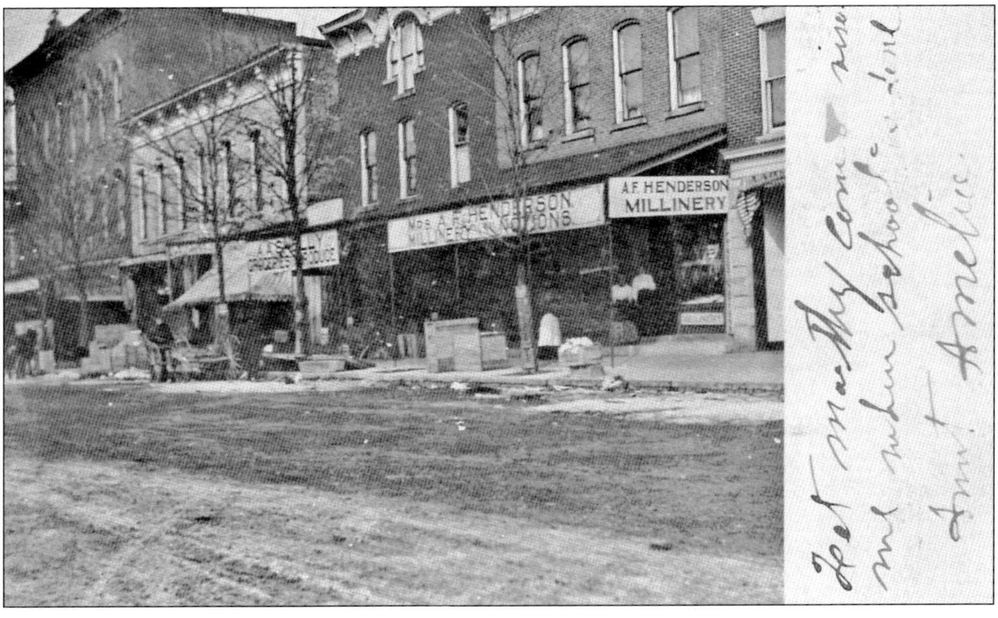

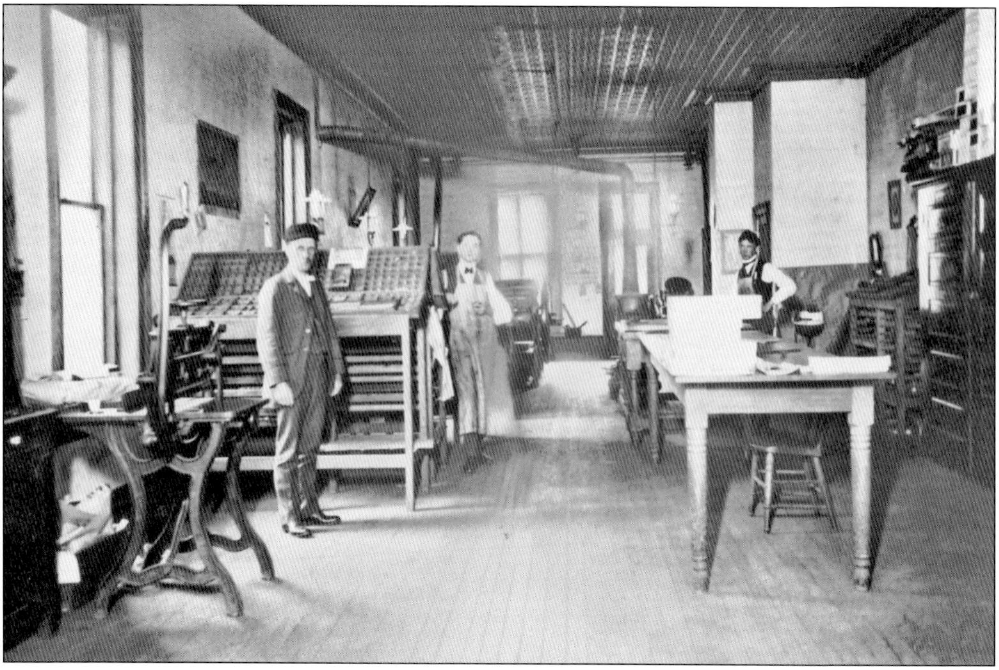

Newspapers and banks are important to community life. Reynoldsville received daily city papers by mail in the 1860s, but none were sold on the streets until the railroad arrived in 1873. The *Star*, first issued on May 11, 1892, changed to the *Reynoldsville Star* in 1942. The final issue was set to type in 1992 after the 100th anniversary issue was published. Brockway, Brookville, and Punxsutawney also had weekly papers. Barter worked for the early pioneers, but entrepreneurship after the Civil War made banks a necessity. About 1900, Brookville's Main Street had three banks in a row. By 1921, the Brockwayville Bank had become the First National Bank in a new building (below) at the southwest corner of Fifth Avenue and Main Street. During the Great Depression, several banks in the county failed. (Above, RHS; below, BAHS.)

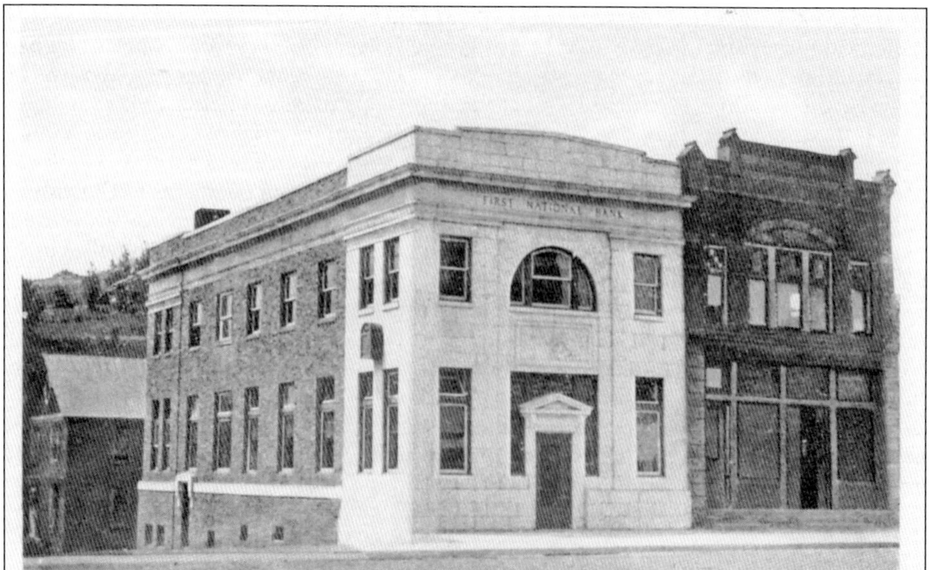

Four

Business and Industry

Before recorded history but verified by archeological evidence, Native Americans had trade routes running north-south and east-west across the area that became Jefferson County. Men of European descent traded goods for furs. The land on which Jefferson County is situated was purchased from the Native Americans as part of the "Last Purchase" of 1784. It became available to be deeded to speculators and settlers. The settlers harvested the timber, then created water-powered sawmills where they squared the timber which was rafted down the waterways to market, then floated it downriver to market. Others came and established gristmills and woolen mills. Millers and woodsmen needed tools. Blacksmiths set up shops. Where people established mills and shops, communities developed.

Cleared land became prime land for farmers, who could supply food and necessities for others. Creeks were used as public highways, residents made them navigable farther upstream, and industry expanded. For nine decades, lumber was a major industry.

Geological surveys published by the commonwealth in the mid-1800s revealed more natural resources in the county. Encouraged by this knowledge, residents reached out to investors to underwrite the building of railroads. Coal mining brought untold riches to landowners and financiers. Lasting six decades, this was the most significant industrial and economic boom ever experienced in Jefferson County. Natural gas, another local resource, was harnessed in the 1890s and brought in manufacturing, including the glass industry, which continues to flourish.

Strip mining increased during World War II to supply much-needed coal for the war effort. The Cameron Manufacturing Corporation in Reynoldsville and Sylvania in Brookville employed women to make vacuum tubes and other needed equipment.

Since the 1950s, many factors have had a depressing effect on the county's economy. However, some industries have continued and new industries have developed. Second-growth hardwoods have revived the timber industry, and the completion of Interstate 80 supports economic development. Light manufacturing, tourism, health care, and education continue to employ many.

The quaint and rural nature of Jefferson County's communities and the hospitality of its people make it a haven for tourism, a welcoming place where telecommuters live and work, and an affordable place in which to retire.

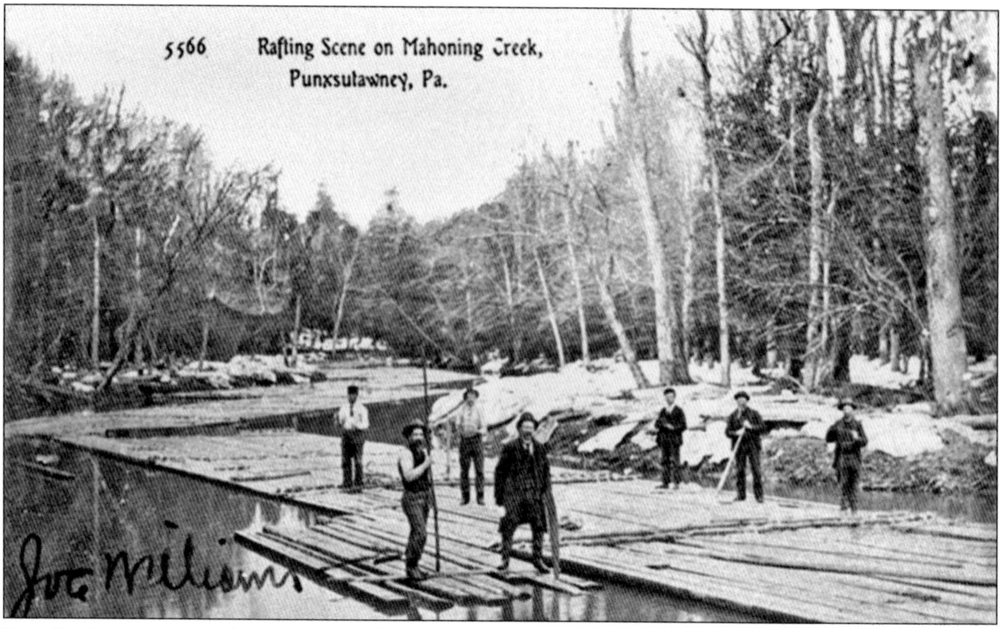

Lumbering was a major industry throughout the county in the 1800s. Square timber rafts, pictured near Kremkau's Dam at Cloe, near Punxsutawney, transported lumber in 1898 by way of Mahoning Creek, a designated public highway since 1808, to the Allegheny River and markets in Pittsburgh and Cincinnati. The clear-cutting of timber opened land for farming and the development of industry. Although the Honorable Albert Cole Hopkins of Lock Haven was a member of the Fifty-Second as well as the Fifty-Third US Congress, his true calling was timber. He purchased the interests of Carrier and Scott in 1881. The mill, two miles below Reynoldsville on the Sandy Lick, employed over 100 men and was known locally as the Hopkins Big Mill. When timber vanished, the town of Hopkins faded away. (Above, PAHGS; below, RHS.)

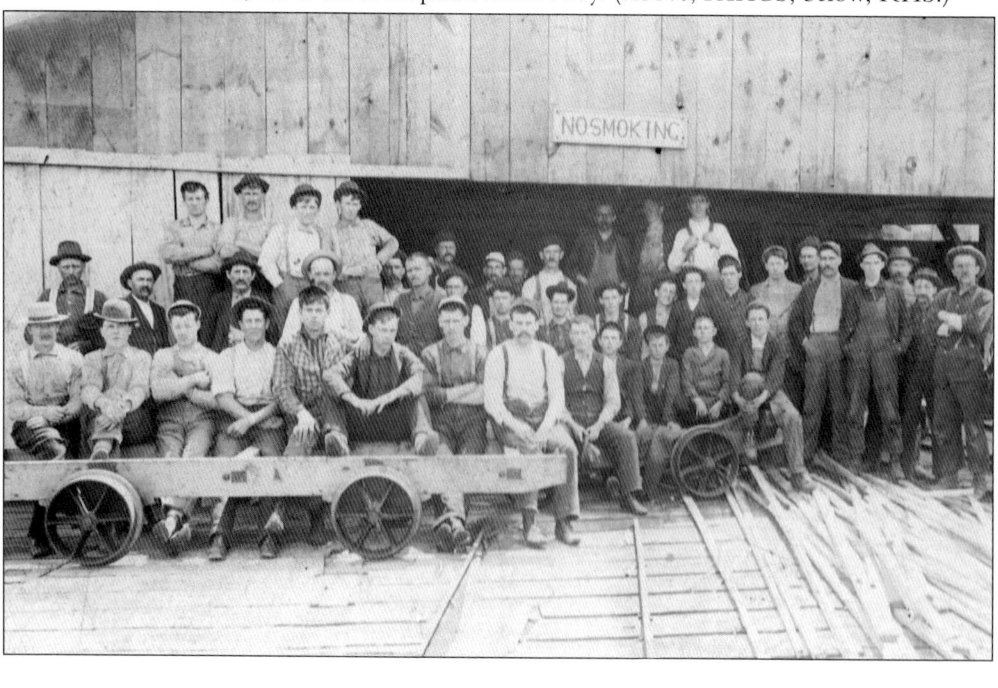

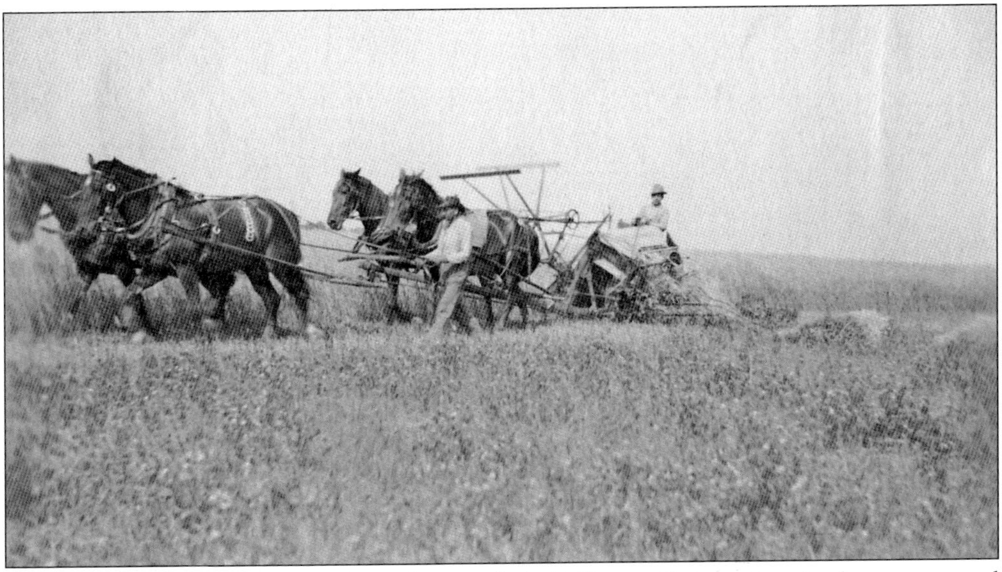

Forestry and farming developed simultaneously in Jefferson County, but the latter surpassed forestry by the last part of the 19th century. Winslow Township and the areas immediately surrounding Reynoldsville Borough were prime locations for agriculture. Farmers raised grains of all kinds, potatoes, and corn, as well as all forms of livestock. Orchards of apples, cherries, and pears were also plentiful in the area, and many of the groves are still visible today. Many families ran small subsistence farms while engaged in other occupations, resulting in their working from morning until late into the night to meet all of the obligations of daily life. During the Great Depression, small farms like these made it possible for many families to survive the economic hardships by sharing the bounty of the land with their neighbors. (Both, RHS.)

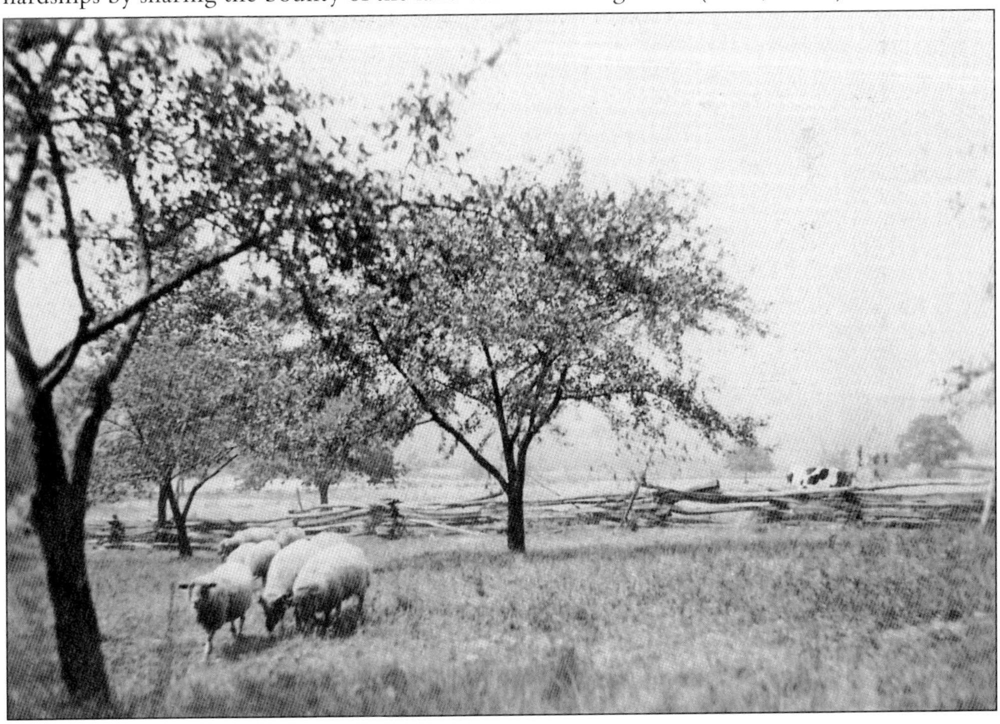

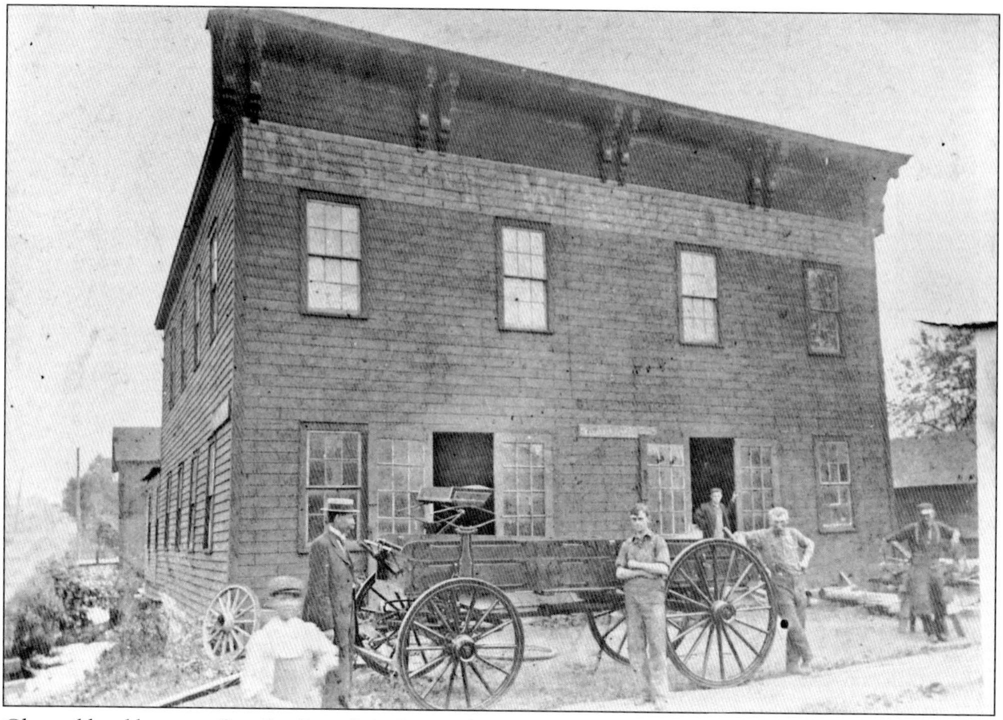

Cleared land became farmland, and timber and grain needed transport. Jacob and Henry Christian Deible owned and operated the Deible Wagon Works (above), founded in 1875, where they manufactured a complete line of carriages, sleighs, and wagons, including a lumber wagon of their own patent. They also managed a blacksmith shop. The first floor housed the blacksmith forge, horseshoeing shop, and woodworking machines. Wagons were rolled up an outside ramp to the second floor for painting. Thomas S. and S.M. McCreight built the Soldier Run Flouring Mill (below) in 1877. Designed by Jerry Myers, it had a capacity of 500 bushels of grain per day and operated on waterpower or steam according to the season. Its size, equipment, capacity, and quality of production placed it among the best in western Pennsylvania. (Both, RHS.)

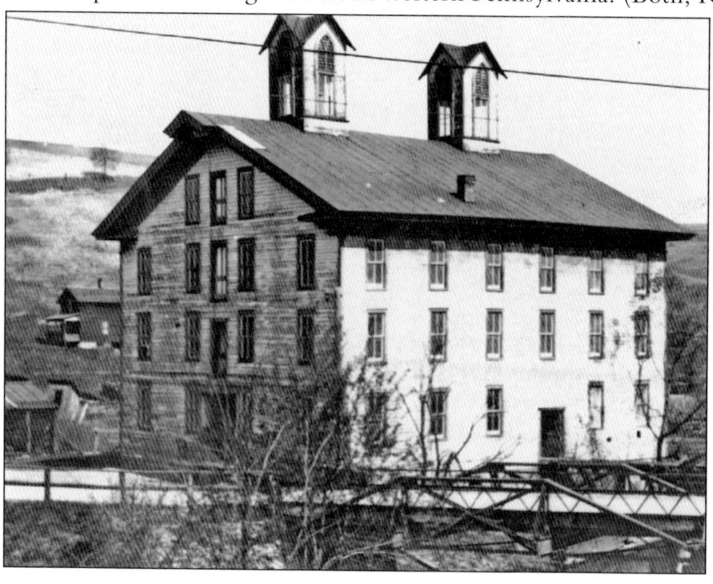

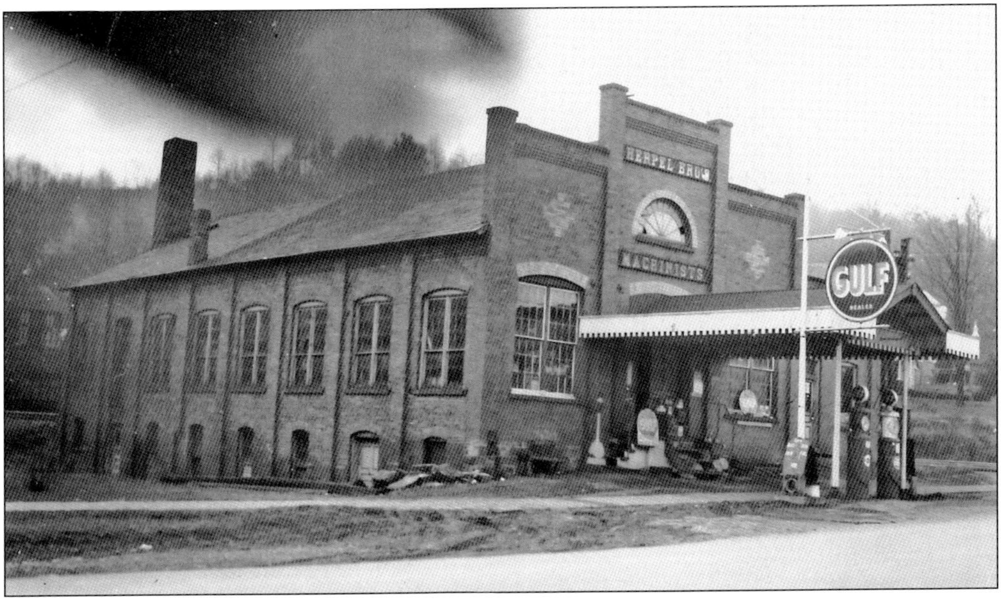

In 1878, D.J. Crowell built a machine shop and foundry (above) in Reynoldsville, where he manufactured heating stoves, mining machinery, steam engines, and coal cars. Its location next to the railroad made it convenient for heavy metal work. The building was later owned by the Herpel brothers. Over the years, the structure has served many purposes, including a gas station. Today, it is the home of the Jefferson County Area Agency on Aging. Ice production was an important industry in the years before electric refrigerators. The Hoffman Ice Company in Reynoldsville (below) cut huge blocks of ice from a pond just east of town, then stored it in large buildings where it was packed in sawdust to keep it from melting. During the summer months, wagons hauled the blocks of ice door-to-door. (Both, RHS.)

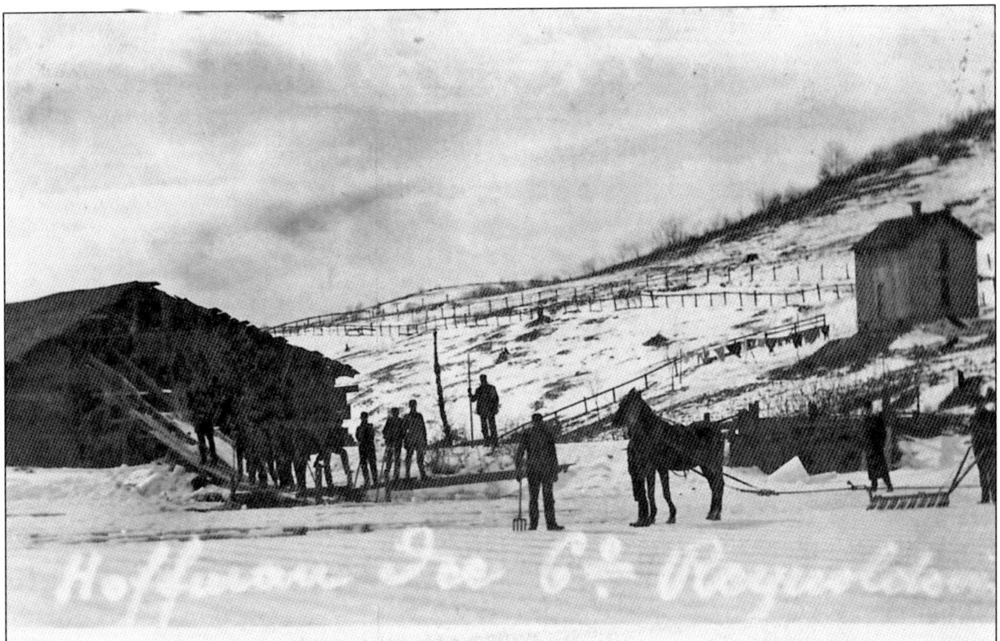

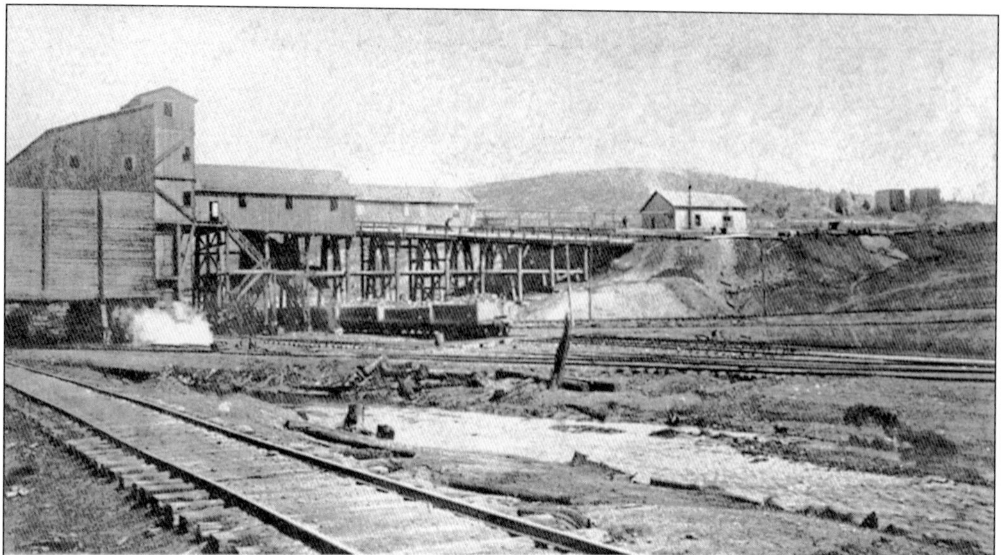

Tipple at Adrian Mines, near Punxsutawney, Pa.

Between 1887 and 1949, the Buffalo, Rochester & Pittsburgh Railroad Company, owned by Adrian Iselin, operated the Adrian Mines (above), the second industrial mine in the Punxsutawney area. Built as a modern model mining community, it set the standard for all of the company's mines developed in Jefferson, Clearfield, Indiana, and Armstrong Counties. Adrian Mine's post office was named Delancey in honor of Adrian Iselin's grandson. The Elk Run Shaft (below), part of the Adrian Mines, was 14 by 28 feet and 160 feet deep. Constructed by Hans Olson, the shaft was completed in nine months and was fully timbered and partitioned into three divisions: one for hoisting coal, one for pumping out water, and one for air to be driven into the mines. (Both, PAHGS.)

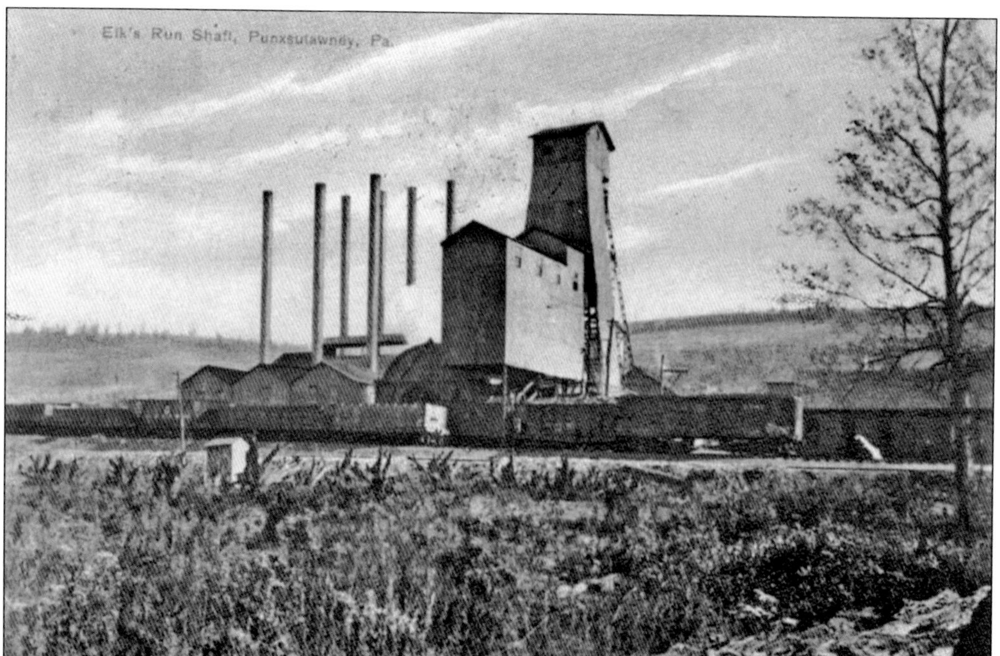

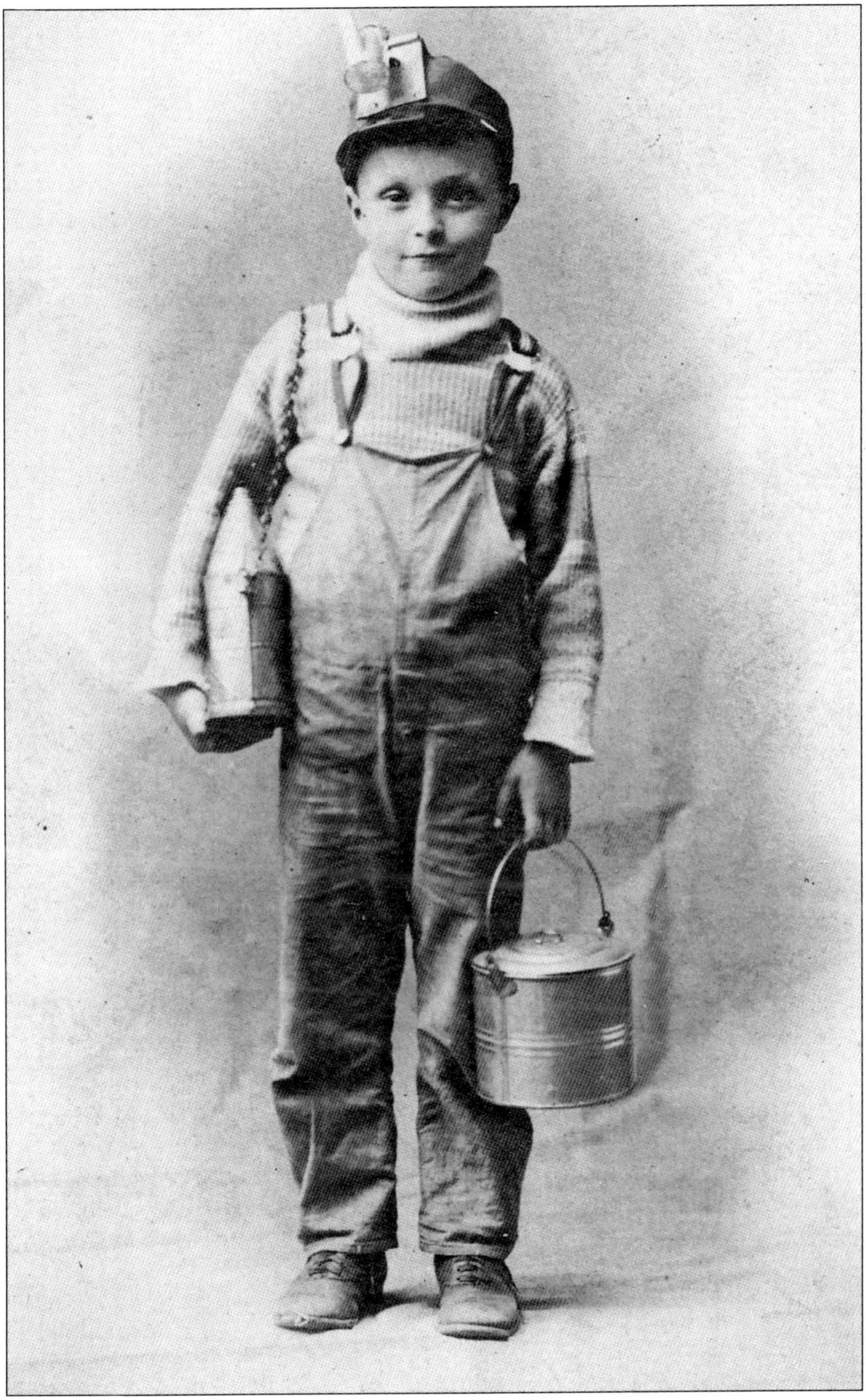

Many small boys, like Ted Burns, followed their fathers into the mines. It was common practice for miners to instruct their sons in the methods of extracting coal. Whether it was removing shale in the breakers or negotiating small tunnels, their jobs were demanding, often involving 10-hour shifts. The Keating-Owen Child Labor Act of 1916 put an end to most, but not all, of this activity. (RHS.)

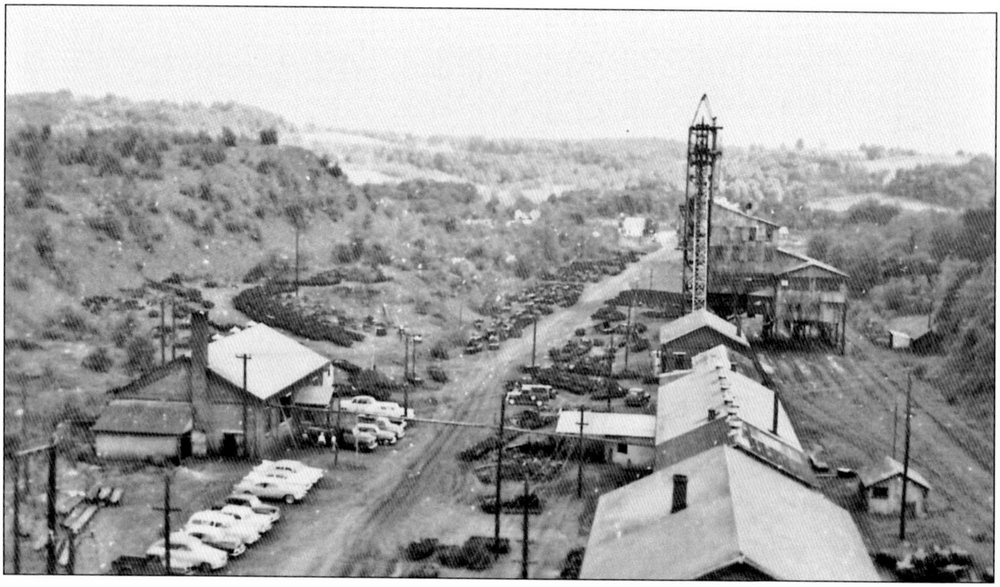

Construction on the Northwestern Mining & Exchange Company's mine at Kramer began in 1922. The mine was engineered and designed with safety in mind, and every consideration was taken to make it one of the most modern and efficient operations possible. In spite of an outstanding safety record of more than a million and a half man-work hours without an accident, two explosions took the lives of nine men on March 31, 1937. Between 1922 and 1959, the Kramer Mine (below), at the village of Stump Creek in Henderson Township, employed over 1,600 people, making it the largest employer in the history of the township. The Upper Freeport coal ranged in thickness from one to six feet. Kramer was a modern deep-shaft mine that used electricity to power the operations. (Above, RHS; below, PAHGS.)

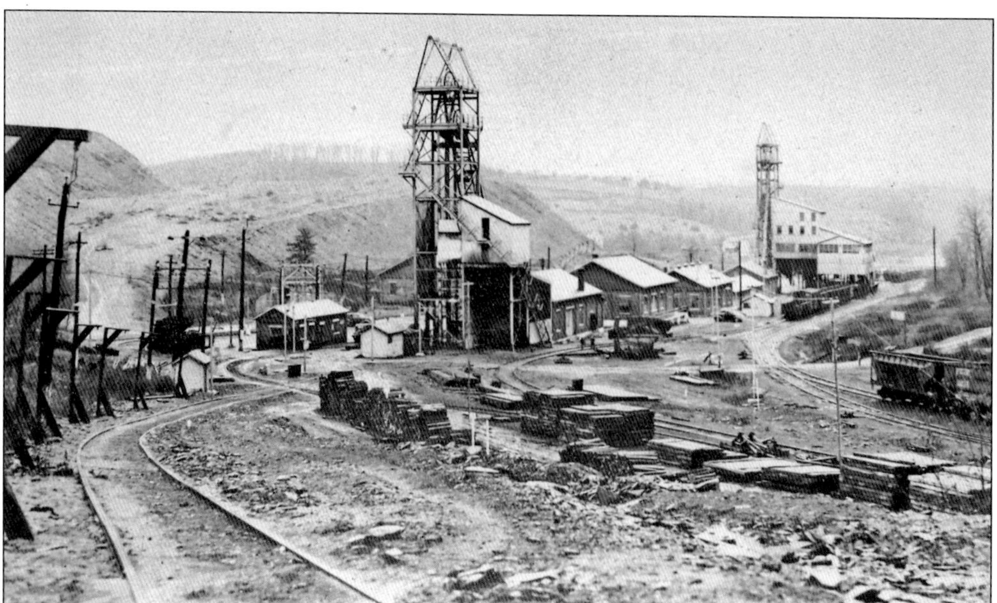

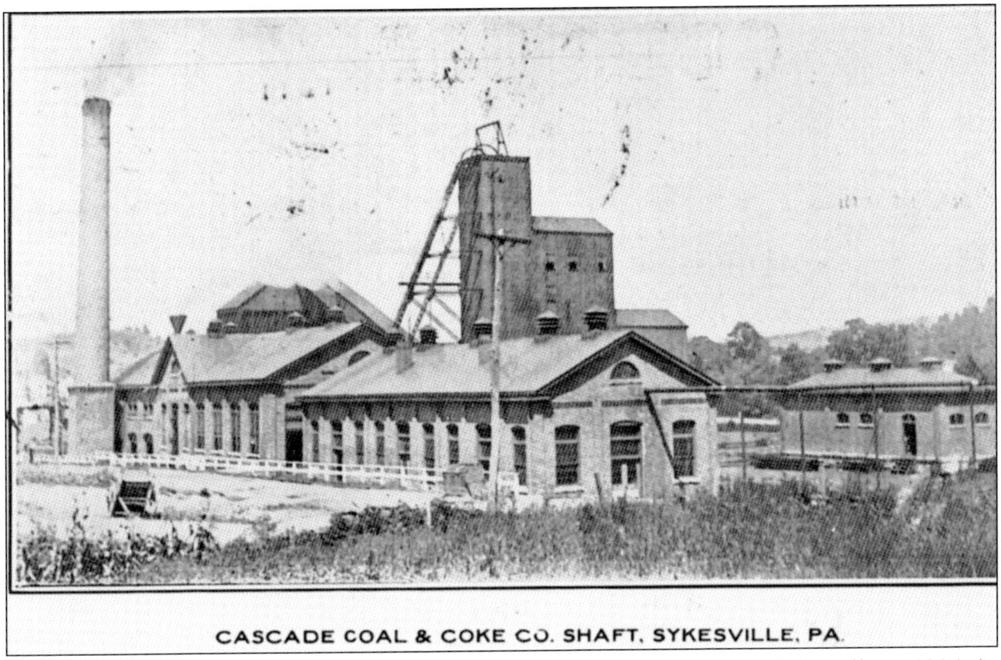

The Powhattan Coal & Coke Company (above) opened a new mine at Sykesville in 1904, in an area known throughout world markets as one of the region's best coal pockets. Under new management in 1905, the name changed to the Cascade Coal & Coke Company. Most of the output was used to manufacture coke at the company's huge coke plant nearby. At the peak of its production, 500 men were on the payroll, undoubtedly the largest industry in Sykesville. On July 15, 1911, a devastating accident tragically took the lives of 21 miners. The funeral procession through Sykesville was a solemn event. Surrounded by rock faults on all sides, the original pocket of coal embraced some 10 billion tons and was eventually worked out and abandoned in 1939. Many of the miners were able to find work in neighboring coal mines. (Both, RHS.)

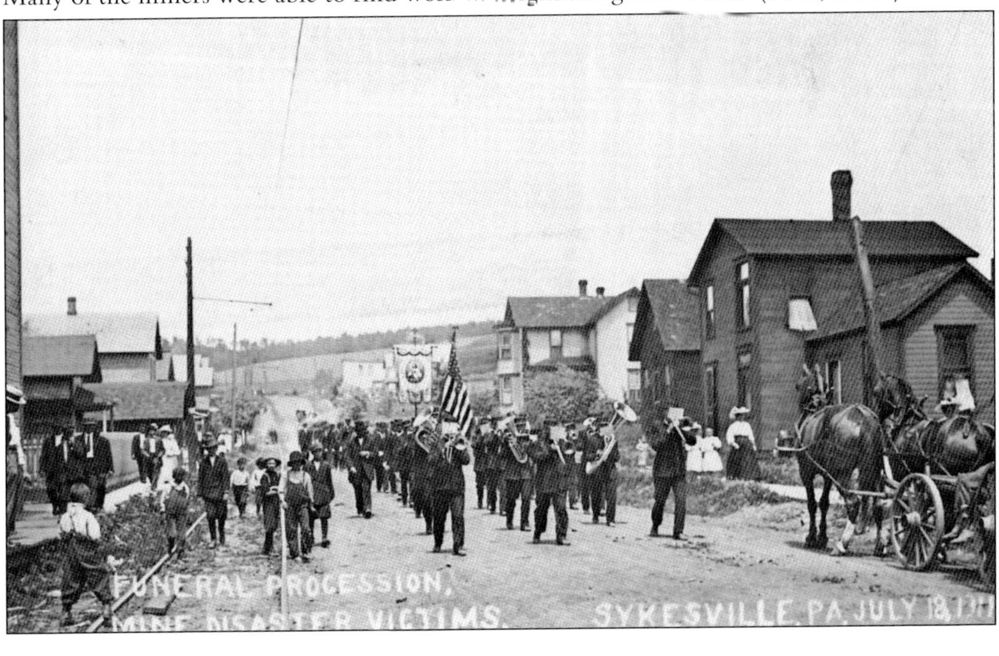

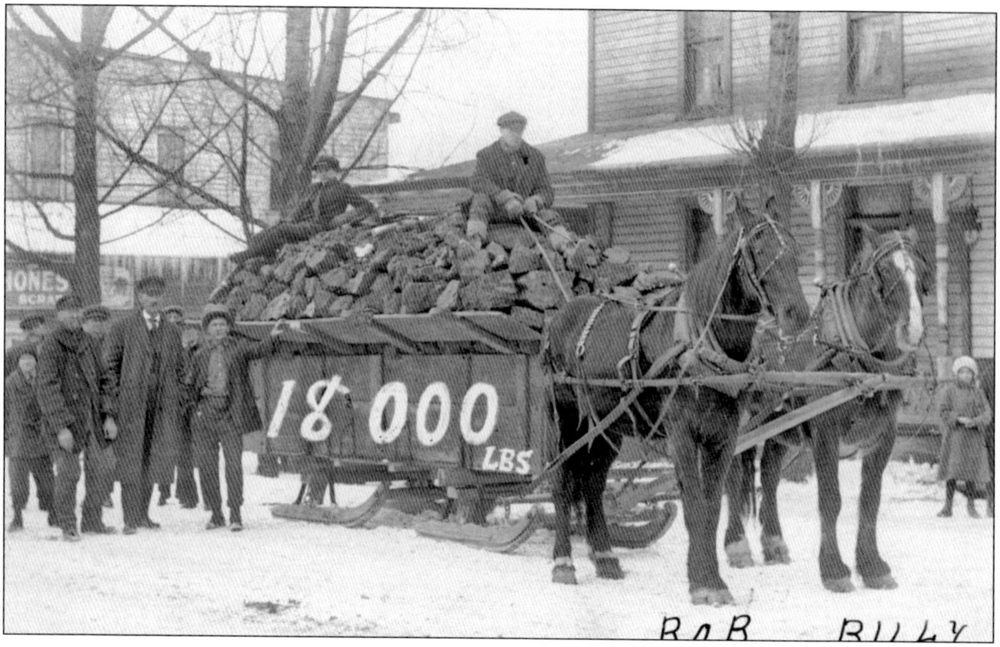

In 1917, the county shipped coal by rail as part of the war effort. Mines on the west end of Brockway competed for the biggest load, including William Key's Pine Grove Mine on Kearney Road and the mine of Frank Lemmon, as illustrated in the image above of a heaping bobsled heading east toward the Pennsylvania Railroad. Photographer James Kester, who more than likely took the photograph, lived in the house behind the horses. The West Clarion Mine, seen below, used mules to haul out the coal until 1913, when the company built an electric plant at the mouth of Oyster Run, about 7.5 miles east along Little Toby Creek. It closed in 1917, after which the coal was hauled out of the Granville Mine, about 1.5 miles to the southeast. (Both, BAHS.)

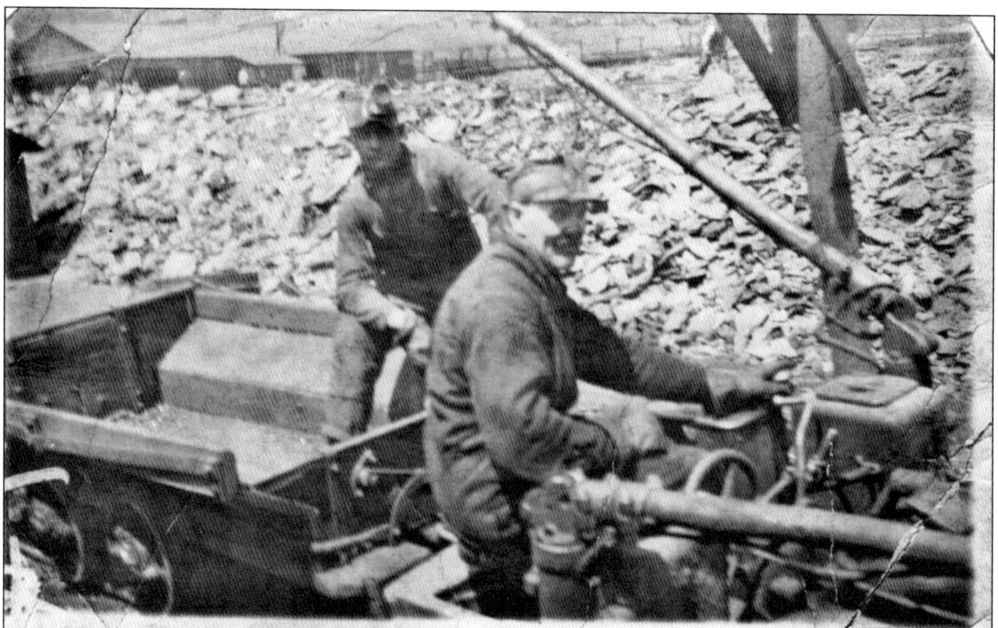

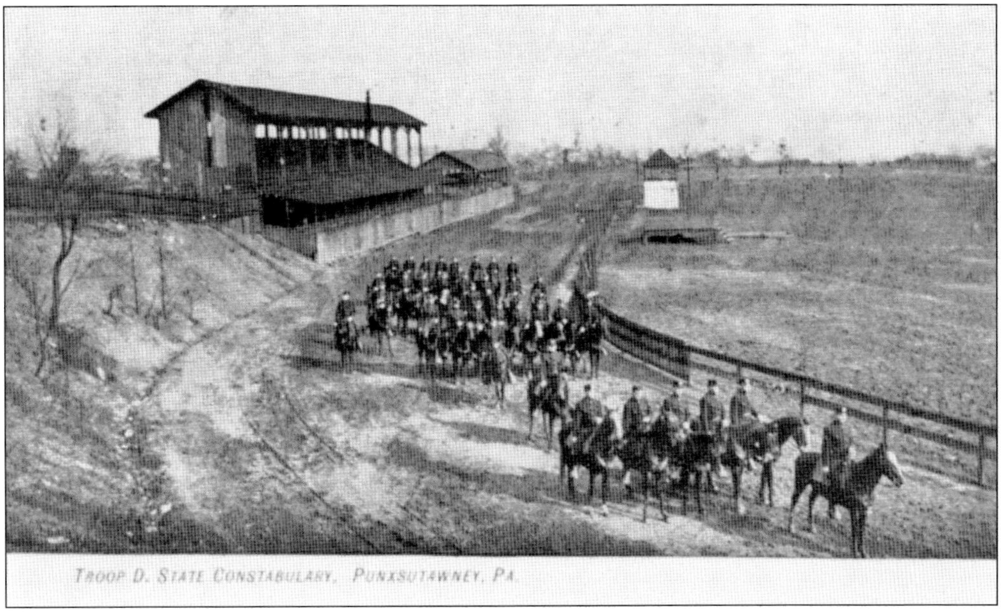

Troop D, State Constabulary, Pennsylvania's rural police force (above), arrived in Punxsutawney in December 1905. Under Capt. J.F. Robinson, its assignment was to serve central Pennsylvania, where the expanding coal industry and related social unrest frequently disturbed the peace. Equipped and trained, the officers participated in their first mounted drill before the public. In a 1906 action in Florence, a nearby mining town, two Troop D members were killed by criminal fugitives. They were the first two members of the Pennsylvania State Police killed in the line of duty. Riker Yard, a facility of the BR&P Railroad in Punxsutawney (below in 1919) was equipped with machine and blacksmith shops, a power plant, a coaling station, a cinder pit, and a water tank. There were eight miles of railroad tracks for storage and classification and a roundhouse with a 105-foot turntable. Riker passed to the Baltimore & Ohio Railroad in 1932, and in 1969, fire destroyed the roundhouse. (Both, PAHGS.)

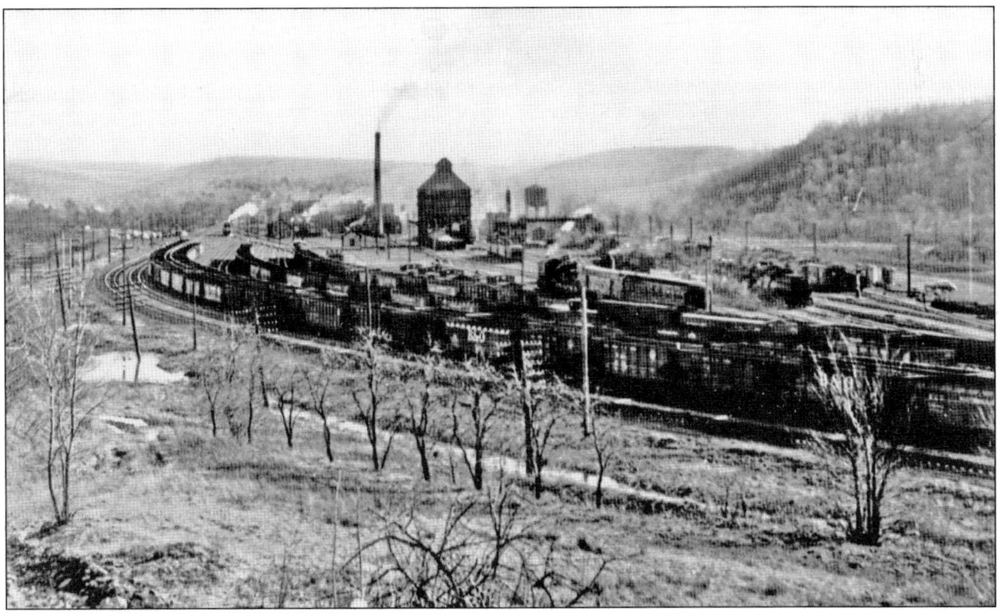

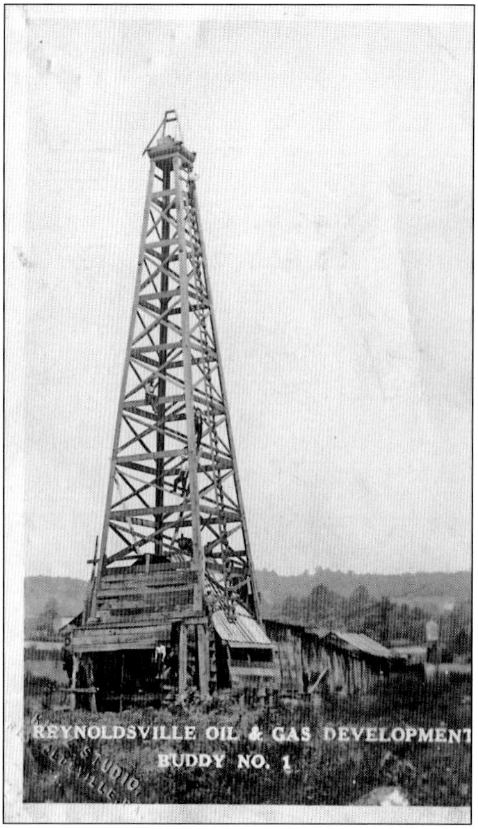

The discovery of oil at Drake's Well in 1859 prompted a frantic search for petroleum in western Pennsylvania. Wells like the one at left sprang up, but few yielded any oil. An unsuccessful oil well drilled by the Sandy Lick Oil Company in 1866 produced salt water instead. A distillation process extracted salt from the water, and the Reynoldsville Salt Works hauled this salt to Kittanning by wagon. (RHS.)

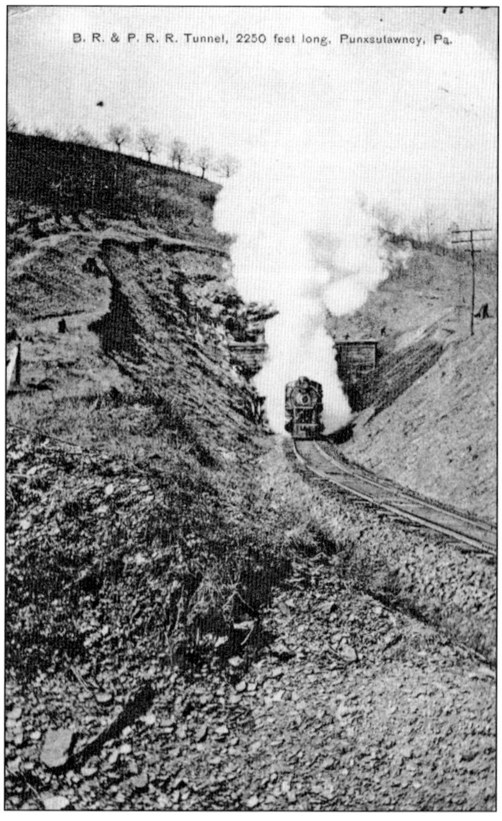

Digging through hills made rail travel easier. When the BR&P Railroad extended its route from Punxsutawney to Pittsburgh in 1899, the half-mile Simpson Tunnel near Sportsburg (pictured) enabled trains to run from Buffalo to Pittsburgh in eight hours. The tunnel is still used today. (PAHGS.)

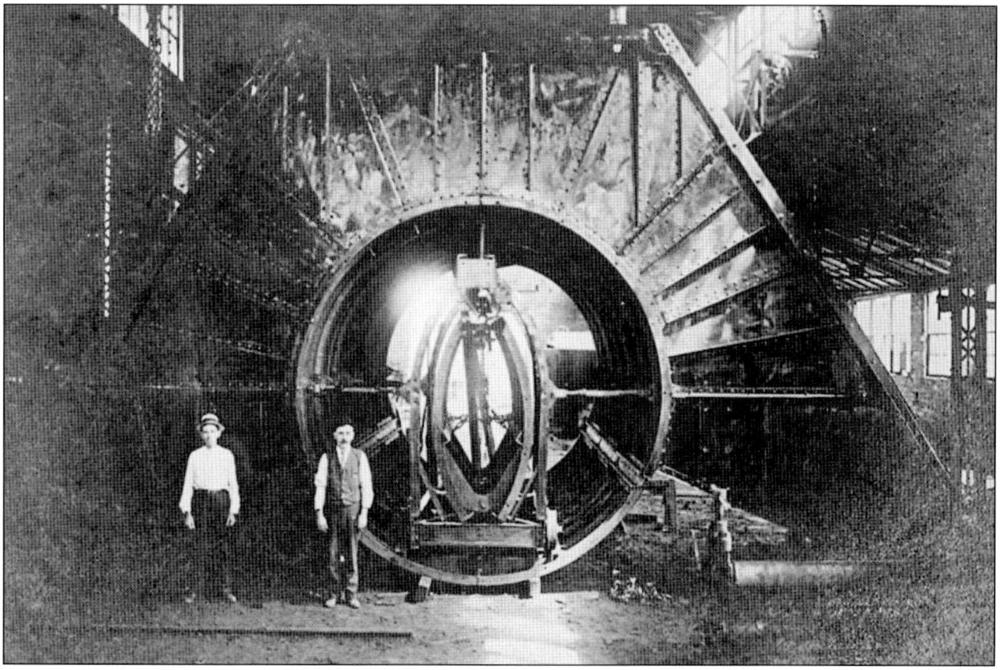

In 1910, the Blaw Collapsible Steel Centering Company in Reynoldsville was a hub for manufacturing fabricated steel forms used in concrete work. It had grown out of the suspended American Production Company, locally known as the "Steel Plant," and revived an interest in an abandoned mill. The plant manufactured the steel concrete forms used in building the Panama Canal. Rail traffic was not without danger. On July 3, 1913, engine no. 403 of the BR&P Railroad crashed into the rear of engine no. 328 and its string of 60 freight cars while the latter was waiting on the track to pull onto one of the Riker north yard tracks in Punxsutawney. The crew jumped off, and no one was injured. (Above, RHS; below, PAHGS.)

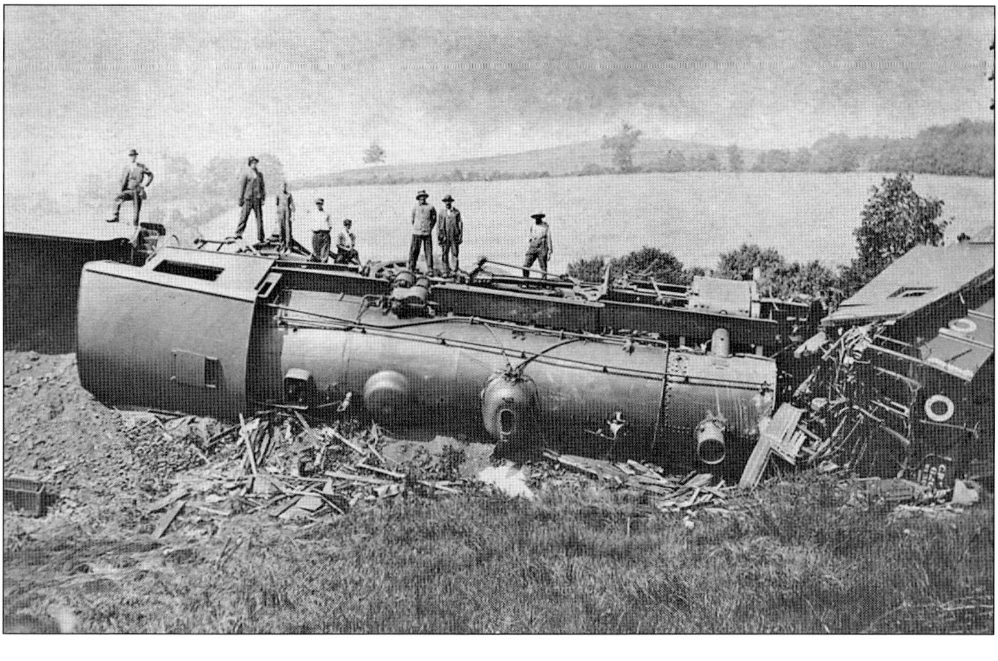

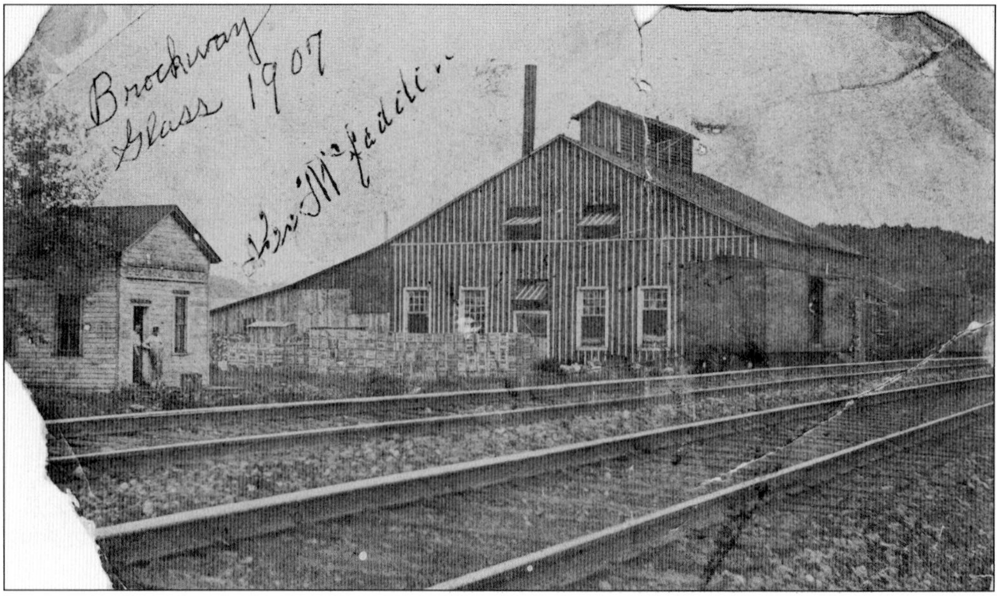

For more than a century, Brockway Glass has been one the county's most important industries. The Brockwayville Glass Company (above) began production in 1897 but failed due to poor equipment. It floundered under a variety of operators until 1907, when local businessman Hugh B. McCullough and 12 experienced bottle-makers from Olean, New York, purchased it for $34,000. The first bottles were made in the old renovated building, with packing boxes stacked against the factory wall. "Operators and boys" of the Brockway Machine Bottle Company take time out for lunch in 1908 (below). Seated on the ramp leading to the boxcar are, from left to right, Mike Costion, Robert Prindle, Curt Butters, Robert Cole Sr., Norman DeVallance, Jayce Edwards, Norman Prindle, Herbert Adams, Albin Lindholm, "Pete" McVehil, and John Marsden. Standing are, from left to right, Tom Quinn, Emory Coyle, George Nieoff, Charles Ausprung, and Guy Arrowsmith. (Both, BAHS.)

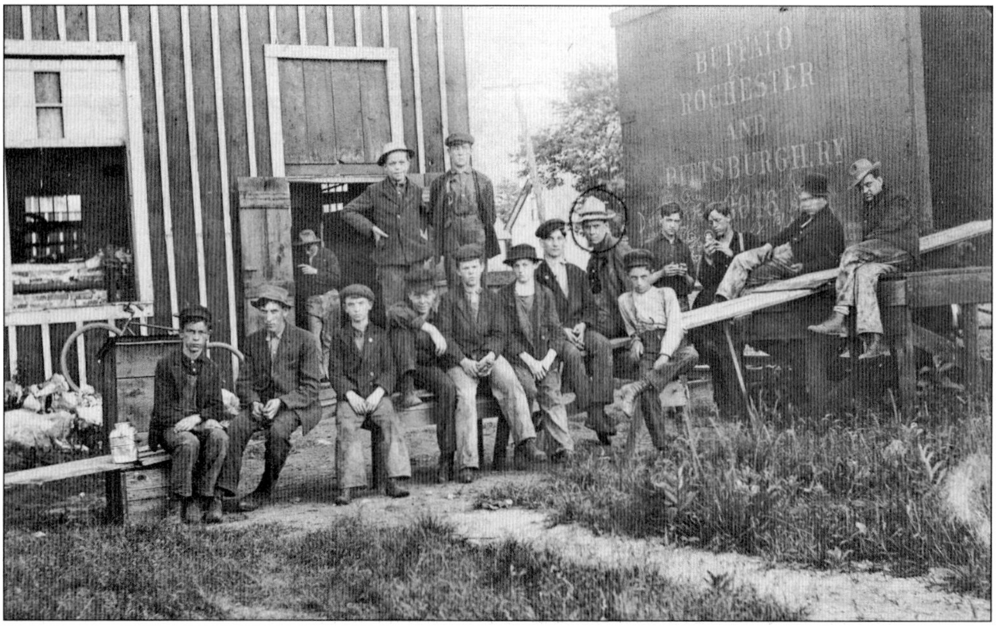

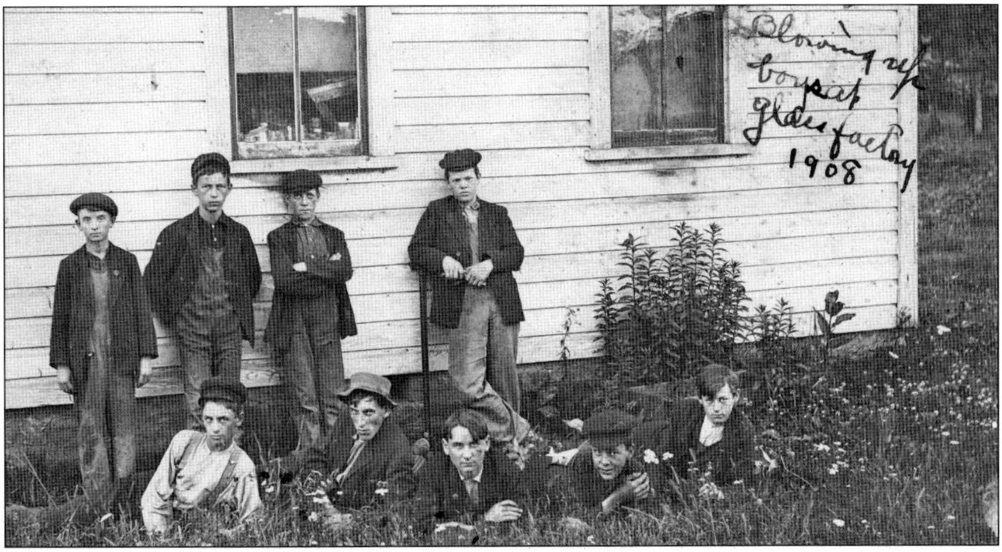

Blowing glass was part of the production process used to make thousands of early bottles. Above, the "blowing up boys" of the Brockway Machine Bottle Company take a break, leaning against the office building. Ranging in age from 14 to 17, these boys were part of the workforce in 1908. From left to right are (first row) Albin Lindholm, Robert Prindle, Floyd Chittester, Robert Coyle Sr., and Jayce Edwards; (second row) Curt Butters, Mike Costion, Charles "Bright Eyes" McQuone, and Norman DeVallance. Below, inside the machine shop are, from left to right, Russell, Earl, and Alex McFadden; John Harding; and Dave R. Cox. Alex McFadden, Harding, and Cox were three of the original 12 investors of the company. In 1933, the Brockway Machine Bottle Company and the Brockway Sales Company merged to form the Brockway Glass Company. (Both, BAHS.)

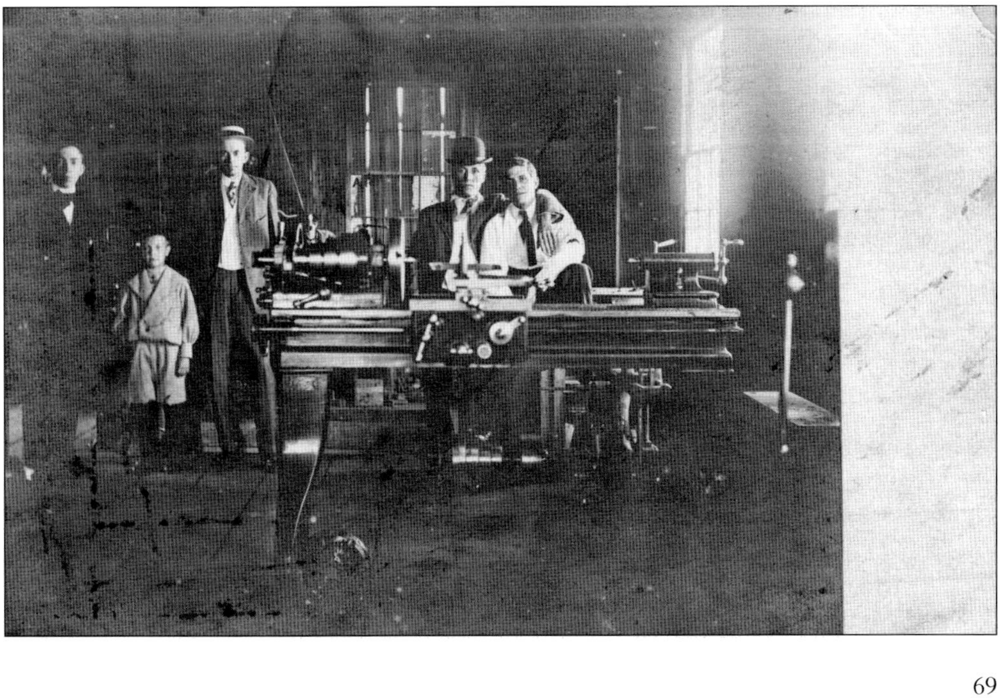

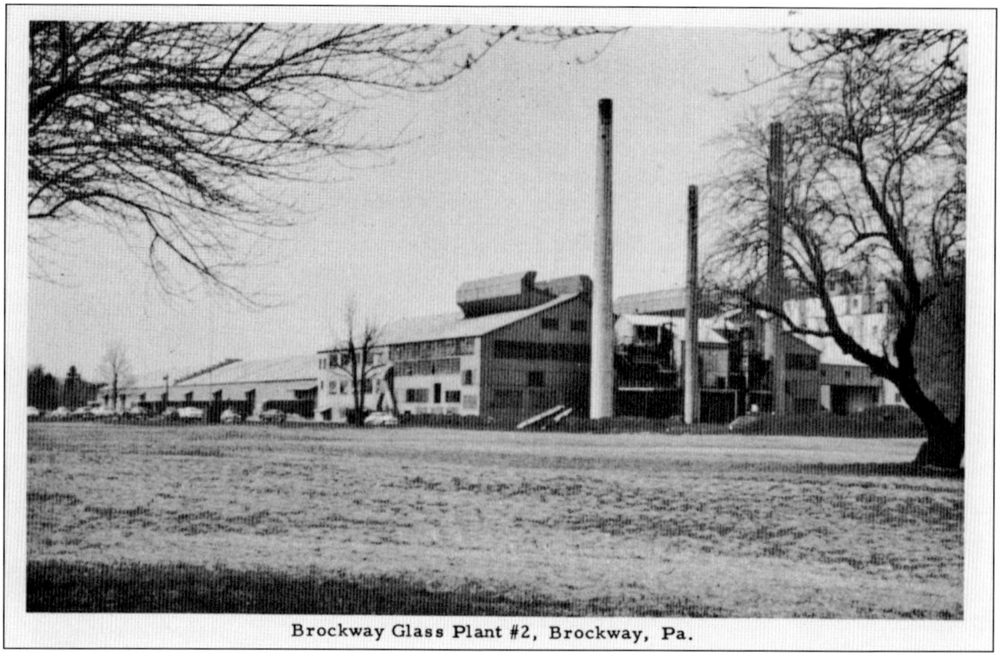

Brockway Glass Plant #2, Brockway, Pa.

In 1940, Brockway Glass broke ground for a second factory on land purchased from William Moore in Crenshaw, Pennsylvania, east of Brockway on US 219. Between 1947 and 1964, the company purchased plants in Lapel, Indiana; Freehold, New Jersey; Rosemount, Minnesota; Danville, Virginia; and Washington, Pennsylvania. In 1964, the purchase of six former Hazel-Atlas container plants doubled the company's size, and by the 1980s, the company had become the second-largest glass manufacturer in the world. Brockway Glass Plant 1 is shown in this c. 1950 aerial photograph. The plant sits between US 219 (upper portion of the photograph) and the B&O Railroad (lower portion), formerly the BR&P, the same site as the 1907 Brockway Machine Bottle Company factory. This glass plant is still in operation today as Plant 18 of Owens-Illinois Glass Company. (Both, BAHS.)

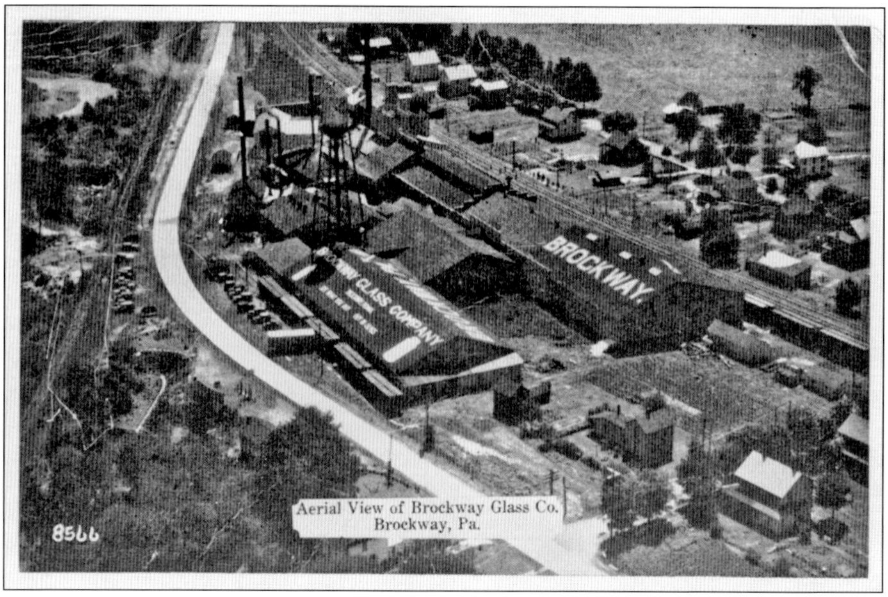

Aerial View of Brockway Glass Co.
Brockway, Pa.

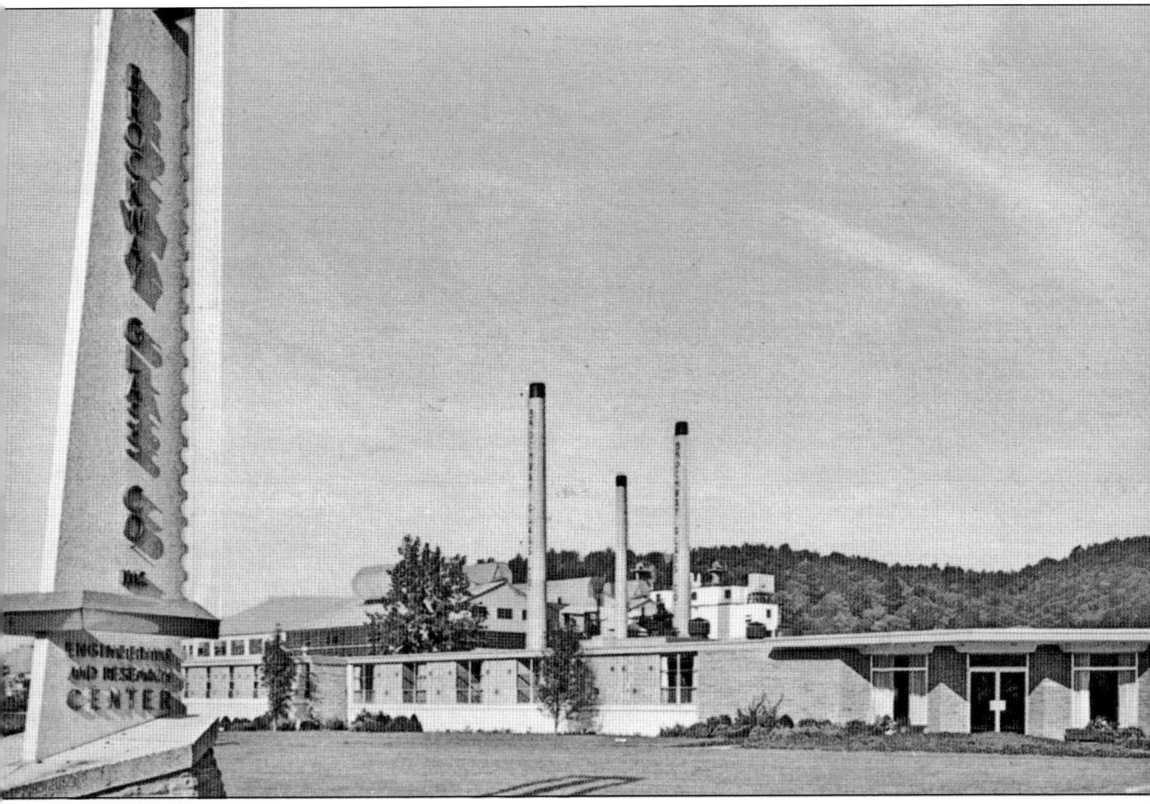

Brockway Glass employed 2,200 people in its two production plants, corporate headquarters, and the engineering and research center in Crenshaw and Brockway (above). In 2016, the obelisk sign was moved to the Taylor Memorial Museum to commemorate the glass industry and its importance to Brockway's growth. Sand, soda ash, and limestone were readily available when the Brockwayville Glass Company began. In the 1920s, land tests in the Sugar Hill area found clay that produced very fine brick, tile, and pipe. Dr. H.E. Kilgus invested in the Brockway Clay Company. The plant prospered during the Great Depression's public works programs. Employment peaked at 270 people in the 1960s. The availability of cheaper and lighter plastic pipe and environmental laws requiring natural gas, not coal, led to the company's demise. The factory burned to the ground in 1999. (BAHS.)

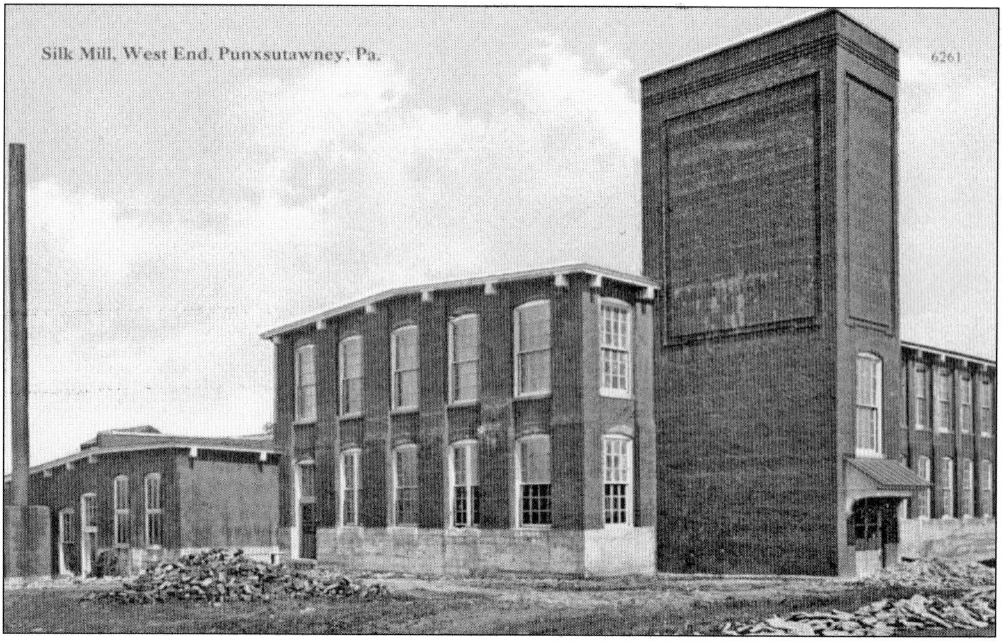

The United Textile Corporation of Allentown opened a silk mill (above) in 1909 in Punxsutawney that operated until the 1930s. The chamber of commerce purchased the building during World War II, and the Jefferson Textile Company processed and sewed heavy canvas for military use. In 1948, Pramco, a large shirtwaist manufacturer, used the building to make ladies' blouses, skirts, and slacks, providing employment for women in the area. The Lauderbach-Barber Grocery Company (below) built a four-story brick building in 1909 at North Findley and Cherry Streets to house its wholesale grocery operation, which served coal company stores and family grocery stores in villages in the Punxsutawney area. Area brick companies supplied the bricks. The Jefferson Grocery Company occupied the building and continued the wholesale grocery business from the 1950s until 1964. (Both, PAHGS.)

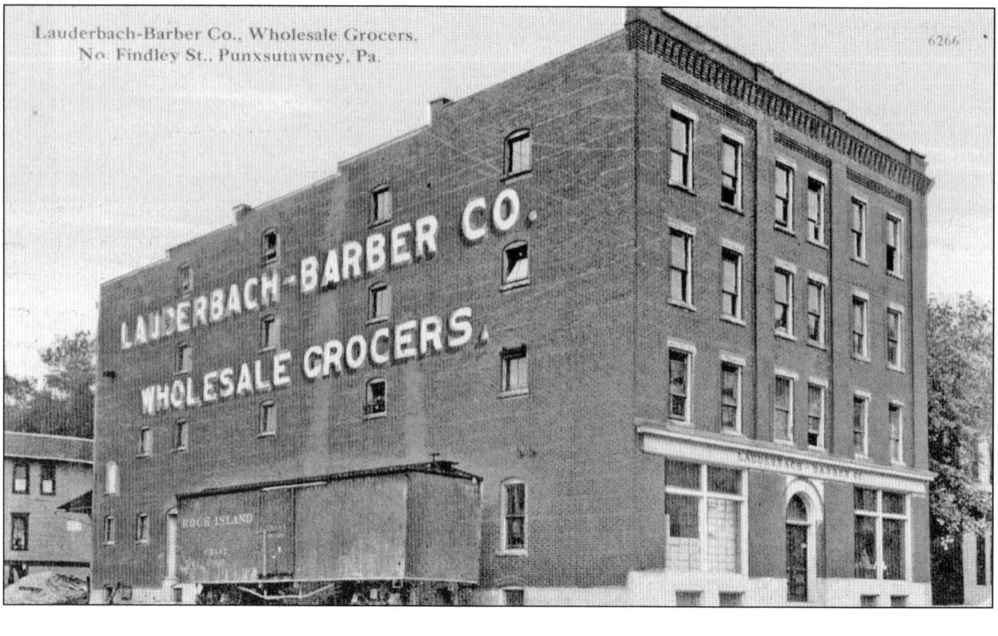

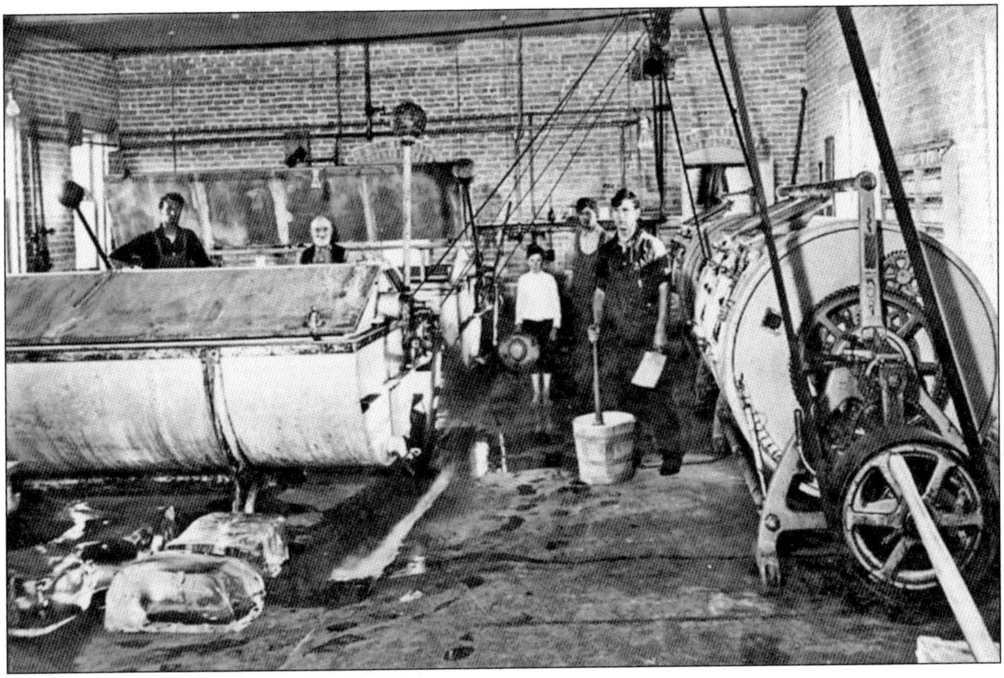

Before 1880, Christian and Conrad Haag operated a brewery dug out of a Punxsutawney slate rock hill. The brick Punxsutawney Brewery, operated by Joseph Baumgartner, replaced it in 1896. About 1900, Bernard Schneider, a former partner of Baumgartner, began the Elk Run Brewery (above). Notice the large ice cakes in front of the Elk Run Brewery workers, pictured in 1901. Many years before Prohibition, hundreds of licensed distilleries and probably many more unlicensed distilleries made whiskey in Pennsylvania. Rye grew well in the state's rocky soil. The Reynoldsville Distilling Company (below) produced Blue Ribbon Pure Rye Whiskey in 1906. (Above, PAHGS; below, RHS.)

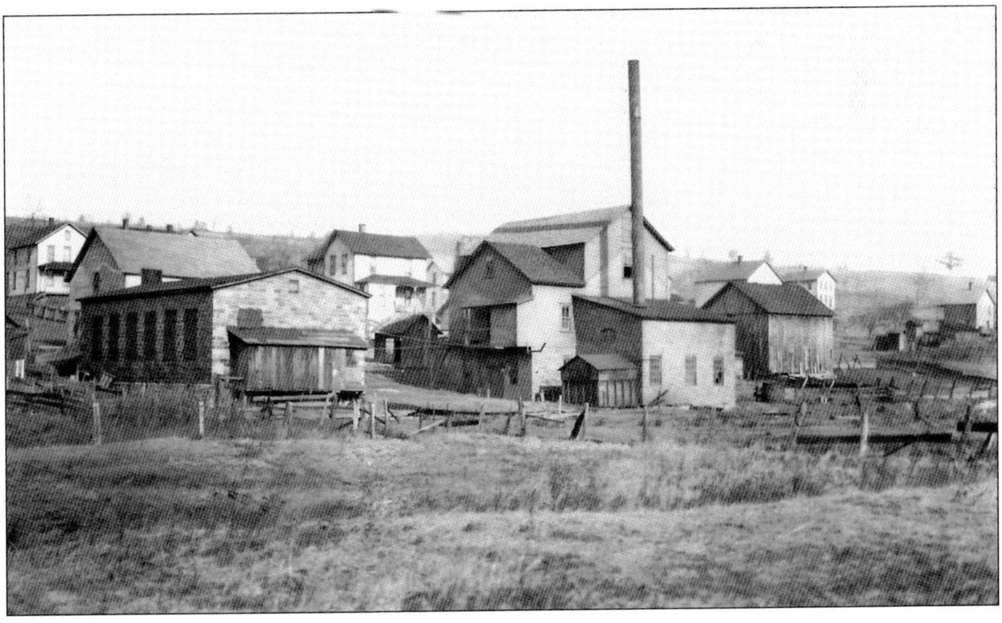

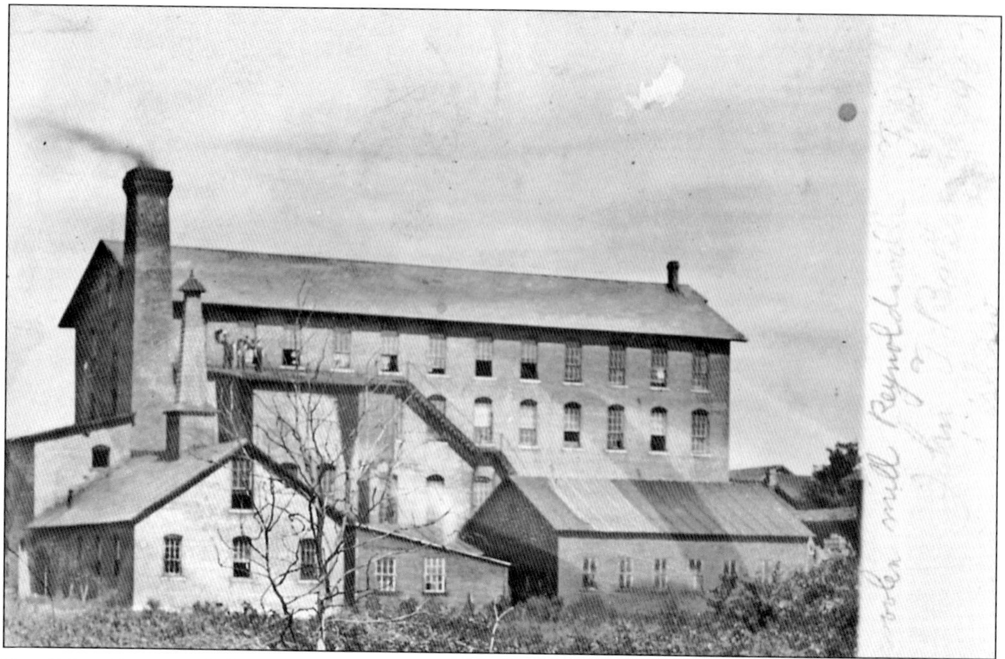

Small locally owned factories were abundant at the beginning of the 20th century. In the mid-1880s, G.W. Sykes and G.H. Allis were the proprietors of two woolen mills in Reynoldsville, one (above) on Jackson Street. The building later housed a macaroni factory, a tallow plant, and the Reynoldsville Silk Fabrics Corporation. Two silk mills, two woolen mills, a haberdasher, and a tannery gave Reynoldsville an edge on the clothing industry. Factories boomed in Brookville, too. Southeast of town (below), a woolen mill, the Brookville Glass and Tile plant, and the Deemer Furniture Factory formed an industrial park. Nearby, the Twyford Motor Car Company made automobiles for several years, and smaller factories made trucks, ladders, and a multitude of other products. (Above, RHS; below, JCHC.)

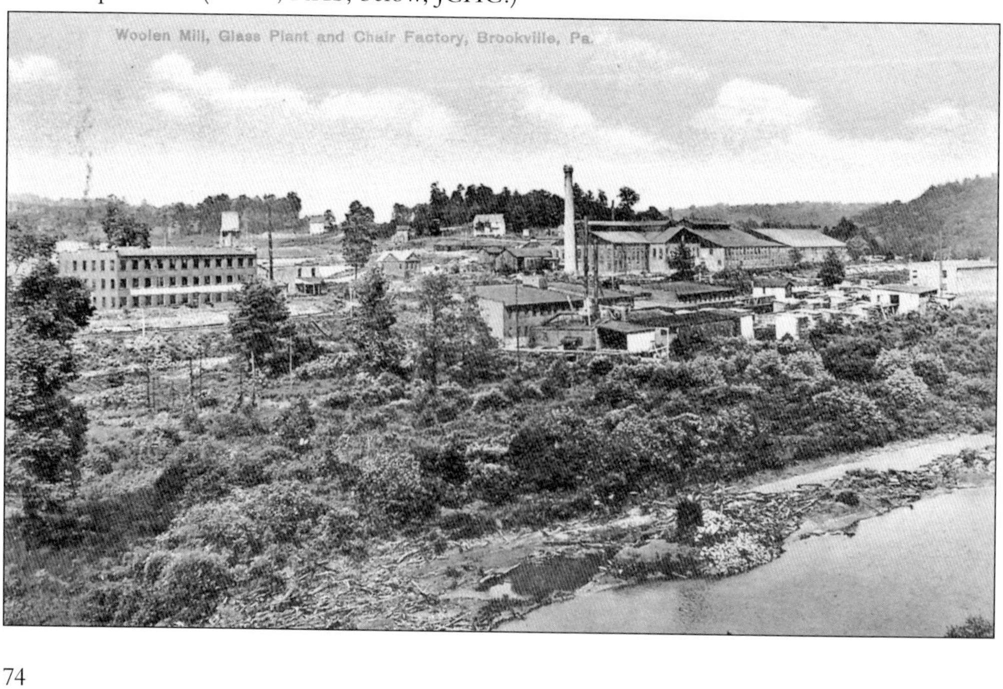

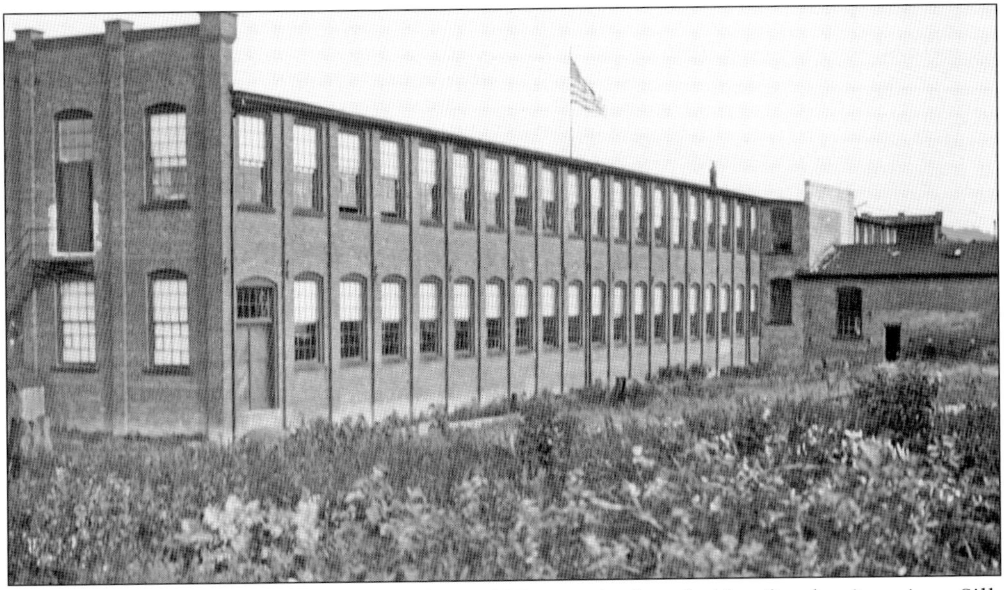

The Enterprise Silk Mill (above), built in 1897, was the leaseholder for the American Silk Company. This industry had been solicited by stock subscription and supported by Reynoldsville businesses and citizens. In September 1901, Thomas T. Haggerty, national organizer for the United Mine Workers, helped orchestrate a strike brought on by wage inequality. Huge crowds gathered on Main Street. A parade with marching bands led the way to Centennial Hall, where heated lectures foreshadowed an inevitable strike. By month's end, harassment and violence were followed by arrests and fines. Nonunion workers provoked demonstrations at the mill, resulting in more arrests. Noted labor activist Mary Harris "Mother" Jones arrived and spoke on behalf of unions in general and textile workers in particular. An agreement to end the five-month strike was reached in February 1902. (Both, RHS.)

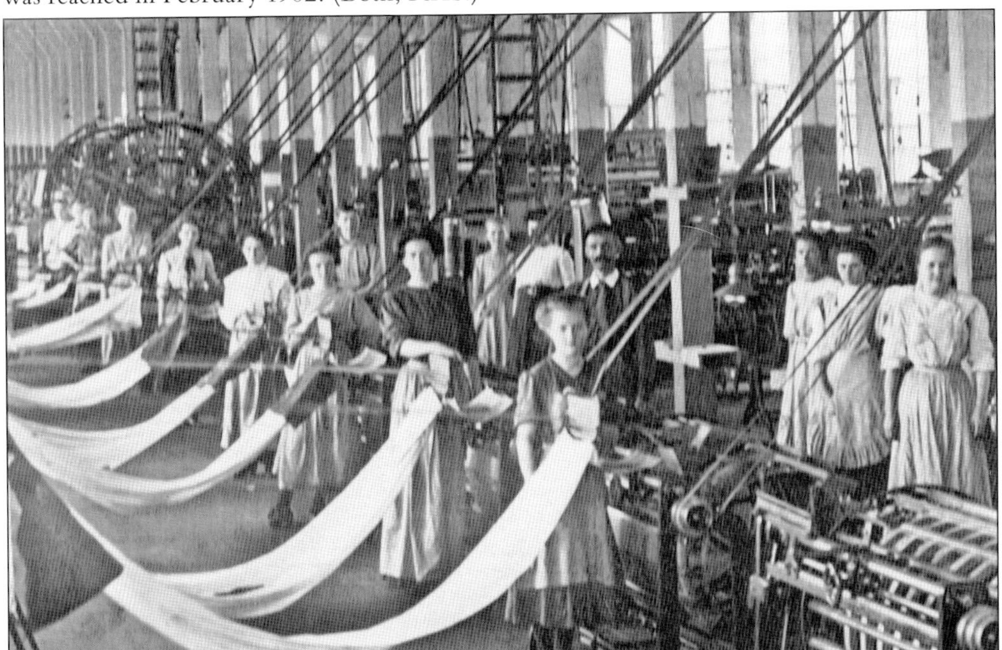

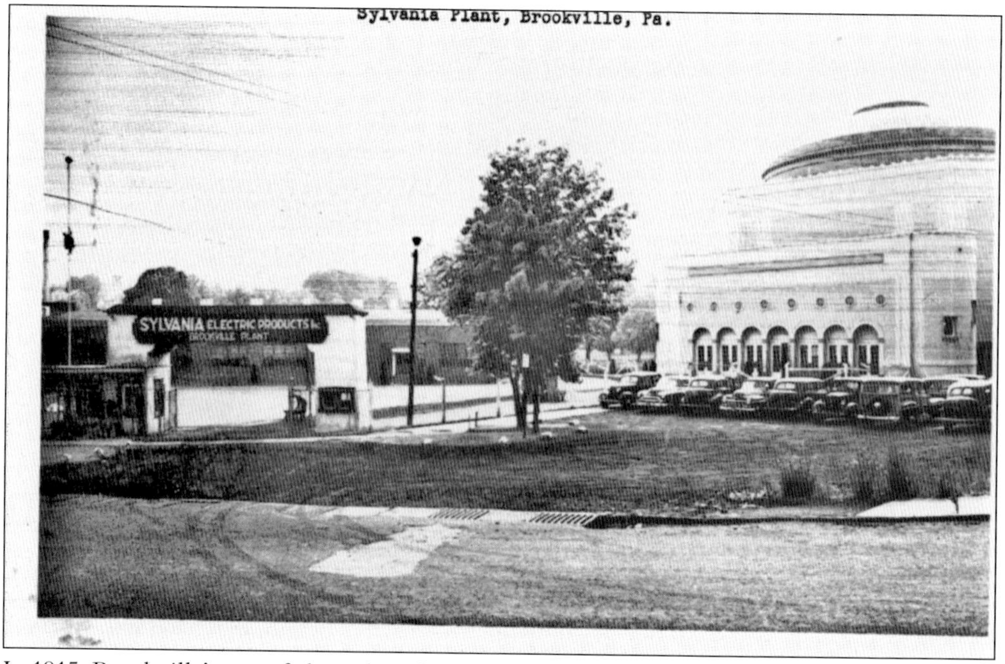

In 1915, Brookville's town fathers chose land near the fairgrounds for an auditorium. Walls were up when World War I began. Roofed at war's end but rarely used, people called it the "White Elephant." Except when the courthouse underwent renovation in the 1920s, it still was rarely used until World War II began. The Sylvania Company (above) moved in and produced vacuum tubes into the 1960s. Today, the building houses a small machine shop. Reynoldsville's Cameron Manufacturing Corporation (below) produced surgical and dental supplies but became active in the war effort. The work was kept secret until later, when it was revealed that the company had made parts for proximity fuses, which played a major part in the aerial battles of the war. At its height, Cameron employed over 600 people. (Above, JCHC; below, RHS.)

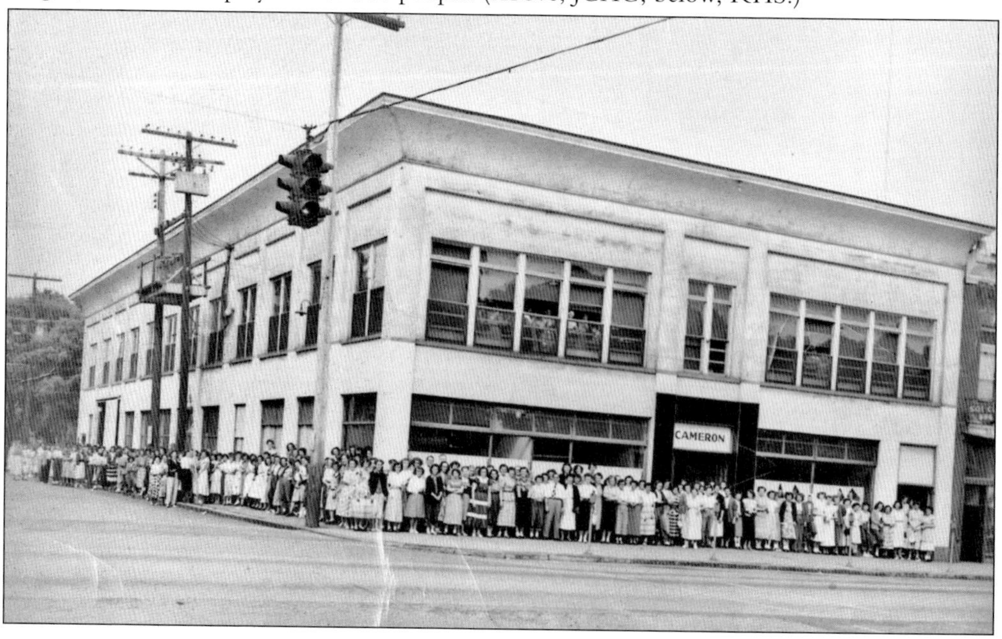

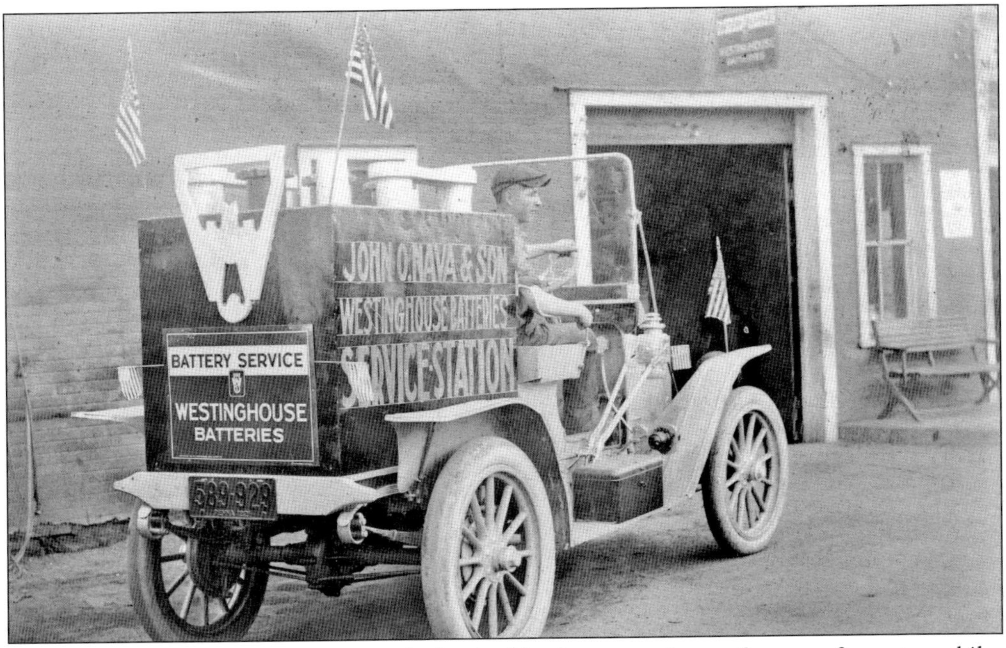

Ford's automobile inspired R.E. Twyford to build a factory and manufacture a few automobiles in Brookville. He exhibited them in Pittsburgh and New York City, then declared bankruptcy in 1908. John O. Nava was more successful with his endeavor. In the 1920s, he purchased the old Soderholm Pick Handle Factory in Brockway, where he and his sons Attilio, John, Caesar, and Adam operated a garage, battery factory, and machine shop. They manufactured the Brockway Battery, the first non-buckle plated battery in the industry, and used the truck seen above. Gas stations flourished. Built in 1929, the Delaney Brothers Pennzoil station, pictured below at the corner of Main and Fifth Streets in Reynoldsville, was later owned and operated by Mark Wildauer. Now, this is the Reynoldsville Historical Society's headquarters. (Above, BAHS; below, RHS.)

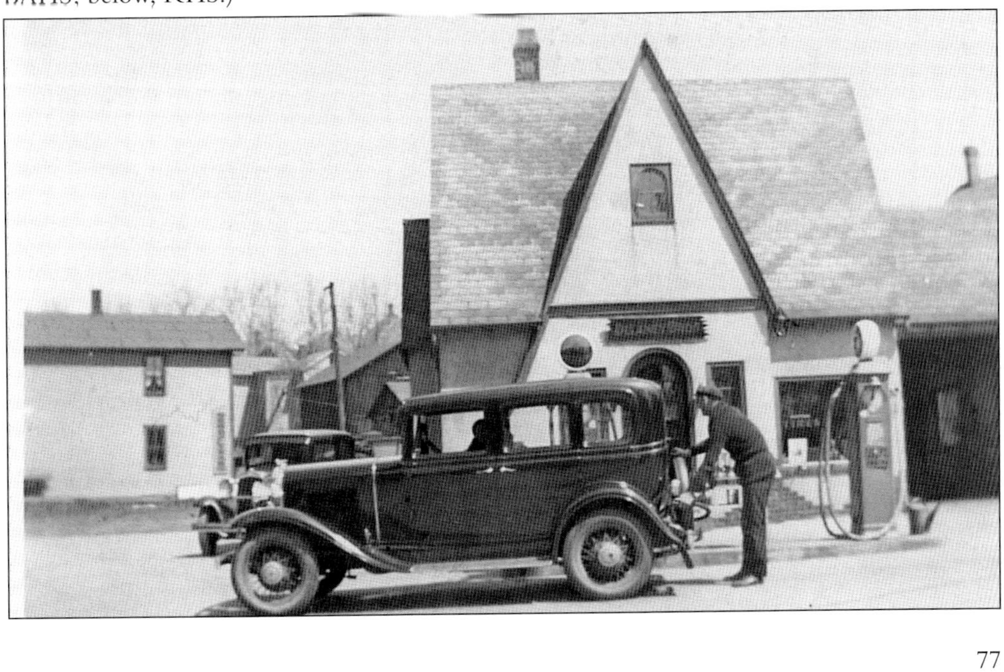

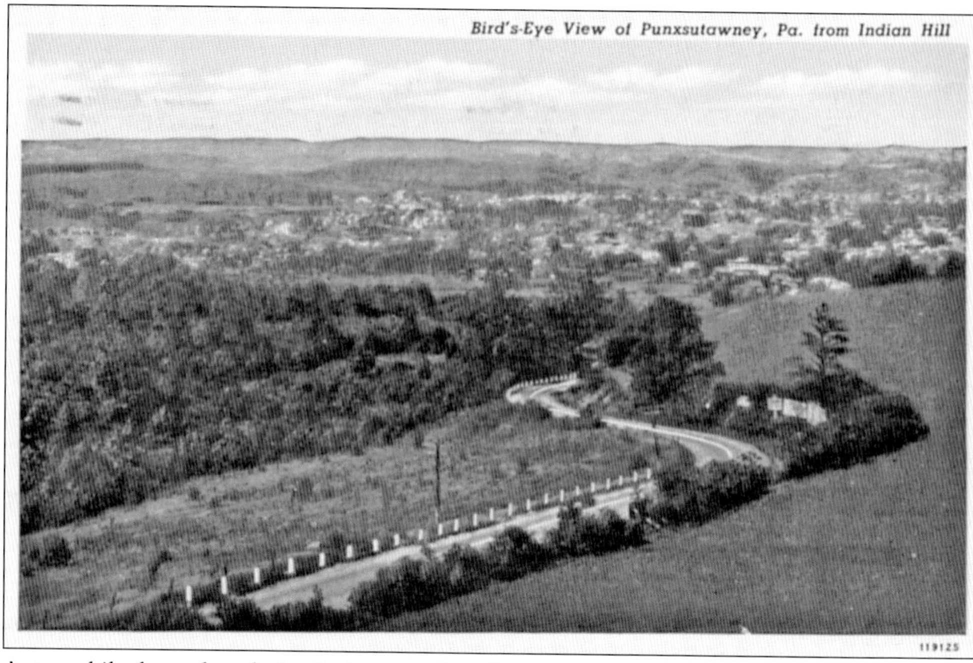

Automobiles brought a desire for improved roads. In 1911, the Sproul Highway Act gave control of 8,835 miles of roads to the Pennsylvania Department of Highways. US 119, viewed from Indiana Hill near Punxsutawney (above), was designated in 1926, allowing for improvements. In 1931, the state legislature passed the Penrose Rural Roads Act to, according to Governor Pinchot, "get the farmer out of the mud." The next big push for improvement occurred between the 1950s and the 1980s, when the federal government built the Interstate Highway System. I-80 extends 2,905 miles from the New York City area to San Francisco. At the ground-breaking ceremony near Corsica, one speaker remarked it was "the beginning of the greatest public works ever undertaken in the county, . . . when done it will bring to this section of the state a new prosperity." The dedication took place at the Milesburg Interchange in 1970 (below). (Above, PAHGS; below, JCHC.)

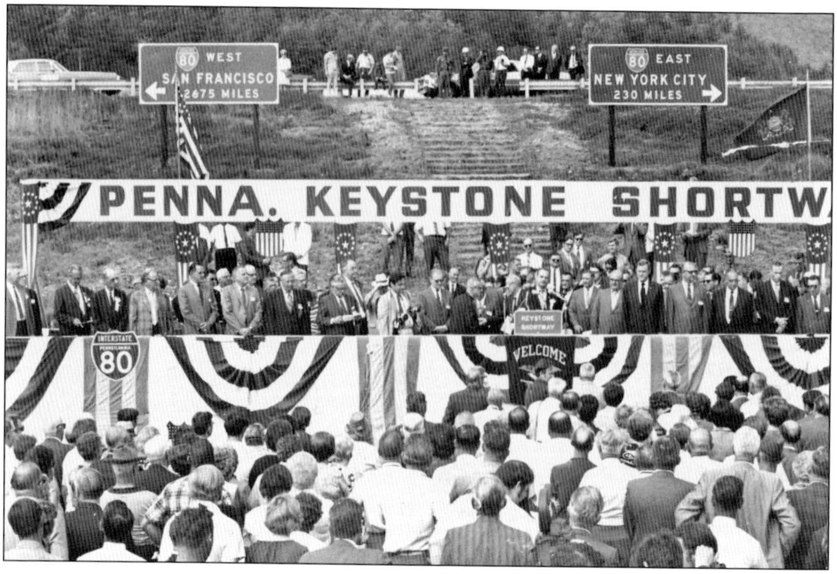

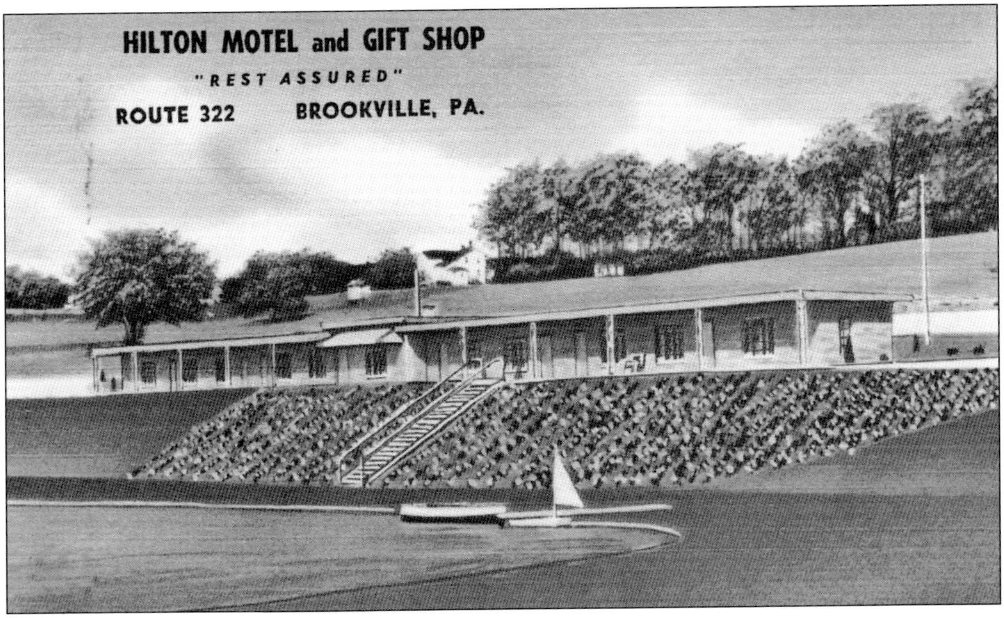

Sherwood Hilton opened the Hilton Motel and Gift Shop (above) in the late 1950s at the intersection of State Routes 28 and 36 and US 322 near Brookville. Within a decade, he had used the parts of three antique barns to build the adjoining Gold Eagle Restaurant in the area that had once been the pond. Shortly after the completion of I-80, he sold both to Rick and Pat Ochs. Like the automobile at the turn of the century, the opening of I-80 in the 1970s became the impetus for many new businesses. Soon a Howard Johnson motel (below), a Days Inn, restaurants, service stations, and a major truck stop developed. Today, businesses that offer goods and services to locals and travelers alike line both sides of State Route 36. The Gold Eagle Inn and Restaurant still stands at the intersection. (Both, JCHC.)

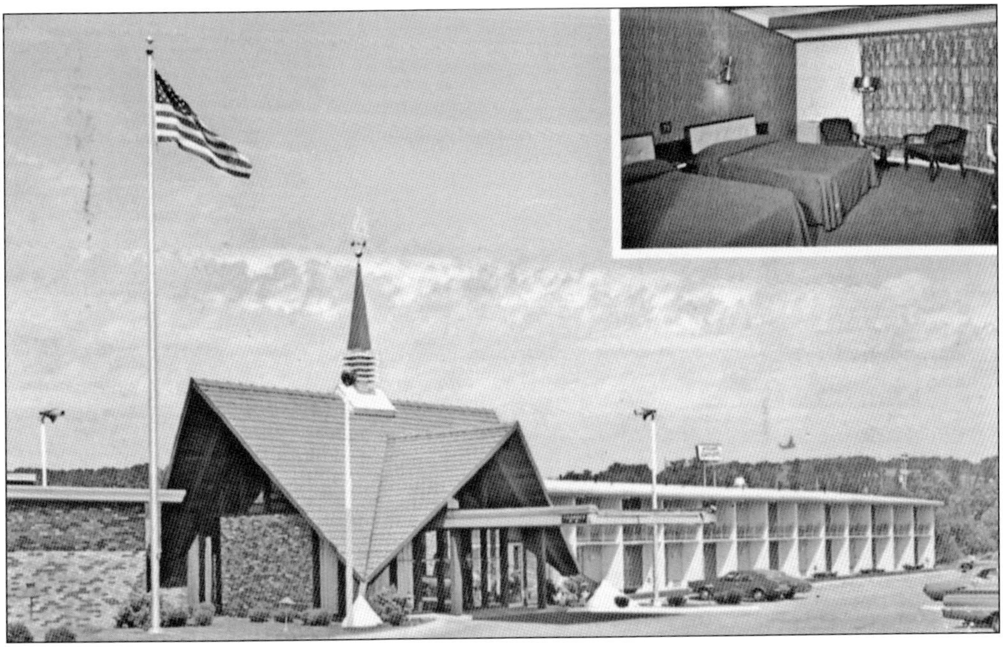

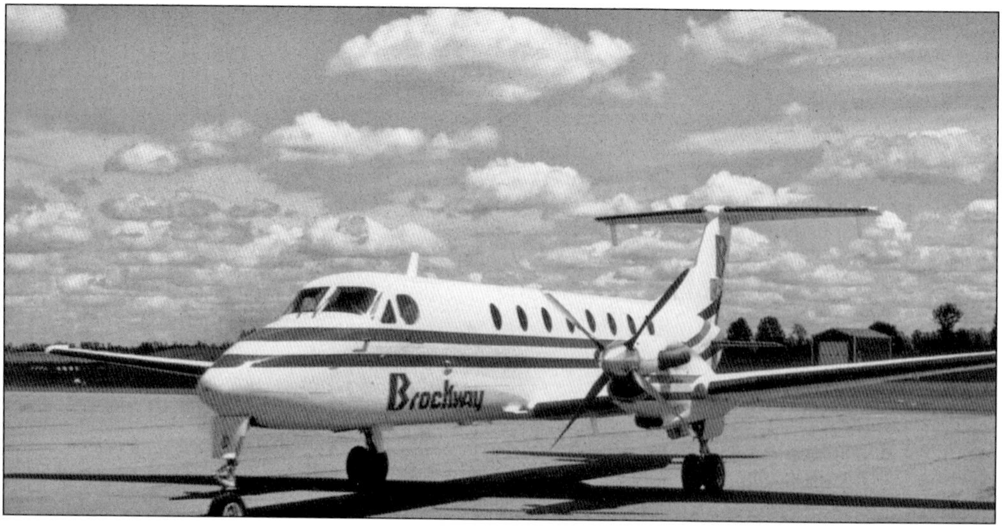

Rail service and better roads improved travel in Jefferson County. So did the completion of an airport in 1960. Brockway Glass built a corporate hangar for its aircraft and later developed a commuter airline service, Crown Airways, which flew from Dubois–Jefferson County Airport to the Greater Pittsburgh Airport. It was designated a foreign trade zone in 2001, and the name was changed to DuBois Regional Airport in 2008. When Gene and Janet Harding married in 1956, she had a degree in economics and political science and had taken a dairy short-course at Rutgers. She moved to Maplevale Farm, a 300-acre dairy farm northwest of Brookville. When I-80 opened, they added a dairy store (below), a bakery, a frozen food distributorship, and a Guernsey Maid Restaurant. Young people eagerly awaited the opening of Burger King and McDonald's. (Above, BAHS; below, JCHC.)

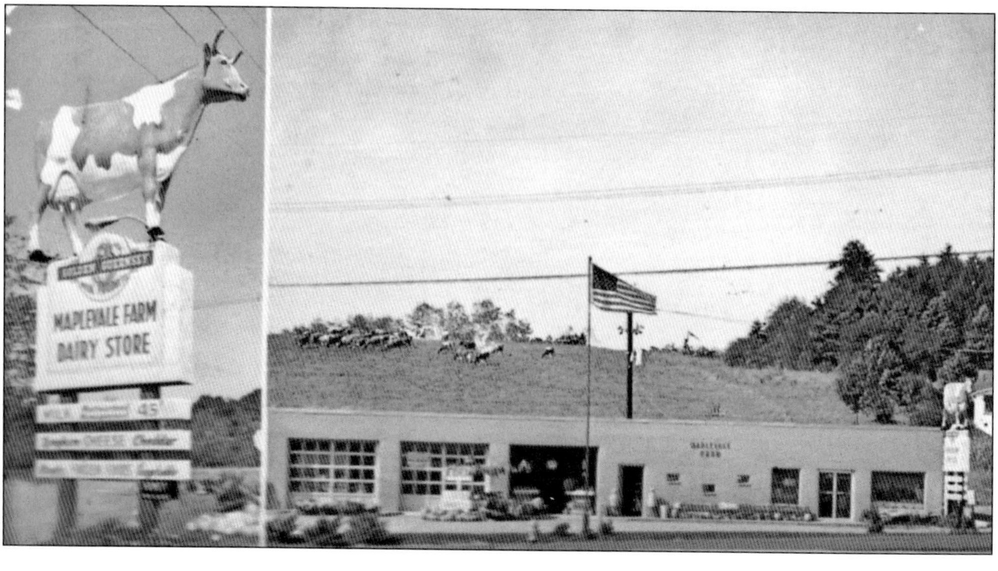

Five

Schools, Churches, and Caring for Each Other

The people of Jefferson County learned, worshipped, and cared for each other even before the county was formed on March 26, 1804. John Dixon taught in a schoolhouse built of rough logs. Today, students attend preschools; schools in five public districts; Roman Catholic, Amish, and Christian schools; a vocational school; the Punxsutawney Campus and Academy of Culinary Arts of Indiana University of Pennsylvania; and BC3, a community college in Brockway.

Churches, like schools, were top priorities. The Reverend Robert McGarragh led services for descendants of Scots Irish Presbyterians as early as 1809, and by 1824, the congregation had built the Bethel Church west of Brookville. Until the mid-1960s, church attendance grew, compelling many denominations to build larger structures. Brookville Presbyterians built in 1904 and Brookville Methodists in 1922. Brockway Presbyterians built a new Colonial-style building in 1964. In the last half of the 20th century, new church groups organized and grew as participation in the traditional or mainline churches began to wane. Today, one finds churches of many denominations throughout Jefferson County.

Commissioners are elected to govern the county. Whether large or small, Jefferson County's municipalities and townships elect mayors, councils, and supervisors to govern and care for the communities. Once, bucket brigades fought fires. Today, volunteers in 19 fire companies fight fires and help during community disasters.

For their physical well-being, early settlers depended upon pioneer women and home remedies, then a long series of doctors came and went. The commonwealth enacted laws pertaining to the practice of medicine in 1877, and doctors formed the Jefferson County Medical Society. The Woman's Relief Corps established the Pennsylvania Memorial Home for Civil War veterans and their wives, widows, and children in 1890 and built a small hospital. A mining company built a hospital in Adrian, and people set up makeshift hospitals during the Spanish influenza pandemic of 1918. By 1919, both Brookville and Punxsutawney had hospitals.

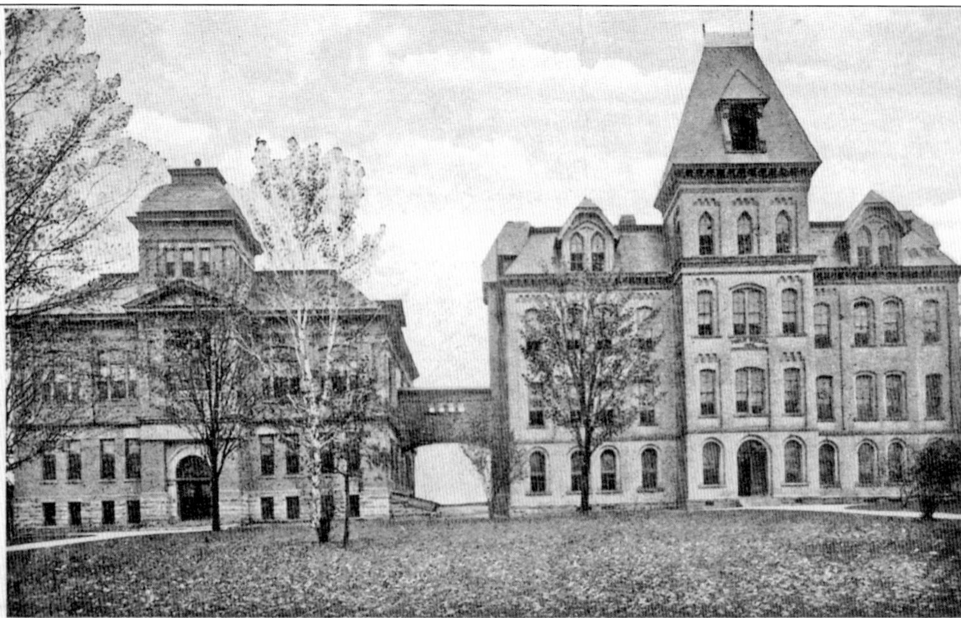

PUBLIC AND HIGH SCHOOL BUILDINGS, BROOKVILLE, PA.

When builders completed Brookville's Central School (above) in 1878, its location north of town became known as "School Hill" or "Knowledge Knob." The building contained 15 classrooms, a band room, and a manual training room. In 1898, builders connected the new Paul Darling Memorial Hall and its four classrooms to the Central School with a second-story bridge. Annexes in 1923 and 1928 (below) added 11 more classrooms, chemistry and physics laboratories, a library, a gym, and a domestic science classroom. The school district completed the present high school in 1961. The Central School, which had become the junior high, was razed in 1966, and Memorial Hall burned in a spectacular fire in 1975. Today, the area has become Northside Park. (Both, JCHC.)

Brookville High School, Brookville, Pa.

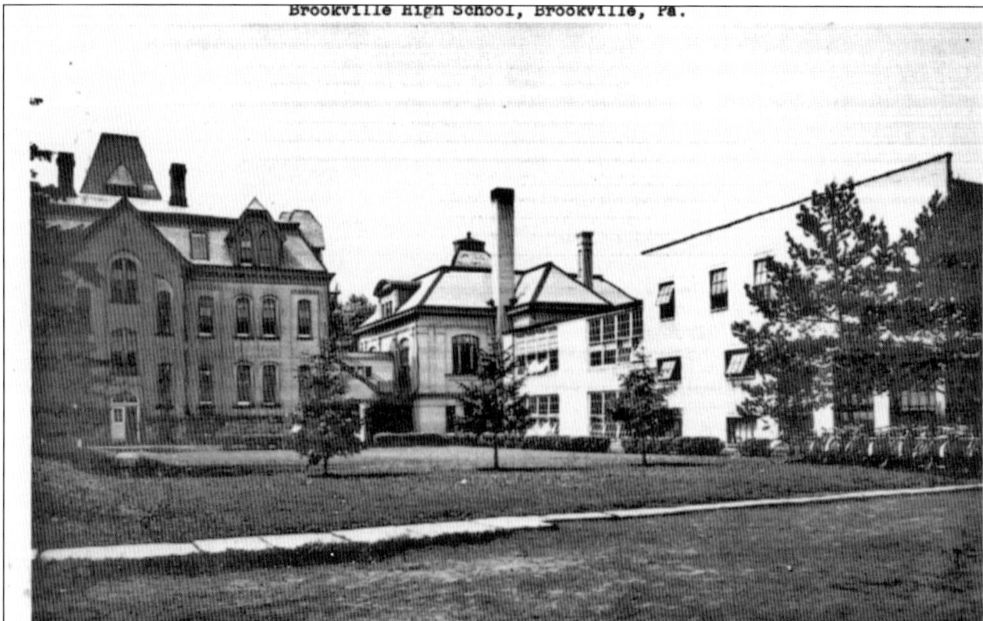

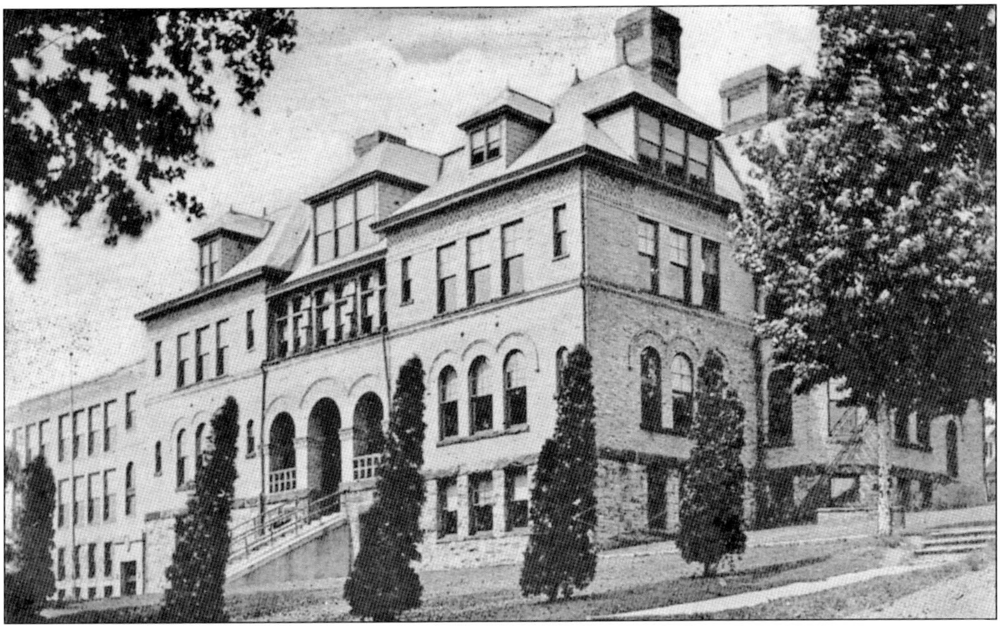

Construction of the Reynoldsville High School building (above) started in June 1895, and it was dedicated on September 4, 1896. It had 14 classrooms, a library, a large auditorium, four extra rooms, an office, and a basement to house a furnace and supplies. This building also served as a hospital during the Spanish influenza pandemic of 1918–1919. In 1924, a $100,000 addition added eight large classrooms, restrooms, corridors, and a large gymnasium. In the early 1900s, the county boasted 13 high schools like the one in Falls Creek (below) and two vocational schools, one in Corsica and one in Washington Township. Brookville, Punxsutawney, and Reynoldsville also had Roman Catholic schools. (Above, RHS; below, JCHC.)

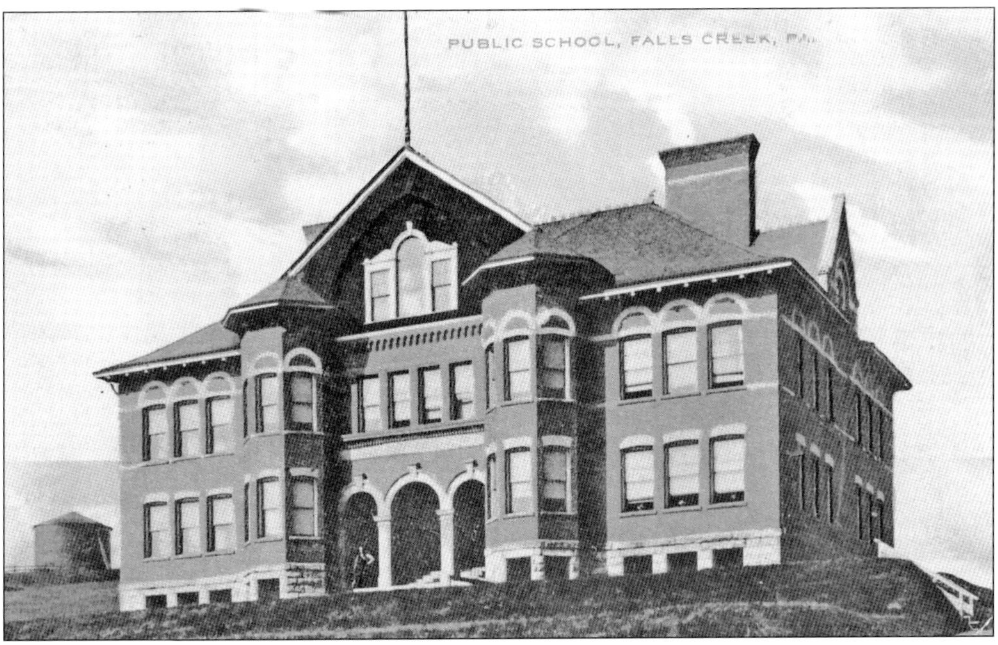

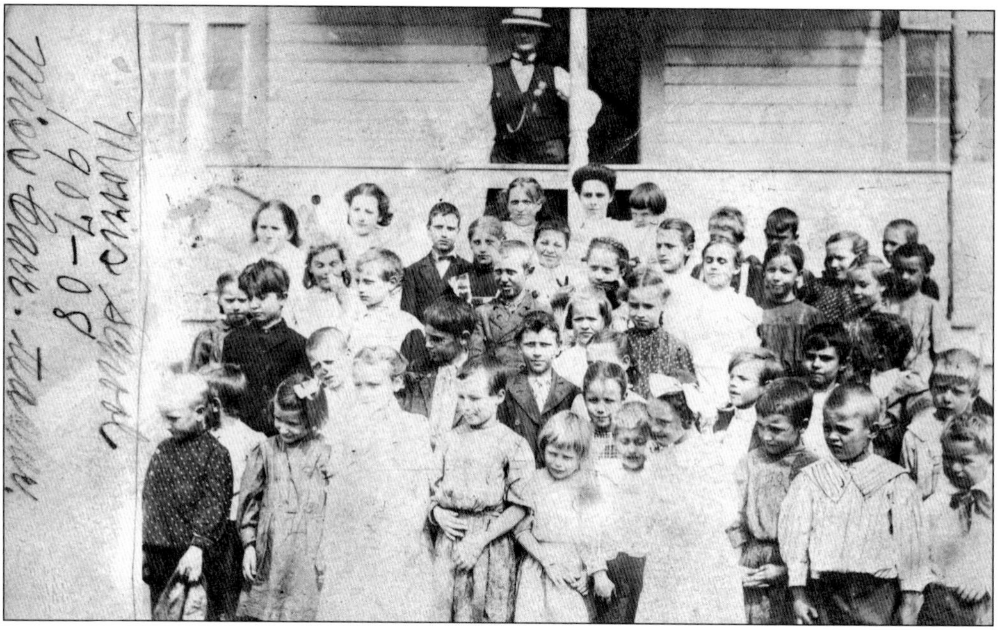

Prior to 1950, townships and municipalities were responsible for education. About 1883, Young Township moved the first Morris School to Walston to serve the children of the mining community. In 1907–1908, this Morris School (above), located on Obed Morris's farm, was a typical one-room school. Over 120 schools were located within what became the consolidated Punxsutawney Area School District in the 1950s. The public school (below) at Clayville (Lindsey) was built in 1890. It served until 1957, when the new West End Elementary School was built. The Punxsutawney Area College Trust purchased the building, and in cooperation with Indiana State College, opened a branch campus in September 1962. The building was razed in 2007 to make way for a new Indiana University of Pennsylvania regional campus. (Both, PAHGS.)

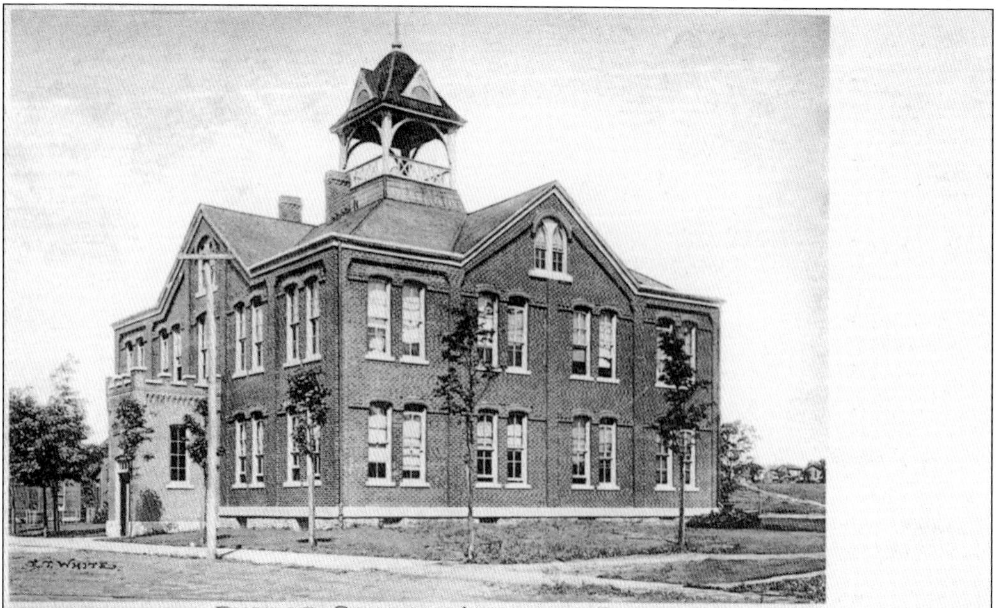

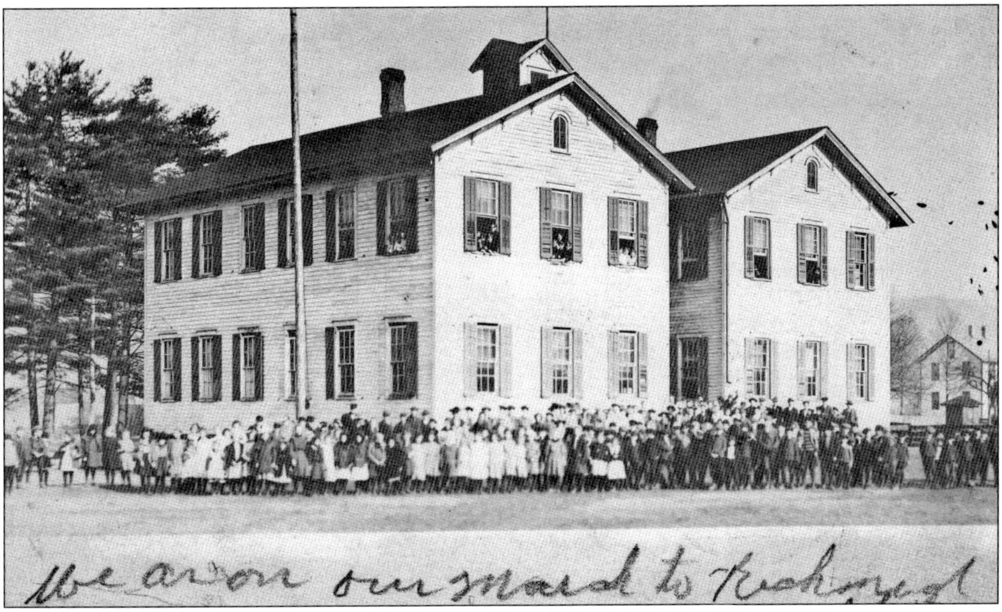

In Brockway, third- and fourth-grade classrooms were housed in a small building to the left of the larger structures (not visible). Others also attended classes in these buildings until 1921. Removed intact for construction of the new school and converted into apartments on Alexander Street, the buildings are still occupied today. Students began classes in the Main Street School (below) on September 10, 1923. There were classrooms on all three levels, as well as modern restrooms, sanitary drinking fountains, and a gymnasium with showers, dressing rooms, and lockers. Folding doors separated the seventh- and eighth-grade rooms and when opened formed an assembly room. Considered one of the most modern and up-to-date school buildings in the state when it was built, this and the Ninth Avenue School closed in 1978 and were razed in 1982. The Council of Human Dignity bought the site for $60,000 and dedicated Toby Terrace in 1983. (Both, BAHS.)

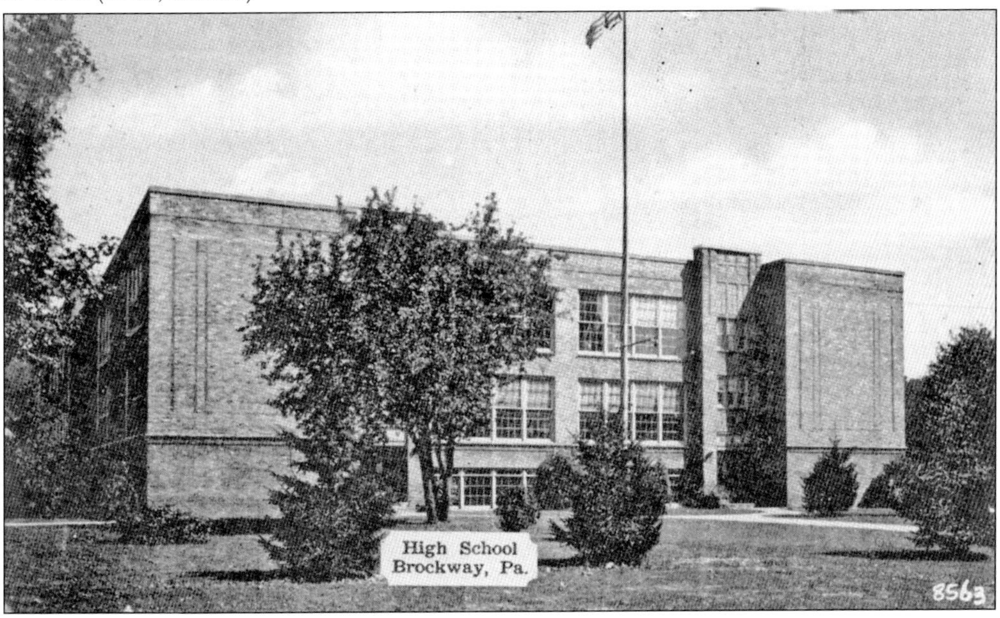

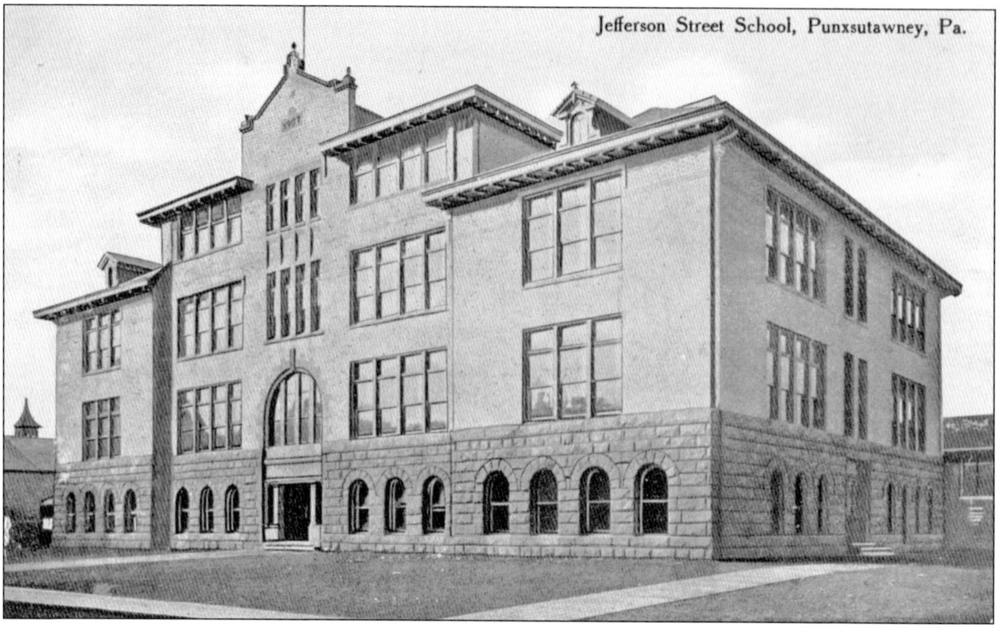

Jefferson Street School (above), the first of three schools on North Jefferson Street in Punxsutawney, had four floors, each accessed by a large, open, double, circular staircase. All students, elementary through high school, went there from 1909 until construction of the Jackson Building. The Art Deco Jackson Building (below) included a 1,000-seat auditorium and gymnasium, was built in 1937 as the high school annex, and was named for Frank S. Jackson, superintendent for 38 years. With the Jefferson Street School, it was the town's high school until 1959, when Punxsutawney Area High School opened. The Jackson Building is now the Punxsutawney Area Community Center. It and the adjacent Weber Building comprised the junior high complex from 1959 until Punxsutawney Area Middle School was built in 1997. Two modern elementary schools, Jenks Hill and Mary A. Wilson, served students after 1950. (Both, PAHGS.)

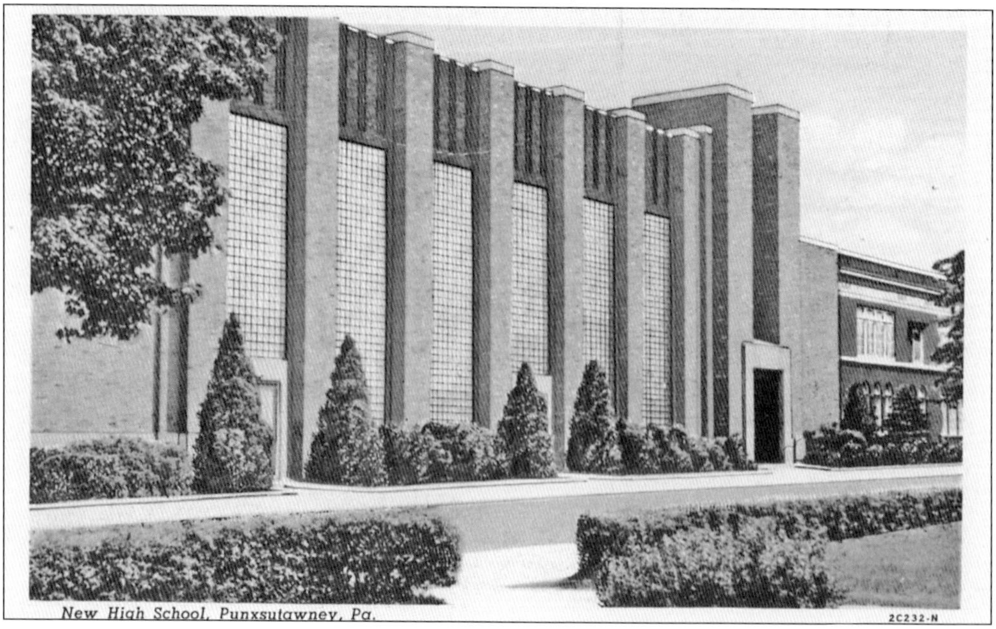

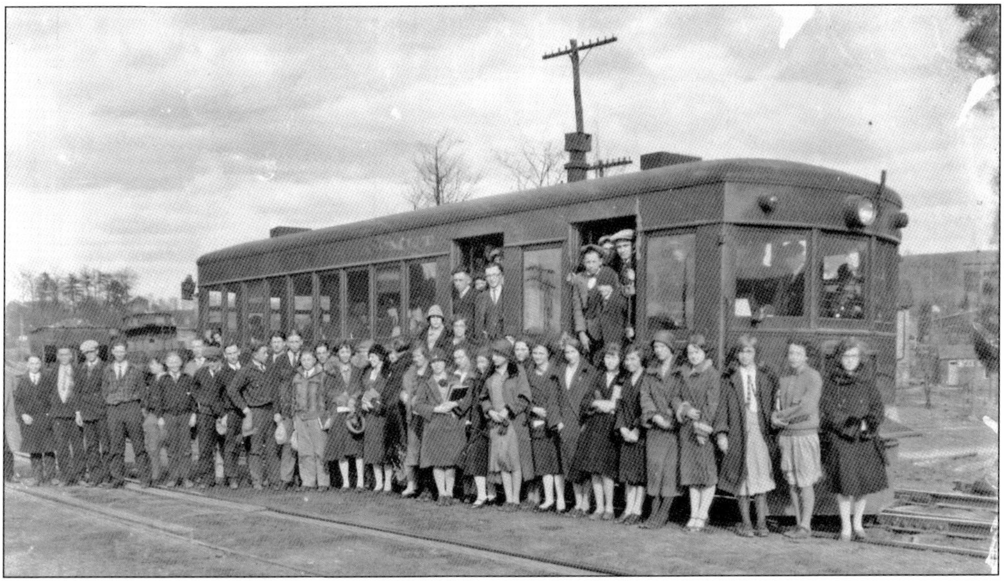

Students from smaller towns rode to Brookville's Central School on the "Hoodlebug," a gasoline-powered tram (above). The Northside Elementary School (below) was completed in 1939 across Barnett Street to the east of the Central School complex, now Northside Park. In the late 1900s, state maintenance regulations made improving Pennsylvania's historic schools difficult and Brookville's Northside Elementary School almost closed. However, preservationists were able to show the state that properly renovated historic schools could actually be safer than new schools. Following renovation, the building won first prize from the National Trust for Historic Preservation and was the featured "poster child" for 2001. Today, Brookville students attend the Northside School for kindergarten, Pinecreek Elementary for the primary grades, and Hickory Grove Elementary for grades three through six, then move to the junior-senior high school building. (Both, JCHC.)

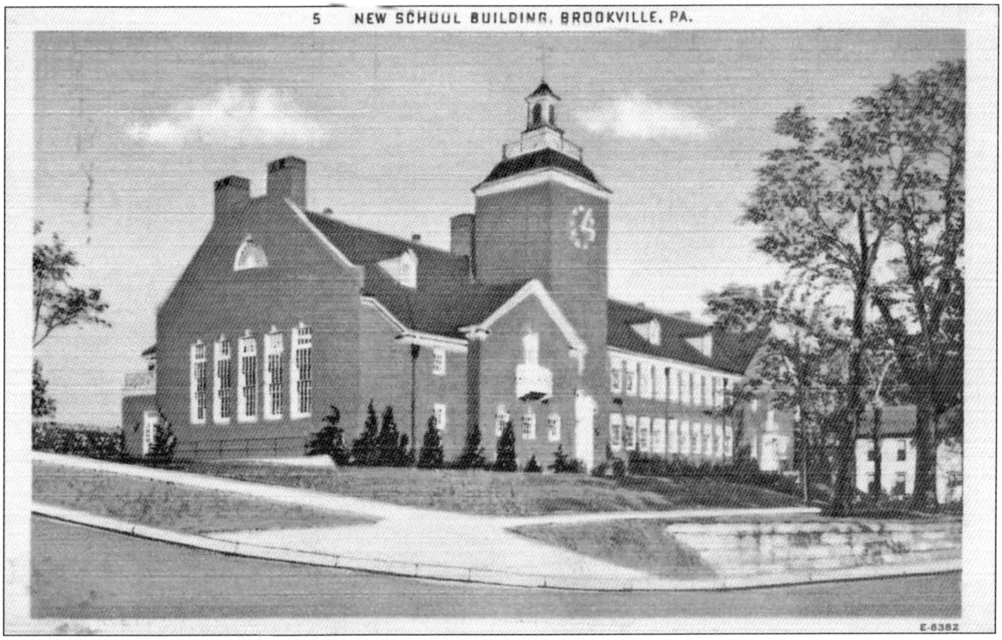

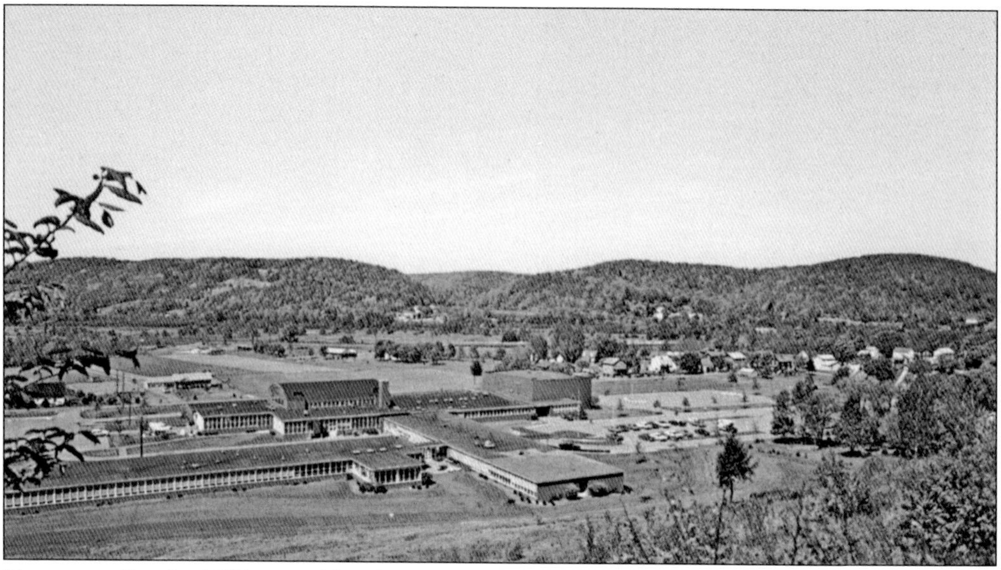

Two years after the 1955 ground breaking, students at Brockway Area High School (above) carried their books from the Main Street School to new classrooms. Representing the best in modern American school architecture in a 1958 exhibit in Switzerland, the project cost $1.7 million. A 1970s addition allowed seventh graders, previously housed in the adjacent elementary building, to move to the high school. Consolidation in the 1950s included an examination of the best way to provide vocational education. The Jefferson County–DuBois Area Vocational Technical School (below) opened near Reynoldsville in 1969 for students from Brockway, Brookville, DuBois, and Punxsutawney. One of the commonwealth's 84 public vocational schools, Jeff-Tech currently enrolls nearly 400 students in 14 career and technical fields. It is comprehensive in that students receive their career training and academic course work all in the same building. (Above, BAHS; below, JCHC.)

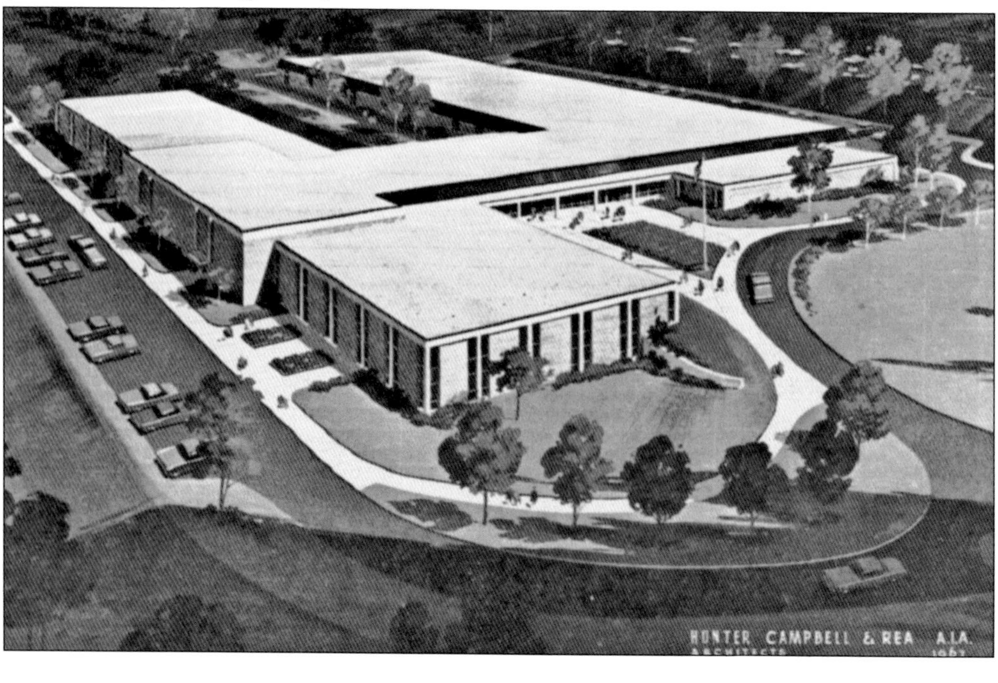

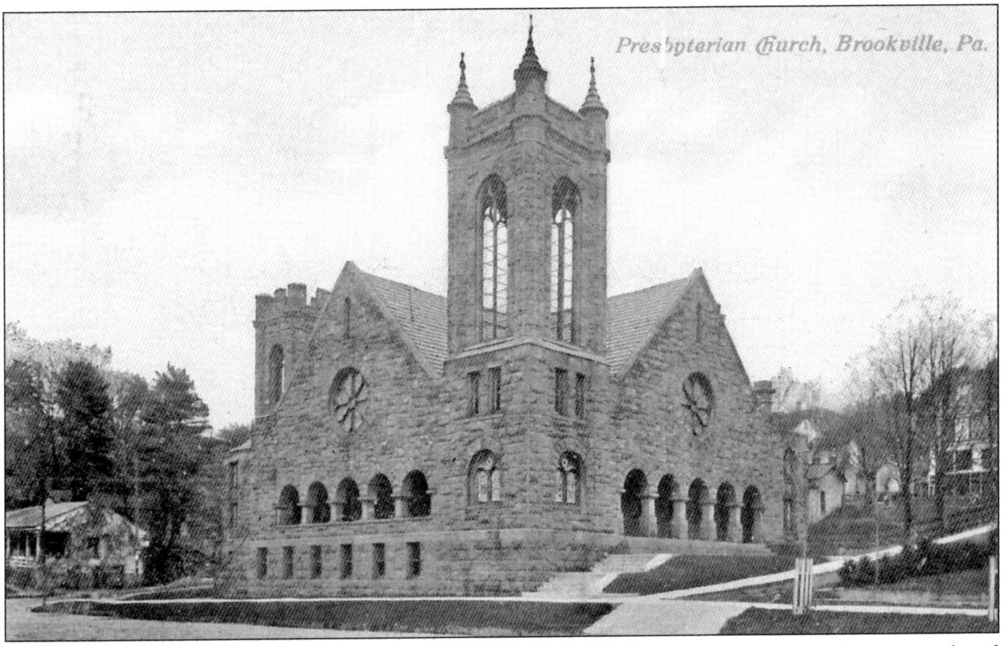

The Scots Irish populated the frontier, and by 1824, Brookville Presbyterians had organized and built Bethel Church west of town. In 1870, they moved into Brookville and built a Gothic-style building. A third building (above) was dedicated in 1905. The Pittsburgh firm of Robinson and Winkler chose the popular Richardsonian Romanesque style. It is built of brownstone, and the roof uses distinctive "Brookville green" tiles. The second Presbyterian congregation in the county organized in 1832 at Beechwoods. An earlier structure was on this same site from 1850 until it was torn down and replaced in 1888 by this church at the intersection of Stevenson Hill Road and Beechwood Road (below). Although several times enlarged and renovated, this building is still used by the congregation. (Above, JCHC; below, BAHS.)

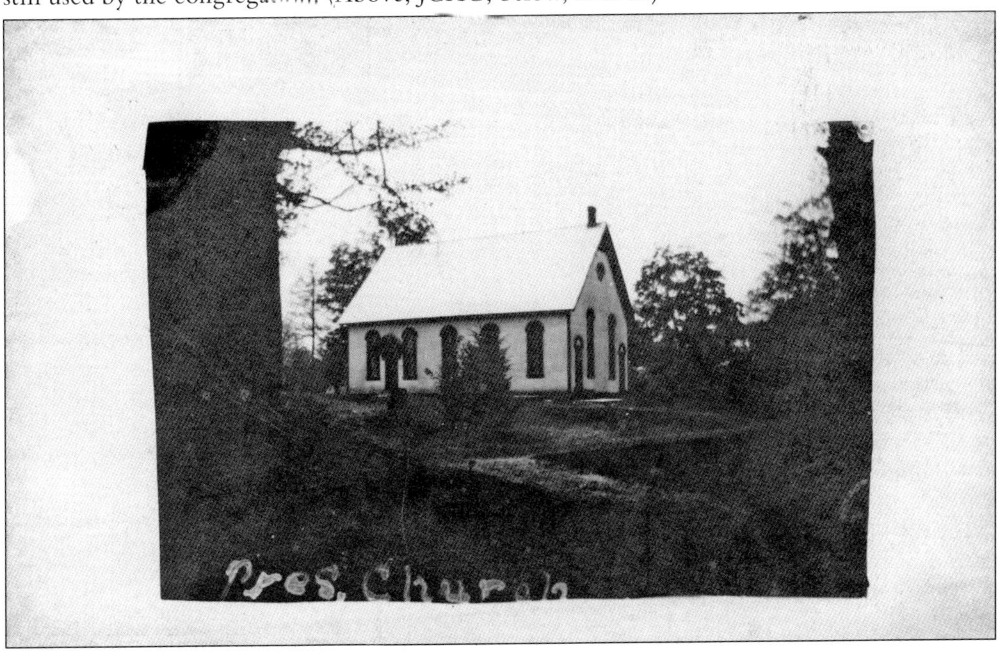

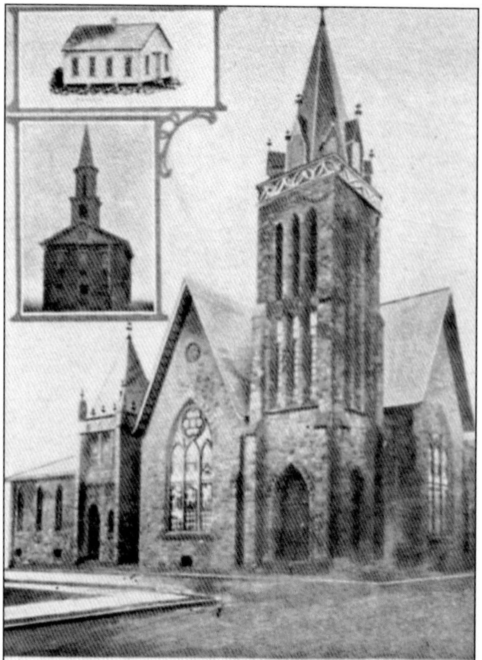

First M. E. Church erected nearly 100 years ago, drawn from description. Second M. E. Church dedicated 1860, now used as Salvation Army Barracks. Present M. E. Church erected 1899. Punxsutawney, Pa.

Punxsutawney's First Methodist Episcopal Church organized in 1812 and occupied the structures at 229 West Mahoning Street, shown in the postcard insets. In 1899, it moved to a Gothic-style building with many stained-glass windows at 301 West Mahoning Street (left). The congregation worships there today. After lightning struck, the steeple was removed. (PAHGS.)

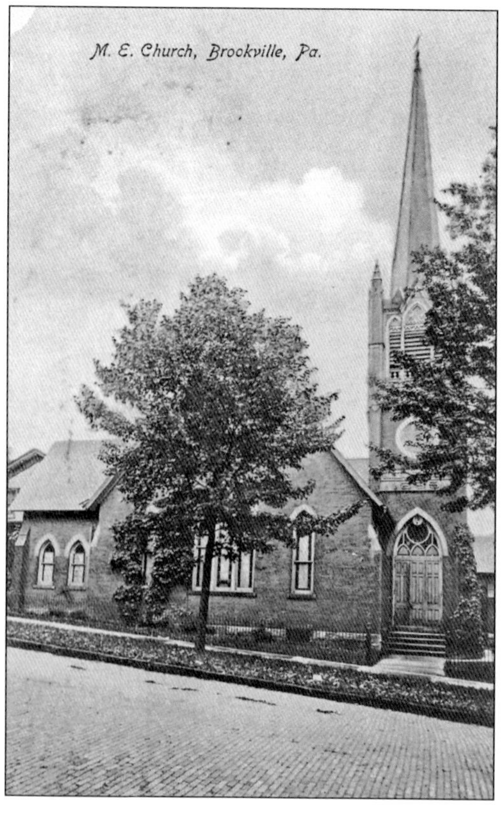

Brookville Methodist Episcopalians built a church in 1854 only to see it burn to the ground two years later. They built another of brick, then sold it to the United Presbyterians when the Methodists decided in 1878 to build a church on the east side of Pickering Street (pictured). The congregation grew, sold the smaller building, and built a larger church on the southwest corner of Jefferson and Pickering Streets, but alas, the new building, completed in 1921, burned down. (JCHC.)

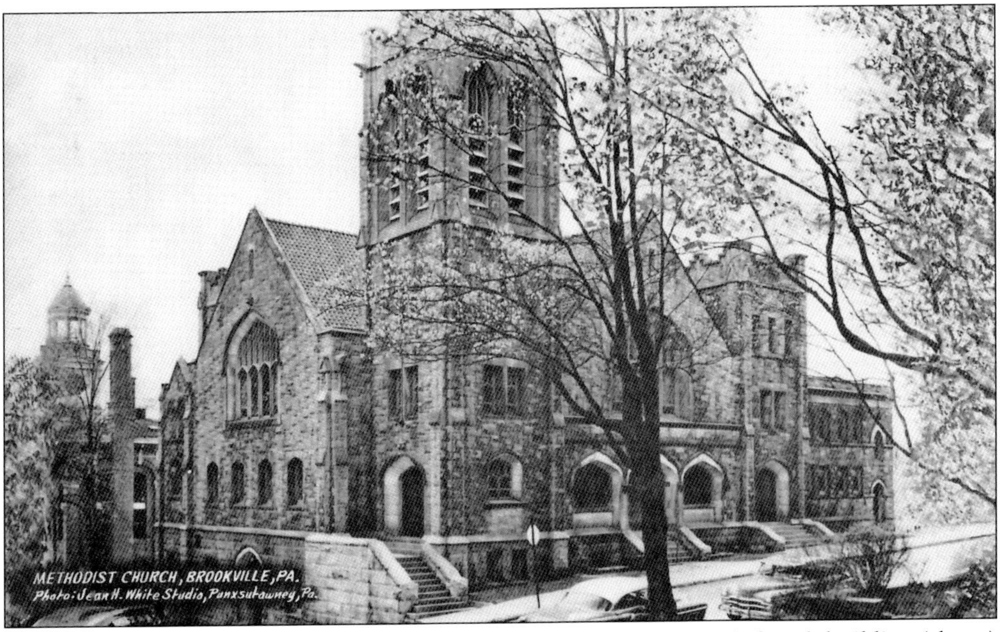

Quickly rebuilt after the fire, the Brookville Methodist congregation's fourth building (above) is located behind the courthouse. Local lumbermen donated lumber to build the Brockway Methodist Episcopal Church in the early 1860s. When the population grew and the early structure became too small, a newspaper article reported that the proposed church would be "strong, sightly, and commodious." The original building was moved and reoriented to face Second Street (now Fourth Avenue). The building (below) was dedicated on January 25, 1891. Separated by folding doors, the new addition could seat 275 and the old portion 225. In 1929, the church was bricked and a basement was added to meet the needs of the congregation. Brockway's Moorhead United Methodist Church is located on the corner of Fourth Avenue and Main Street. (Above, JCHC; below, BAHS.)

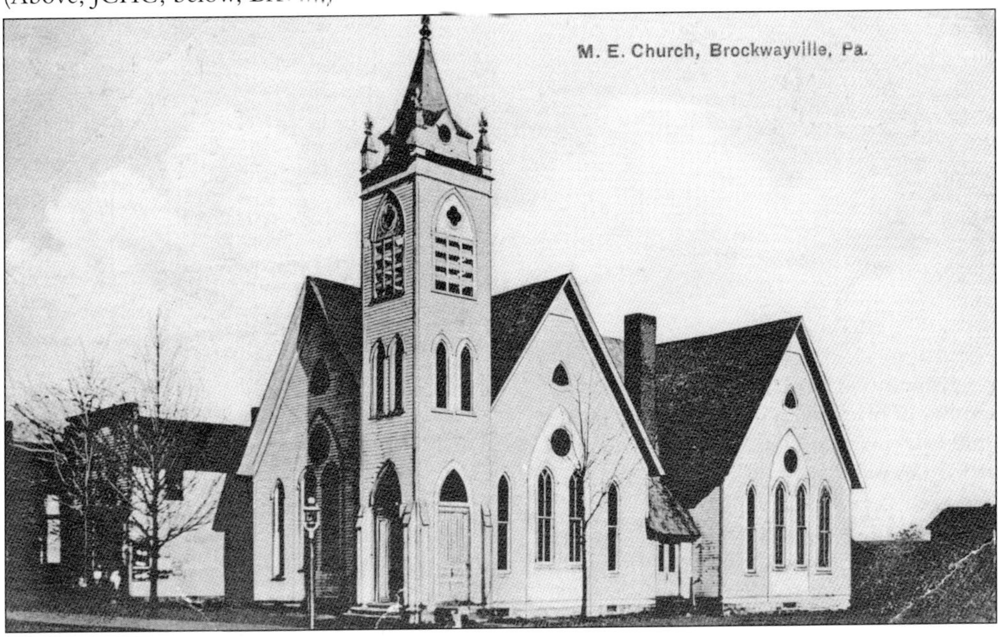

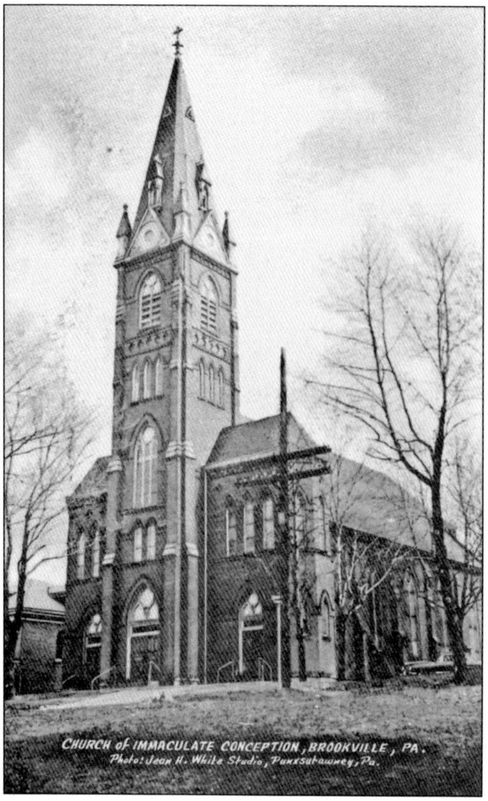

From 1830 until 1871, when Catholic men arrived to work on the railroad, Brookville's Roman Catholic population was small. Rev. Tobias Mullen laid the cornerstone for this building with its gold spire in 1872. The congregation eventually built a residence and two school buildings high on one of the seven hills overlooking Brookville. (JCHC.)

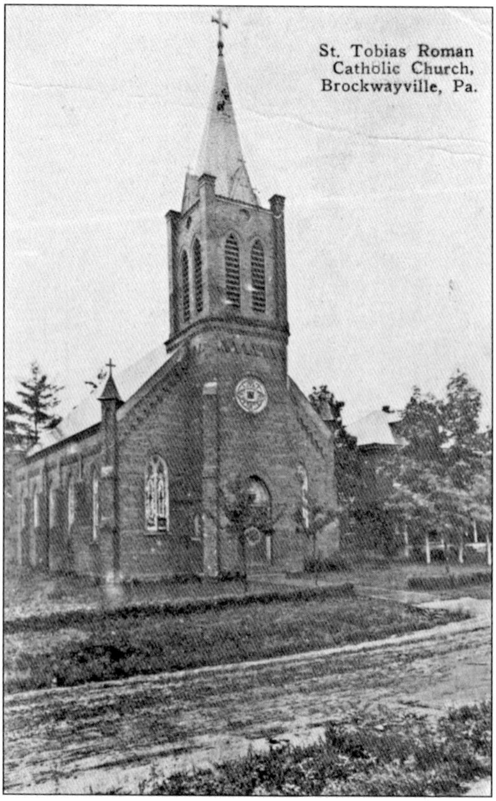

The booming bituminous coal industry of the 1880s brought many Catholic immigrants to the Toby Valley. Many had to walk or ride four miles to attend services at St. Anastasius in Brockport, so in 1899, Tobias Mullen, then a bishop, gave permission for the construction of the building seen here. Dedicated on October 30, 1904, St. Tobias Roman Catholic Church served area Catholics until it was razed and replaced in the 1960s by the present building on Hewitt Street. (BAHS.)

Brockwayville Presbyterians organized in 1884 and built the church pictured here on the north side of Main Street between Seventh and Eighth Avenues. In 1900, Brockwayville had a population of 1,800, with a Presbyterian membership of 300. In 1964, when the congregation needed a new manse and educational facility, it purchased adjacent land and built the present Colonial-style church and education wing. (BAHS.)

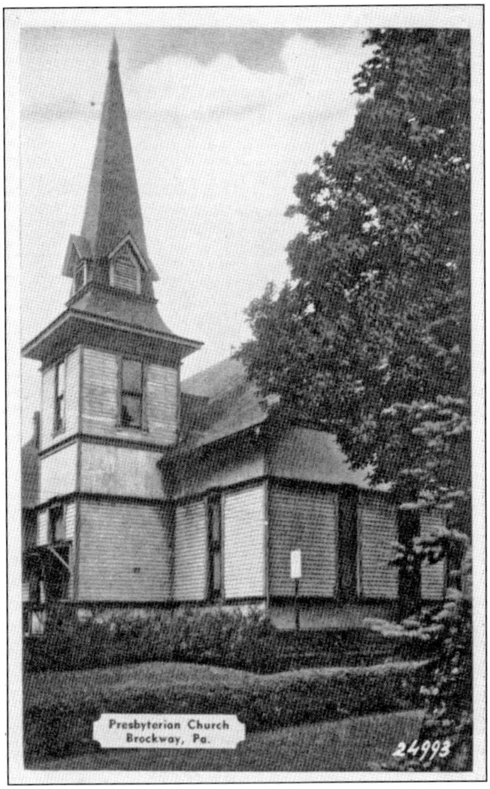

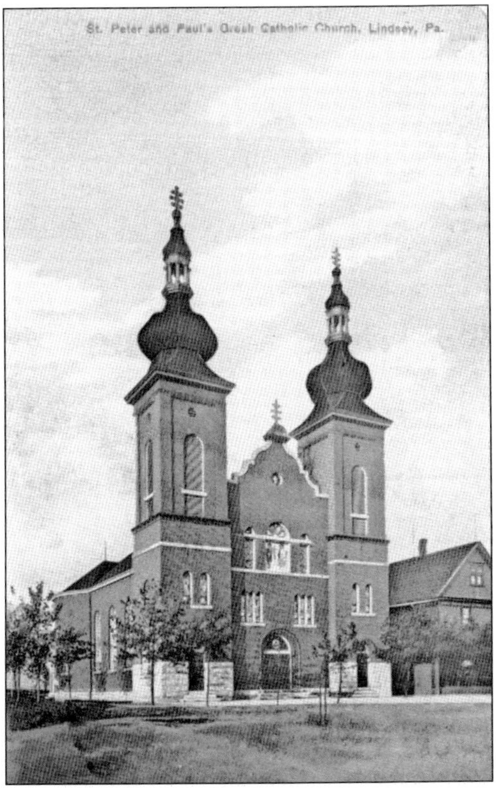

Established in 1893 to serve the many Slavic and Hungarian immigrants drawn to the area's mining communities of Walston, Adrian, and Horatio, the SS. Peter and Paul Byzantine Catholic Church was built at Lindsey. In 1895, the initial frame structure was relocated and replaced with a brick building (pictured) noted for its beautiful iconostasis and other interior painting. Prior to 1923, twin spires replaced the twin domes, a visible hillside landmark in Punxsutawney's West End. (PAHGS.)

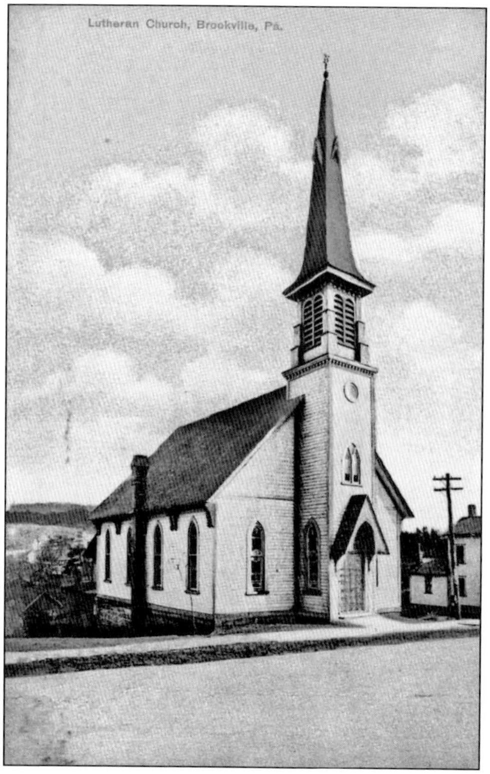

The Grace Lutheran Church structure (at left) is the oldest in Brookville. Built in 1850 and remodeled several times since, the building now includes a preschool. The congregation purchased the home to the north of the original structure and built an addition connecting the two. (JCHC.)

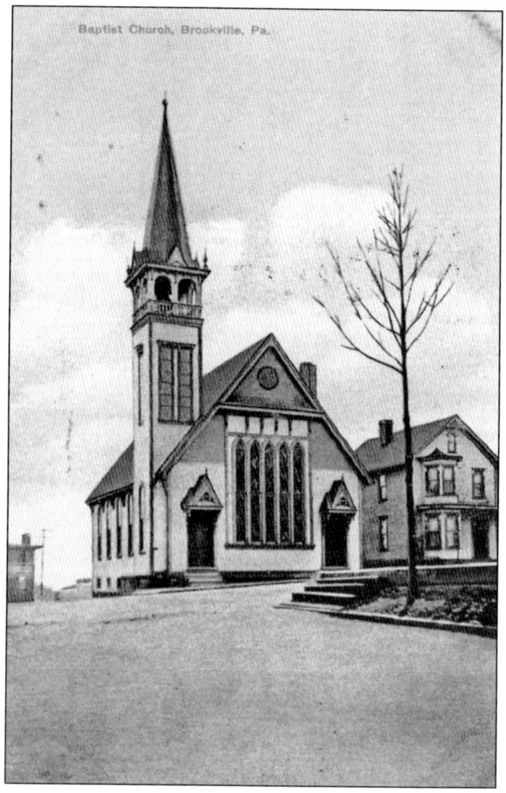

Physician and Baptist clergyman Jonathan Nichols arrived near Brandycamp in 1818, and he and his successors ministered to the Baptists of the county, sometimes traveling to Clarion County to worship at the Zion meetinghouse. Baptist congregations had organized in Beechwoods, Brookville, Corsica, and Punxsutawney by 1840. In 1883, the Baptist congregation in Brookville erected a building (at right) on the corner of Main Street and Mill (now Franklin) Avenue. Lightning struck the building in 1986 and demolished it. The congregation dedicated the present structure on the same location in 1989. (JCHC.)

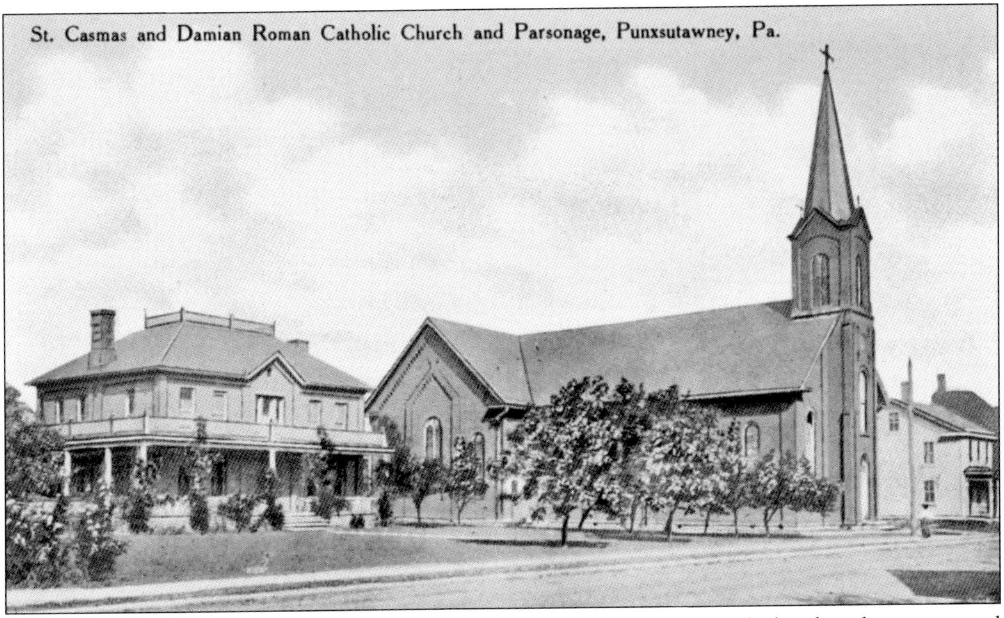

In 1887, SS. Cosmas and Damian Roman Catholic Church, the first Catholic church constructed in Punxsutawney, served as the center for mission churches in area mining communities. A 1941 renovation refaced the exterior of the buildings with sandstone and included niches for statues of SS. Cosmas and Damian (above). The church now serves as the parish for Catholics in the surrounding communities. Pastor Vernon Boyer founded Brookville's First Assembly of God Church (below) in 1952. The congregation first met in an available lodge room, then moved into this building in 1956 and on to a new facility in 1981. This building was the home of Just For Jesus Challenge Homeless Outreach, a charitable organization that provided shelter, food, clothing, life skills, and more to the homeless. The structure was demolished in 2017. (Above, PAHGS; below, JCHC.)

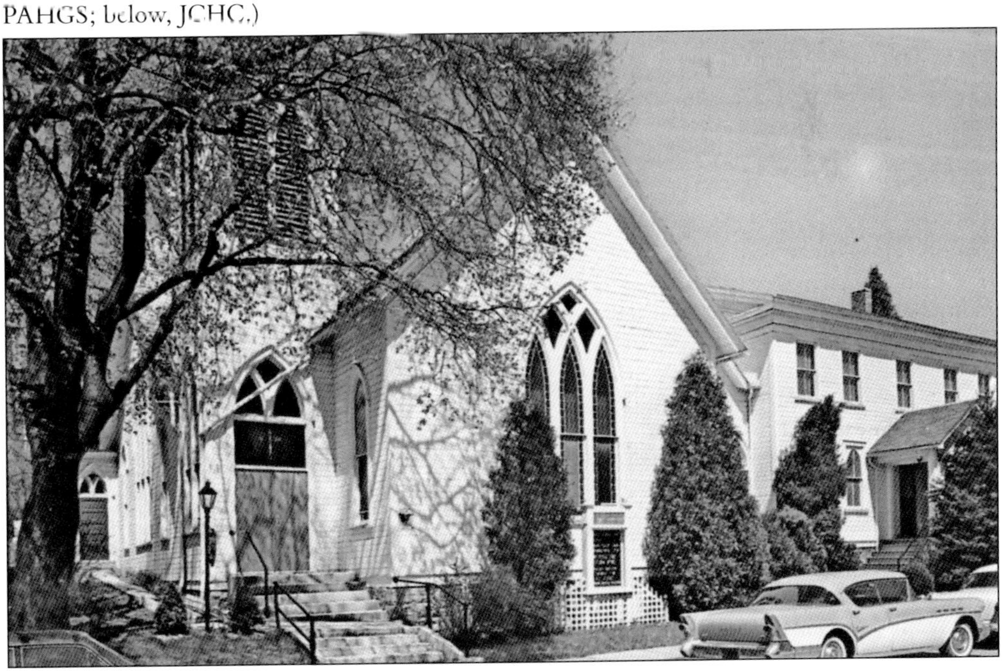

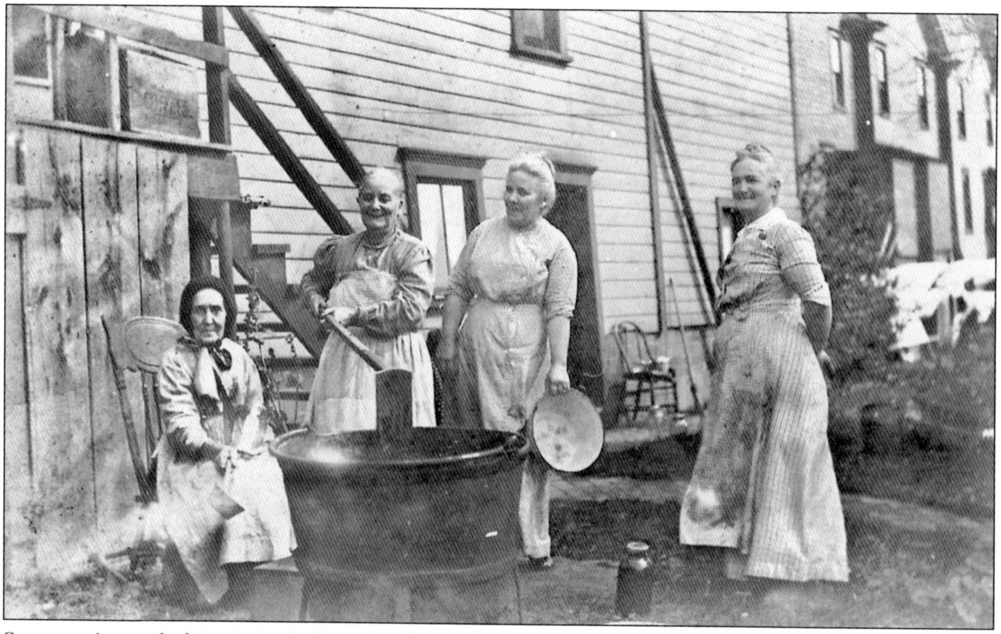

Sanctuaries and classrooms bring people together, and so do times of work and play. Canning vegetables, making apple butter, or rendering lard was more productive when neighbors, like these Reynoldsville women (above), met and shared in the work. As with quilting parties, many hands make light work. Other group activities included corn husking, maple sugar boiling, scutchings, and barn raisings. When children get together, it is usually for fun, not work. Hill Street in Reynoldsville has long held a reputation as the best place for winter sledding. Whether using runner sleds or driving a "set of bobs," the run down the hill for groups like the ones below in the 1930s was always a thrilling experience. In later years, the borough provided barricades, closing off the cross streets to motor traffic. (Both, RHS.)

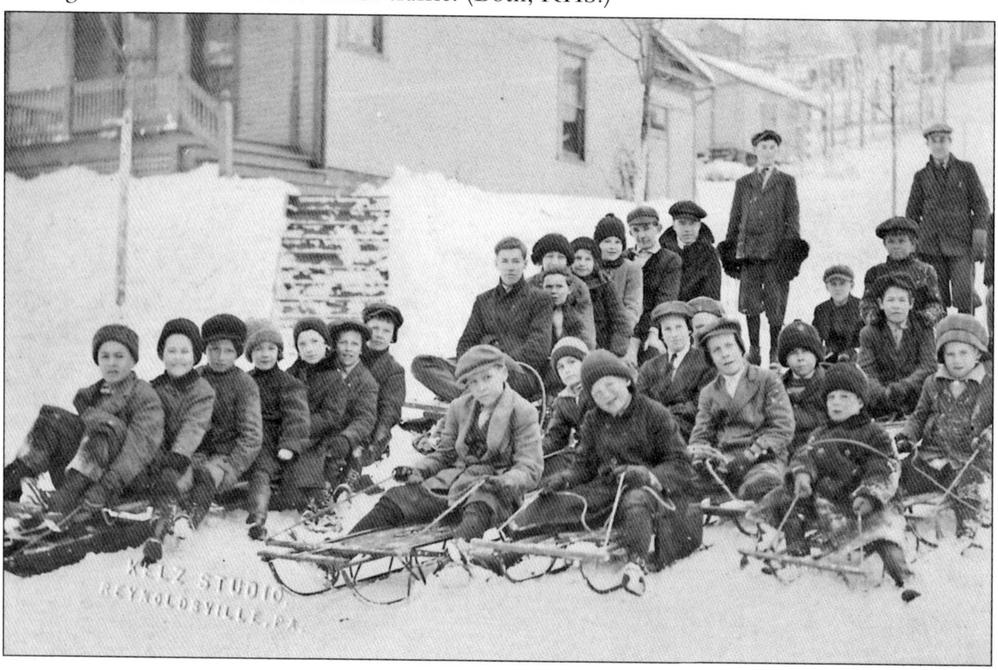

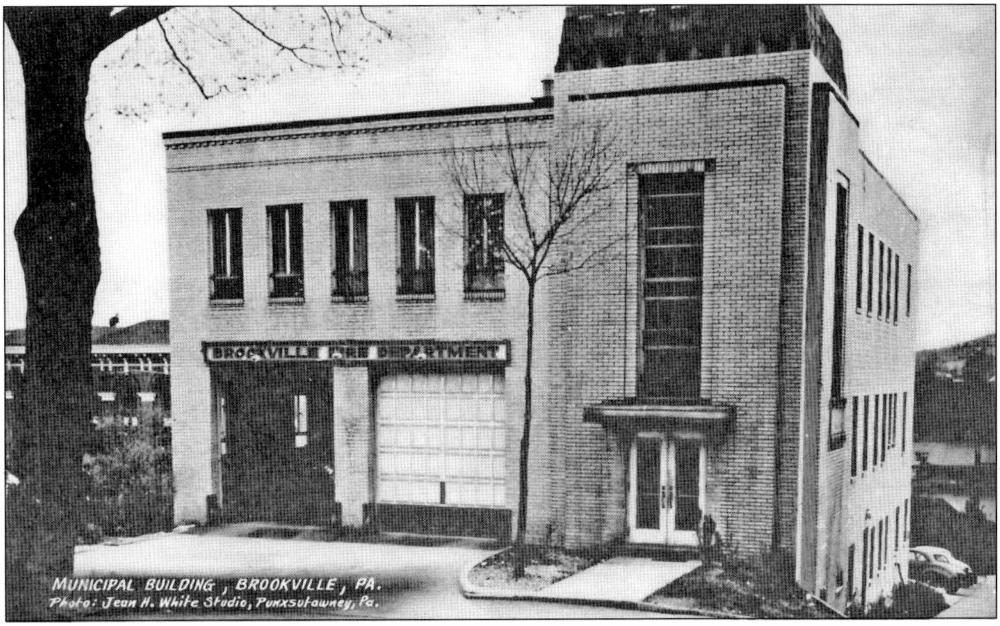

The Brookville Municipal Building (above) housed the police and fire departments and borough offices from the 1930s to 2007. When a fire truck went through the floor, the borough bought the sprawling Pennsylvania Memorial Home (PMH) on the east side of town. Laurelbrooke, a continuing care facility just south of the hospital, had replaced the PMH. Constructed in 1937, the Pennsylvania Department of Highways Headquarters (below) on Witherow Street in Punxsutawney serves as the administrative center for Maintenance District 10-5, Jefferson County. The approximately 96 people employed at this facility maintain or oversee the work of contractors engaged in the maintenance of the 576 miles of state highways and 296 bridges within the county. (Above, JCHC; below, PAHGS.)

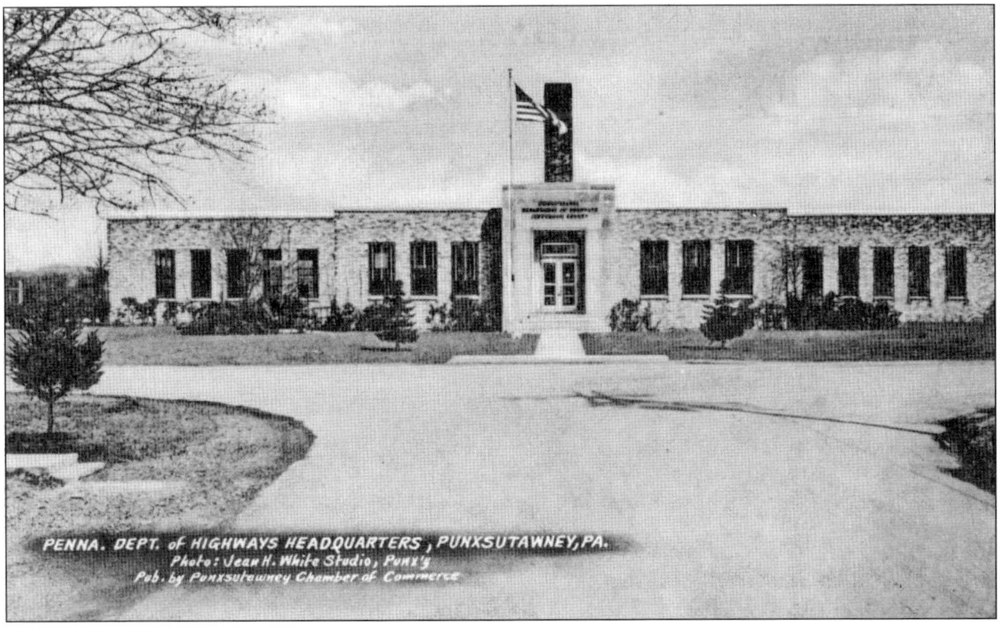

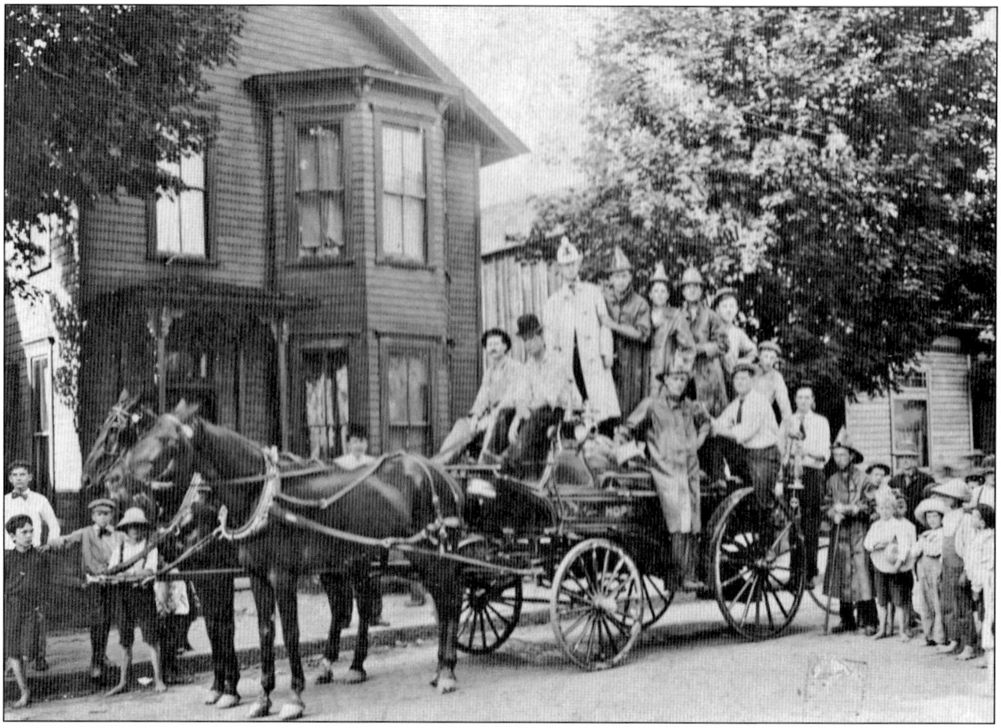

Reynoldsville's original fire company organized in 1875 and consisted of little more than buckets and ladders (above). It added an extinguisher, and in 1888, the establishment of the Reynoldsville Water Company made the utilization of hoses a reality. In 1899, due to requirements for membership in the Pennsylvania Volunteer Fireman's Association, the company officially changed its name to the Hope Fire Company. Gasoline torches used to thaw frozen water pipes caused two major Brockway fires. The 1911 fire consumed the large general store managed by R.W. Beadle & Co. in the Moorhead & Bond (Excelsior) Building. Fighting the fire with a hose cart and buckets, the Brockway Volunteer Hose Company realized its need for the DuBois steam pumper (below). A second fire, during the winter of 1923, destroyed many buildings. (Above, RHS; below, BAHS.)

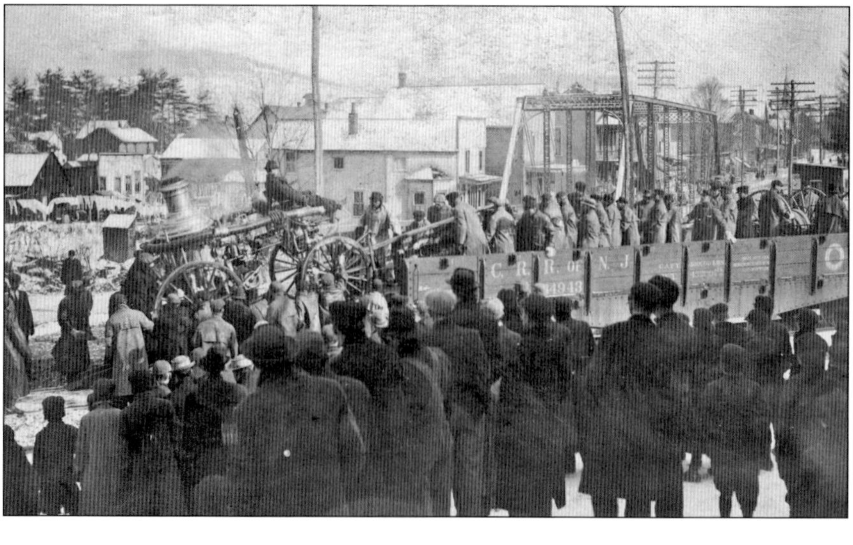

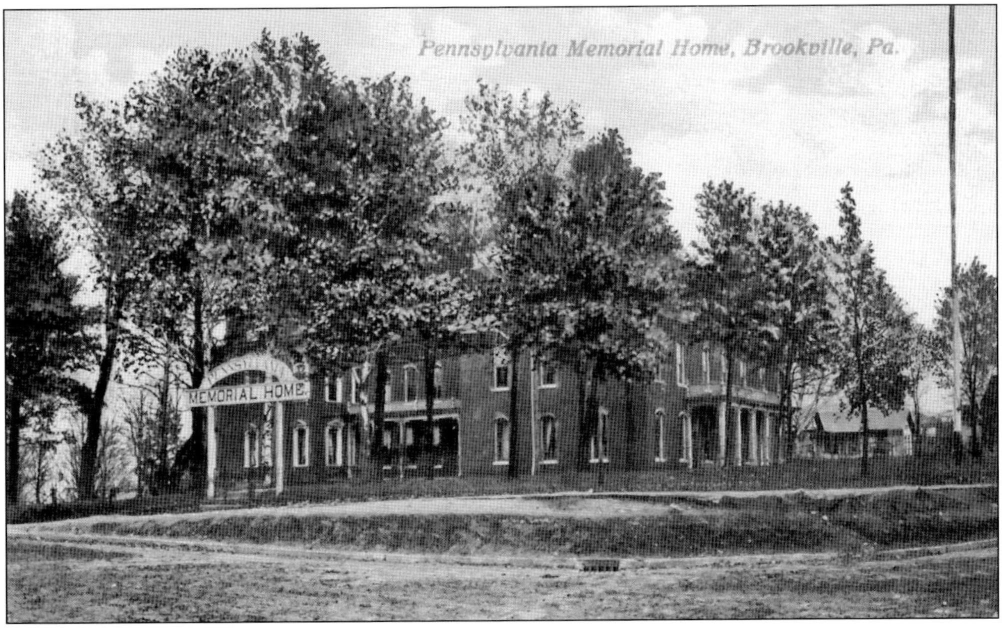

Instrumental in the purchase of the Long Hotel and its adaptation as a home for Civil War veterans and their wives, widows, and children, historian Kate M. Scott remained active on its behalf until her death in 1911. The Woman's Relief Corps (WRC) converted the hotel into the Pennsylvania Memorial Home, a building that, with several additions, offered care for more than a century. A member of the WRC, Scott wrote histories of the 105th Pennsylvania Volunteer Regiment, Jefferson County, and the nurses who served in the war—something she herself had done. In 1910, Scott traveled to Atlantic City for the annual gathering of the Grand Army of the Republic and wrote a postcard inviting her good friend Jennie Pinney to come, too. Scott's history of the nurses was distributed to those who attended. (Both, JCHC.)

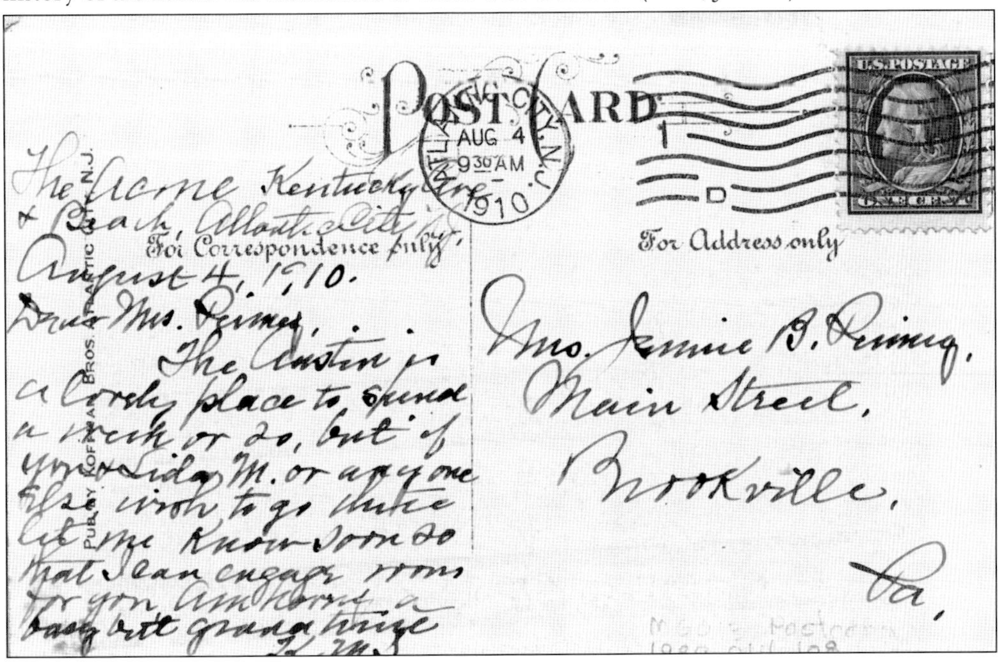

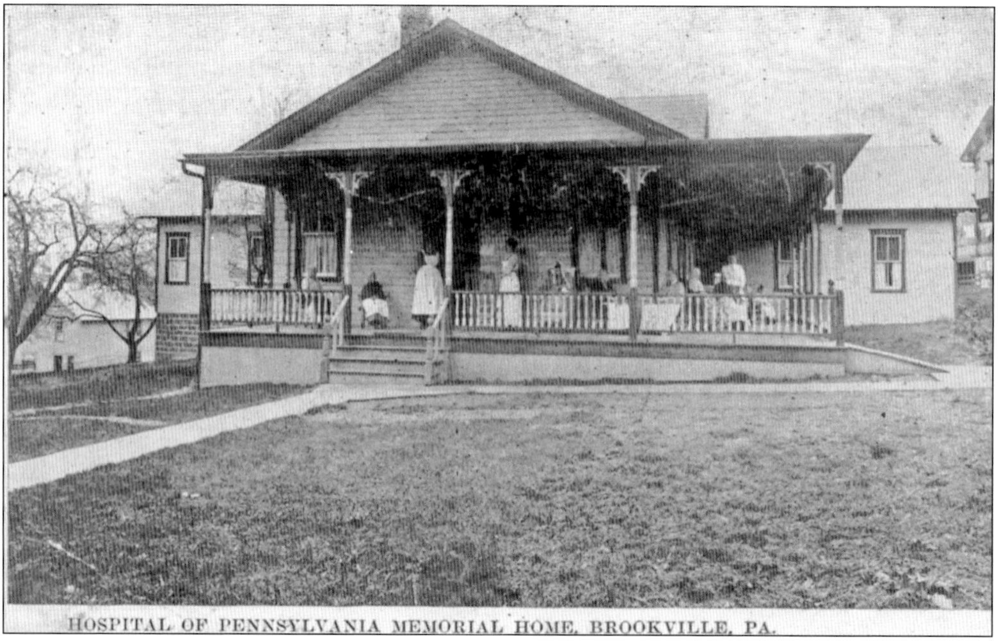

The Pennsylvania Memorial Home maintained an infirmary, or hospital, for residents (above). Ten female residents died in a tragic fire in the winter of 1934. By the 1860s, most large cities and about half of Pennsylvania's counties maintained houses for the poor, but not Jefferson County. Here, the elected overseers of the individual municipalities and townships let out for bid the care of the insane and poor. After a very close vote in 1901, the county purchased 249 acres in Pinecreek Township and built a county home (below), the biggest county project since building the courthouse in 1869. When the new Jefferson Manor opened in 1977, the old building became the service center for county offices, a move eventually deemed illegal, as county offices need to be within the county seat. The building was sold, then razed in 2001. (Both, JCHC.)

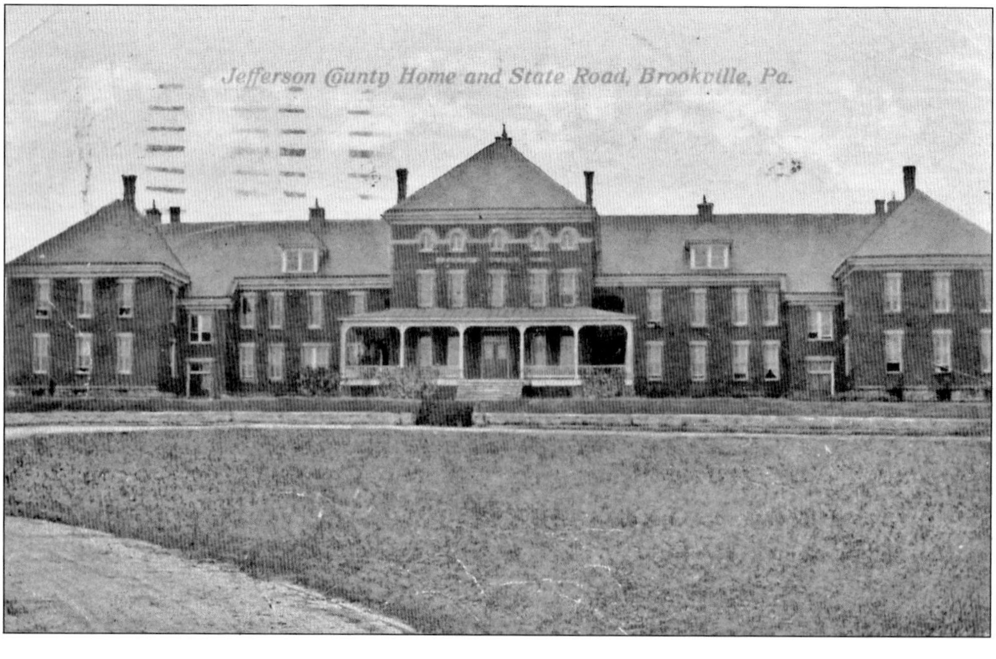

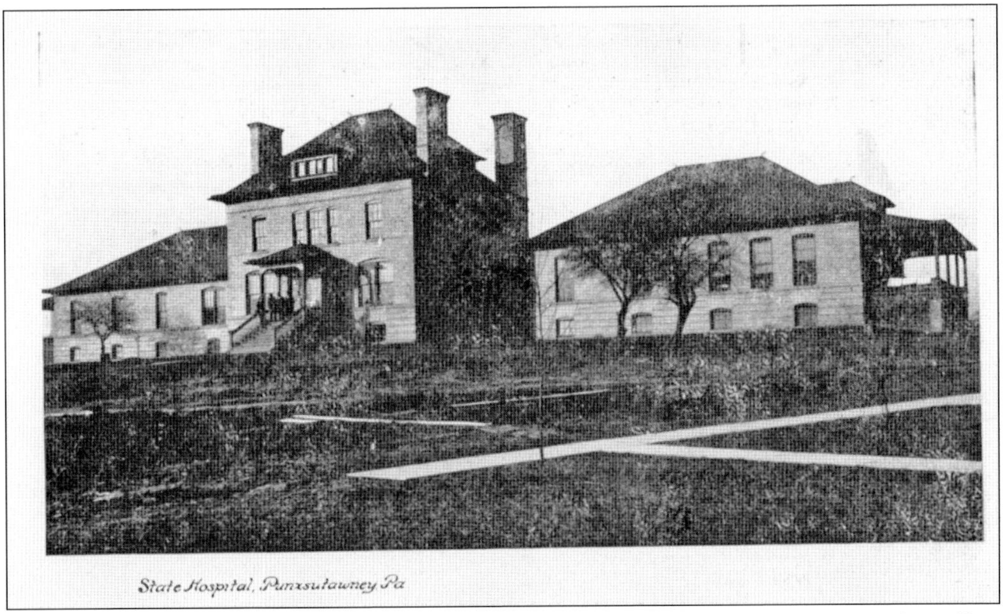

State Hospital, Punxsutawney Pa

Built in 1898 with state and local funding, the new Adrian Hospital (above), on Jenks Hill in Punxsutawney, replaced the original at Adrian Mines, the first medical facility of its kind in rural north-central Pennsylvania. Adrian Hospital served mining communities from DuBois to Indiana before they built hospitals. The hospital continued in operation until the Punxsutawney Area Hospital opened on Hillcrest Drive in 1978. The Punxsutawney Hospital, built in 1907 on Gilpin Street (below), also provided health-care services for the community. These hospitals encouraged a strong medical community in Punxsutawney and offered nurses' training programs, which promised a new career for many area women. The building housed the Clearfield Aviation Institute from 1946 to 1953, later held offices of state programs, and currently contains the Punxsutawney Senior Center, Head Start Program, and private offices. (Both, PAHGS.)

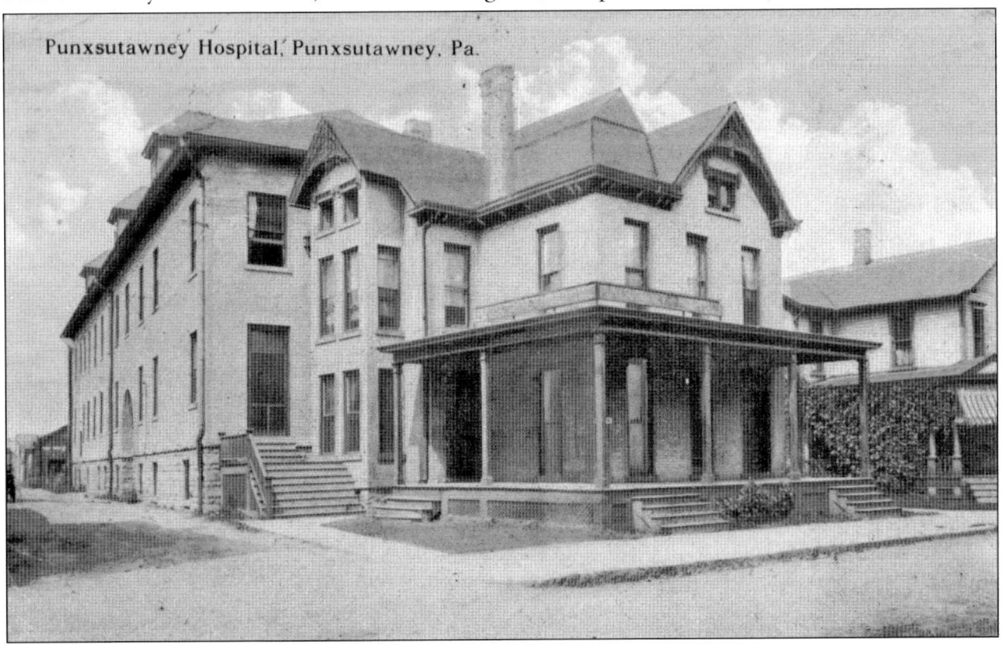

Punxsutawney Hospital, Punxsutawney, Pa.

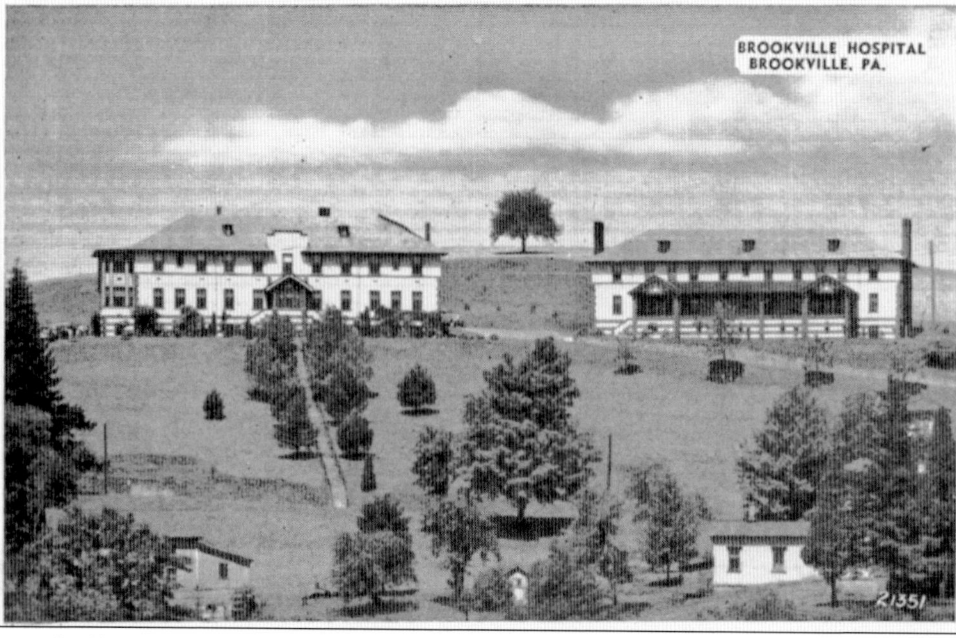

In Brookville at the beginning of the 20th century, doctors made house calls and Dr. Wayne Snyder maintained a small hospital on Franklin Avenue. The community was raising funds when World War I intervened, delaying the opening of a new hospital (above, left) until 1919. The nurses' residence (above, right) was completed in 1929. Headlines claimed the new Brookville Hospital would serve 40,000 people. By 1948, even though there were hospitals in neighboring towns, there was serious overcrowding. The board raised funds to build the Campbell Wing. By 1972, the hospital (below) had expanded several times. Today, it is part of the Penn Highlands Healthcare System. Ambulance and helicopter transport is available to larger hospitals in DuBois and Pittsburgh. A rare fivesome, Dr. Arthur Clifton McKinley and his four physician sons provided a total of nearly 200 years of health-care services between 1908 and 2001. (Both, JCHC.)

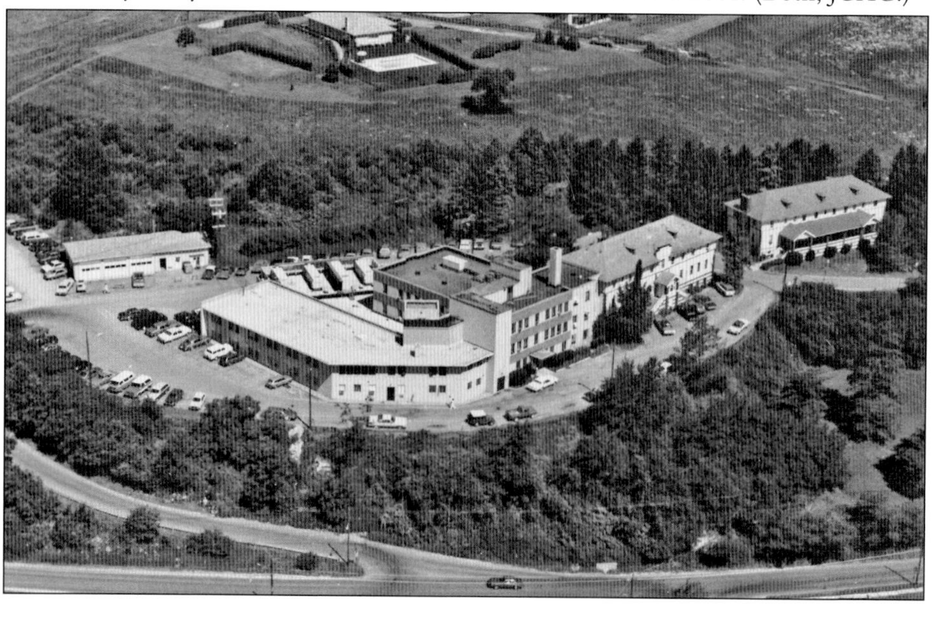

Six

Remember

Posted at the county's borders are signs reading "Come for fun, stay for good," an expression that highlights the possibilities for fun and relaxation that exist in the area and exemplifies the hardworking good people of rural Jefferson County.

Settler life was certainly not easy, yet those first arrivals found time for fun. Fiddlers played and cooks fed those that gathered for husking bees, barn raisings, spelling bees, and recitations.

Following the Civil War, prosperity increased. People played music in their parlors and formed clubs and societies. Lyceum speakers like suffragette Susan B. Anthony came to town, and a president or two showed up for the annual Teachers Institute. The Chautauqua movement traveled to small towns, raised a tent, and provided days and evenings of lectures and entertainments. County fairs, horse races, animal menageries, carnivals, and circuses drew crowds. Traveling shows and troupes of actors arrived and put on plays. As the school year lengthened, young people, too, put on plays, formed orchestras and bands, and organized athletic teams—occasions for people to come together.

Early German settlers brought with them their tradition of Candlemas on February 2, a custom that grew into the annual celebration of Groundhog Day in Punxsutawney. Brockway folks began celebrating the Fourth of July with parades more than a century ago. Reynoldsville's Old Home Week began in 1907 and is still held each summer. During the Great Depression, folks organized the Western Pennsylvania Laurel Festival as a way to draw visitors to Jefferson County, and in 1983, Brookville residents created the annual Victorian Christmas Celebration.

Folks remember good times and try to forget the bad, but tragedy comes to every community, and Jefferson County communities have had their share. Floods swept through them, and fires demolished blocks of main streets. The Great Depression and wars called men and women to serve. Yet people pulled together and moved on, as evidenced by major flood-control projects and the support of the county's 19 fire companies. Coming together in communities in both good times and bad happens in Jefferson County.

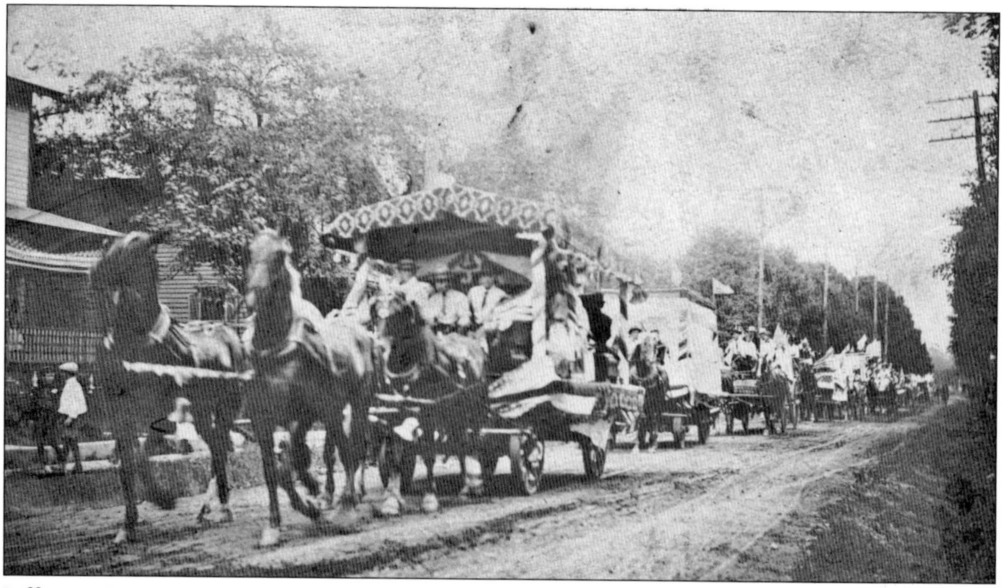

Jefferson County communities have been the sites of many types of parades. Soldiers marched on their way to fight the Civil War. Buggies paraded to cemeteries on Memorial Day. Brockwayville was patriotic and had a sense of civic pride, and its citizens celebrated the Fourth of July in 1907 with horse-drawn floats on dirt roads (above). The float in the foreground above was made by Matt Hutchins and Axel Kalgren and driven by Axel, Matt's employee. More decorated floats with American flags stretched back along Main Street. The year 1907 was memorable for Reynoldsville, too, in that a great celebration in August attracted crowds reliably estimated at over 15,000. People from all walks of life, especially those who had once lived and worked in Reynoldsville, eagerly returned to renew acquaintances and commemorate Old Home Week (below). (Above, BAHS; below, RHS.)

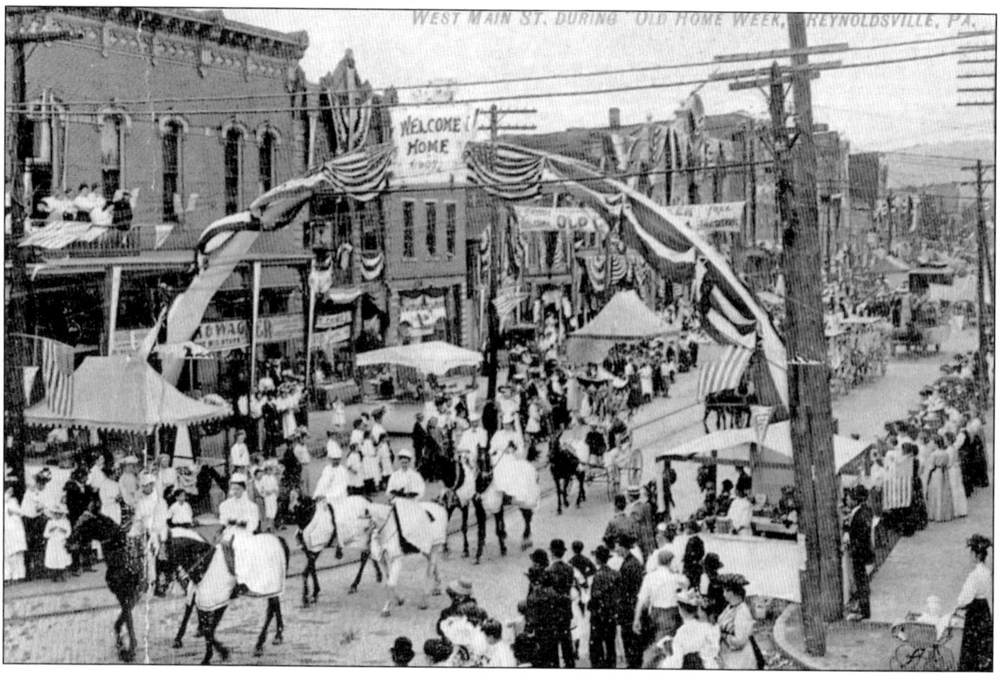

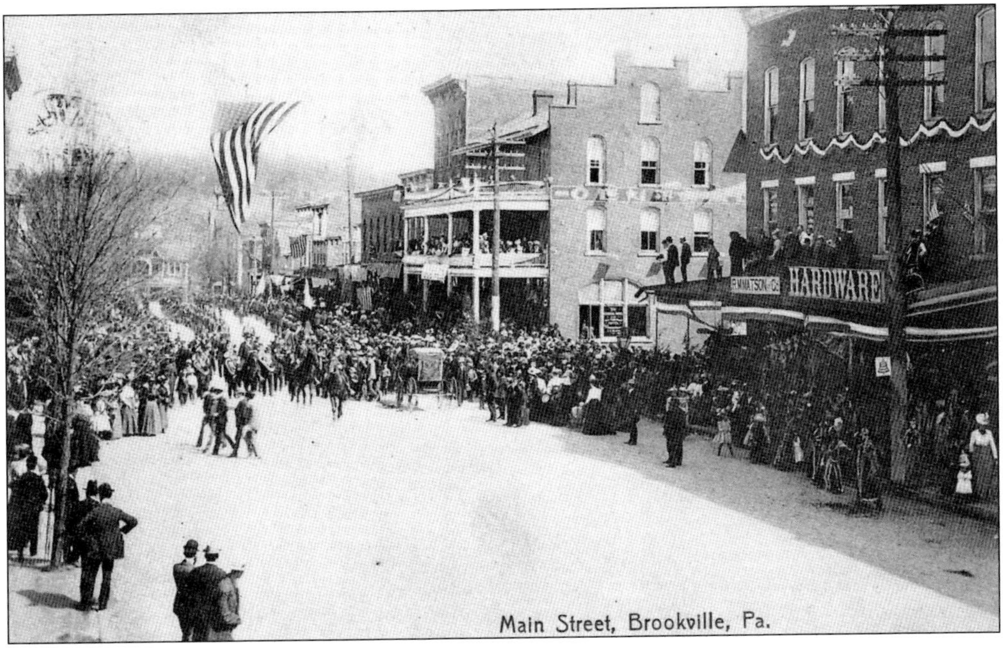

The first Jefferson County Fair, held in 1879 in Rose Township, probably was an occasion for a parade. Soon, county leaders bought and developed property between Brookville's rivers as the Jefferson County Fairgrounds. The grounds included a quarter-mile racetrack, and the annual fairs grew grander and grander. In September 1908, people stood on the porches of Sam Arthurs's Central Hotel in Brookville to watch the parade (above) that was part of the Jefferson County Fair that year. In 1920, Jefferson County–born New York City entertainment magnate Sam Scribner organized and promoted Old Home Week (below) as part of the Jefferson County Fair. Thousands attended. Fairs were held until the Great Depression, then resumed in 1990 at the new fairgrounds near I-80. (Both, JCHC.)

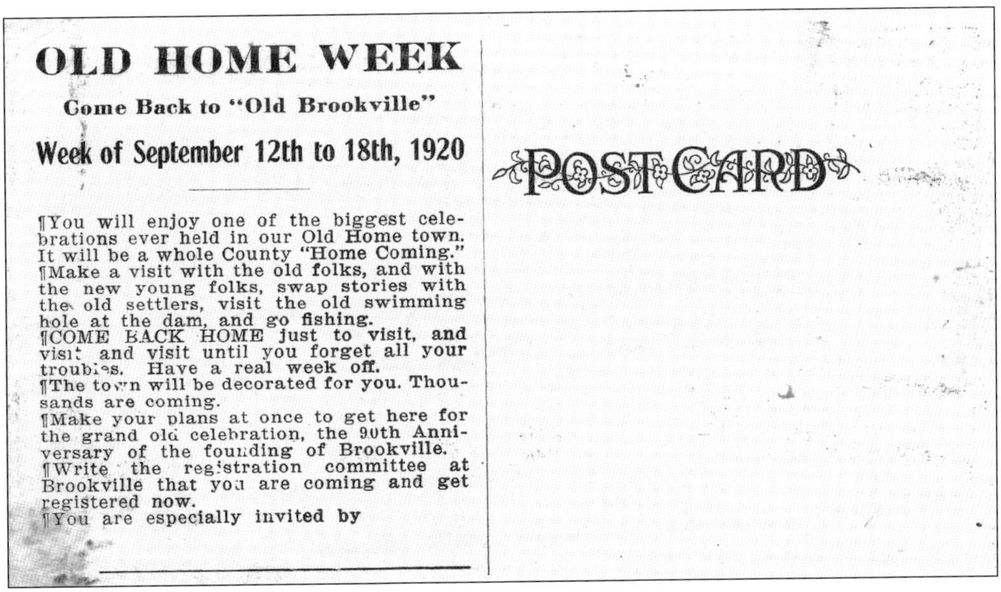

OLD HOME WEEK

Come Back to "Old Brookville"

Week of September 12th to 18th, 1920

¶You will enjoy one of the biggest celebrations ever held in our Old Home town. It will be a whole County "Home Coming."
¶Make a visit with the old folks, and with the new young folks, swap stories with the old settlers, visit the old swimming hole at the dam, and go fishing.
¶COME BACK HOME just to visit, and visit and visit until you forget all your troubles. Have a real week off.
¶The town will be decorated for you. Thousands are coming.
¶Make your plans at once to get here for the grand old celebration, the 90th Anniversary of the founding of Brookville.
¶Write the registration committee at Brookville that you are coming and get registered now.
¶You are especially invited by

POST CARD

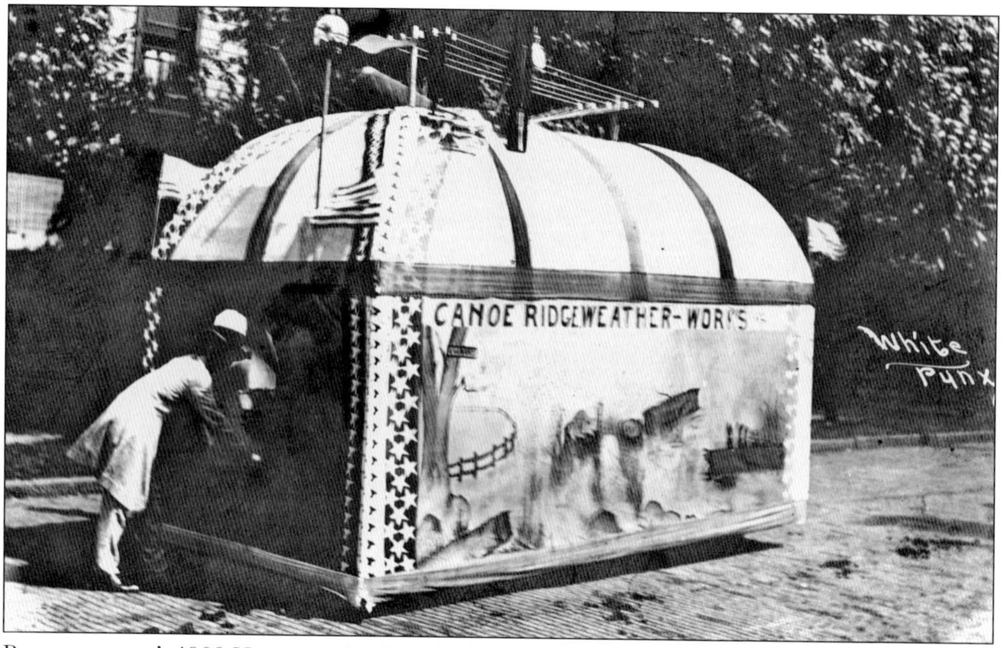

Punxsutawney's 1909 Homecoming Parade featured the Canoe Ridge Weather Works, a satire on the government weather observatory and the allegorical official home of Br'er Groundhog. Designed by C.H. Freas of the Punxsutawney Groundhog Club and constructed by Alonzo Shilling (above), it contained weather murals painted by Frank Boney and Denny Carter. It was driven by Alva Cole, with Shilling disguised as a woodchuck. In 1910, Brockwayville again celebrated the Fourth of July with decorated horse-drawn carriages (below). This celebration ceased until its 1967 revival. Today, people who have moved return to renew friendships, enjoy family reunions, and reminisce. Brockway has kept alive the tradition of remembering who folks are, where they came from, and where they are going. The town celebrated the official 50th anniversary of its Fourth of July festivities in 2016. (Above, PAHGS; below, BAHS.)

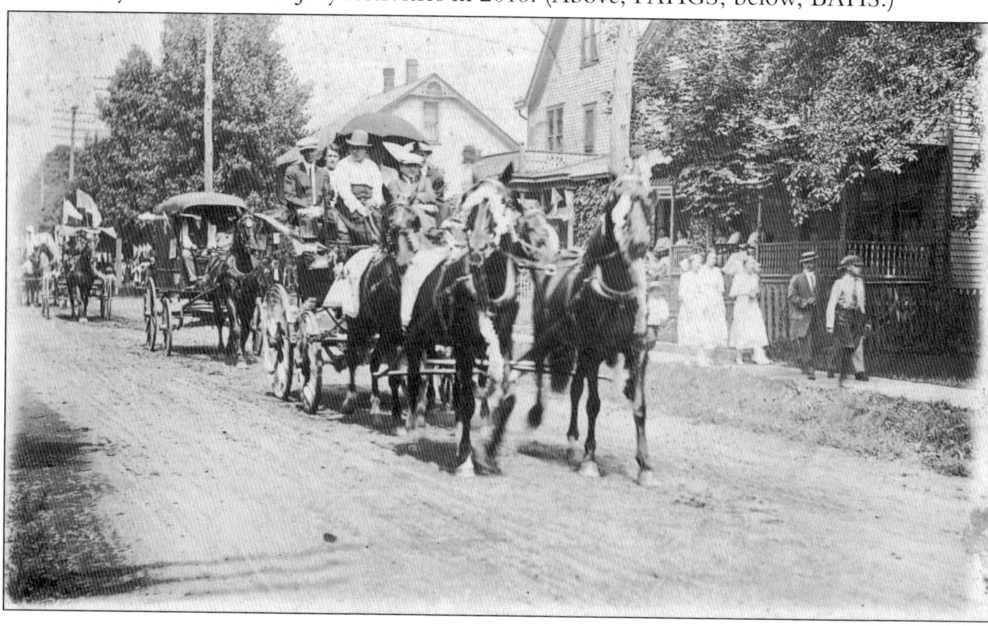

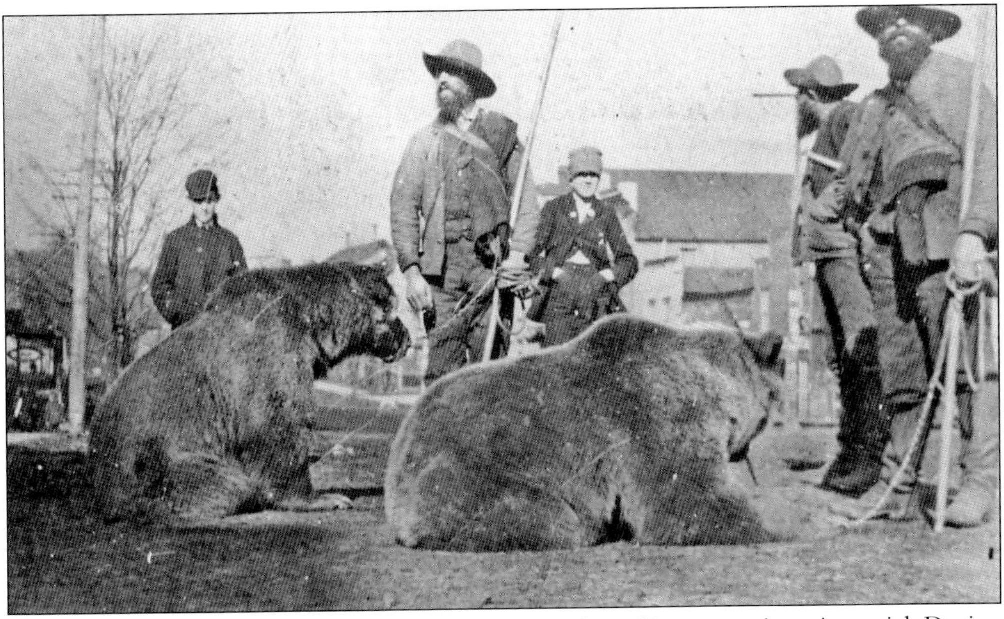

People enjoy local parades, but the arrival of troupes of traveling entertainers is special. During the 1890s, a troupe brought European brown bears (above) to Reynoldsville. Crowds gathered on Main Street, and if enough coin was produced, the men would wrestle the bears. In the evening, men and bears shared sleeping quarters in some shed or barn before traveling on to the next town. L.A. Leathers arrived in Brookville in 1901. He sold groceries, operated a department store, established Brookville Locomotive, and finally moved into the automobile business. Leathers had several Ford dealerships before constructing the Baker Buick Building and establishing the Lakes-to-Sea Motor Corporation in 1923. The interesting image below, printed in reverse, advertises "L.A. Leathers Auto Repairing" and may have been an early way to both advertise and entertain. (Above, RHS; below, JCHC.)

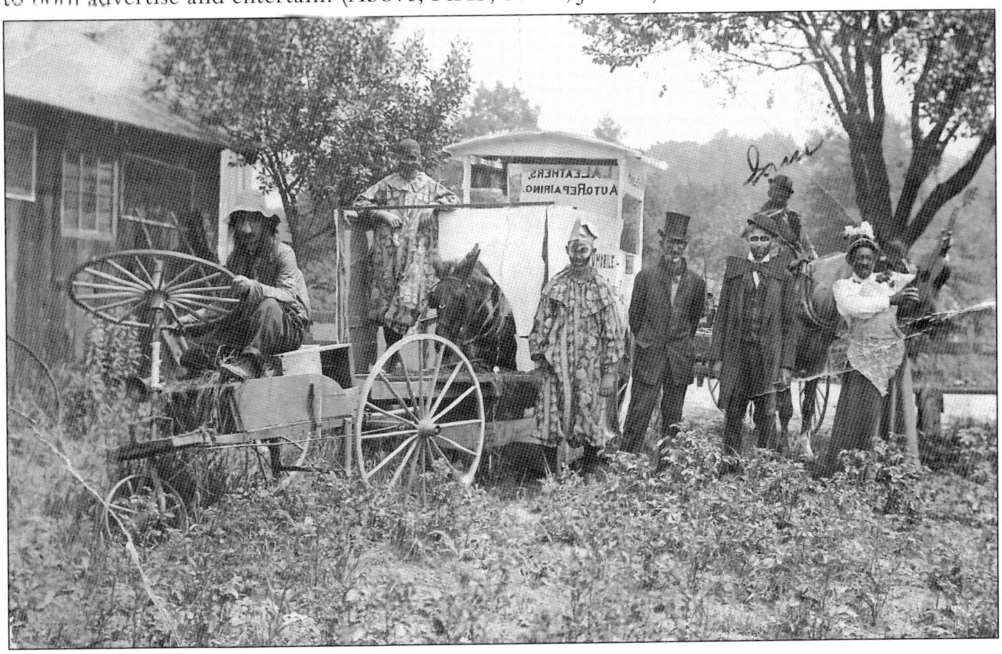

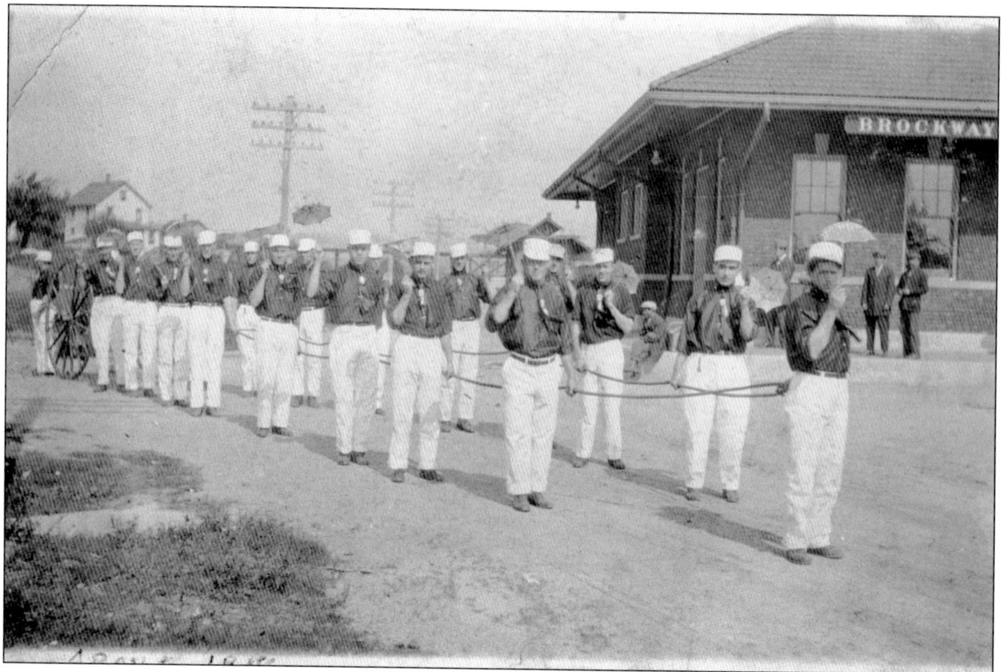

Memorial Day, Labor Day, and times of war call for military parades. The Brockwayville Volunteer Hose Company formed in 1904 and not only fought fires but also participated more broadly in the life of the community. In 1918, members in dress uniform (above) prepare to parade to promote the purchase of Liberty loan bonds. At the end of the columns of firemen is the hose cart, the only piece of firefighting equipment in Brockwayville from 1904 until 1919. In 1921, the company paraded on Labor Day and celebrated the completion of Brockwayville's electrification (below). Other events that day included an airplane landing and taking off from the nearby driving park. (Both, BAHS.)

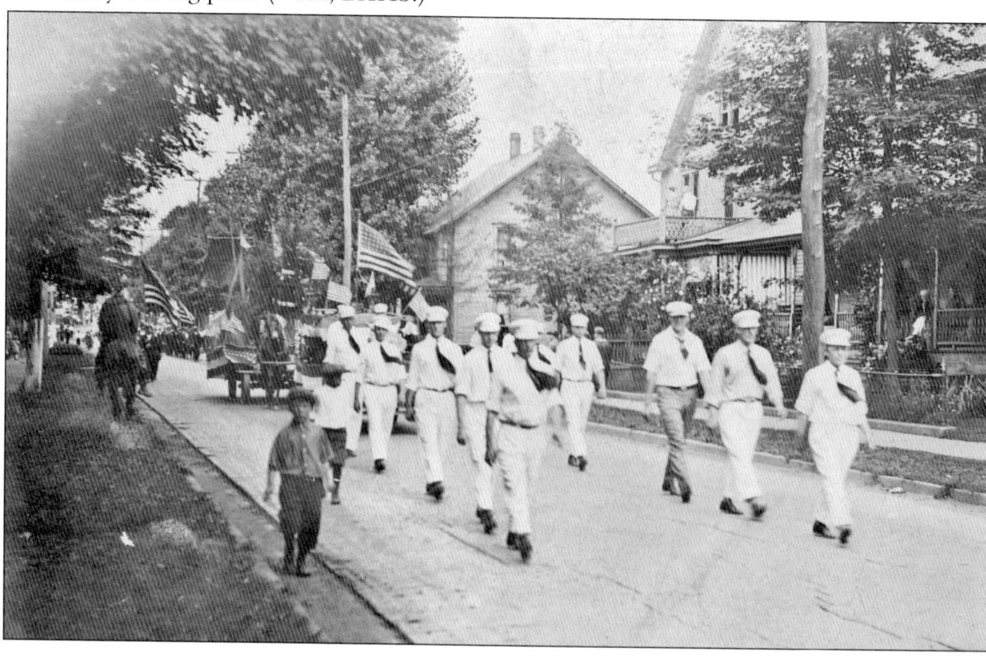

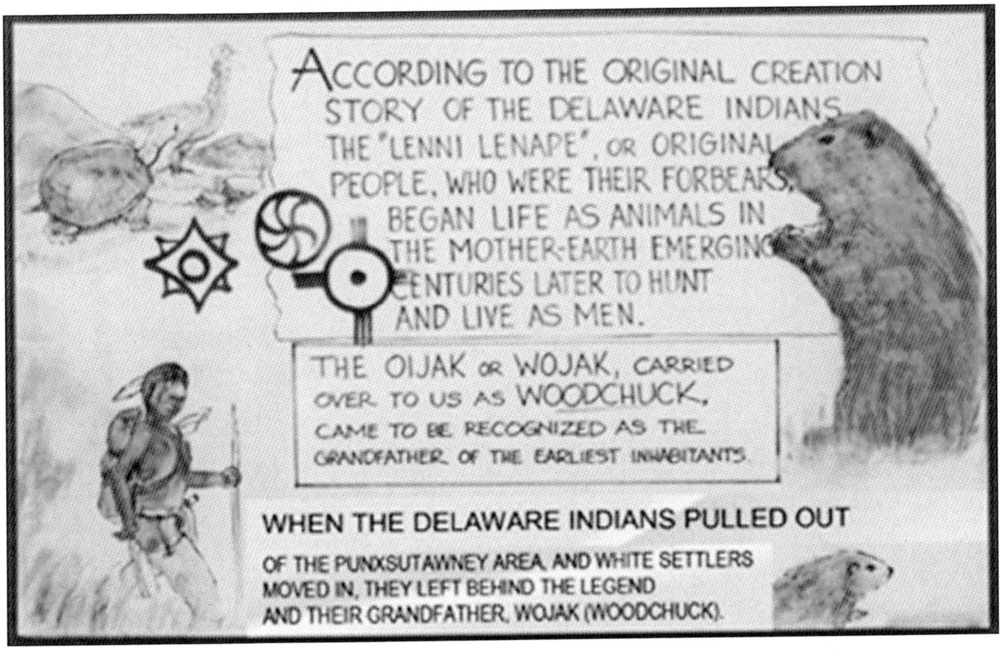

The legend of the groundhog has its roots in Native American traditions. Combined with the German immigrants' method of predicting the arrival of spring based on the weather on Candlemas Day (February 2), this legend led to the annual Punxsutawney celebration of Groundhog Day. In August 1909, Punxsutawney was proclaimed "the Weather Capital of the World" at the town's Old Home Week celebration. The groundhog was the centerpiece of a Weather Parade before Gov. Edwin Stuart. The original groundhog postcard image from 1909 (below) was reprised by the chamber of commerce in 1949 for Punxsutawney's centennial celebration. (Both, PAHGS.)

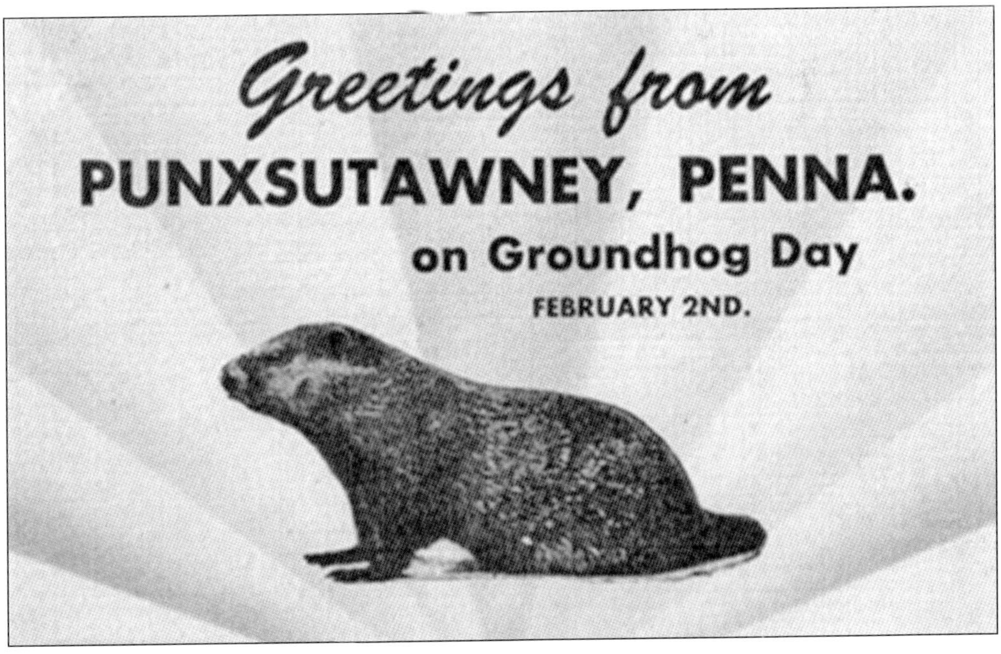

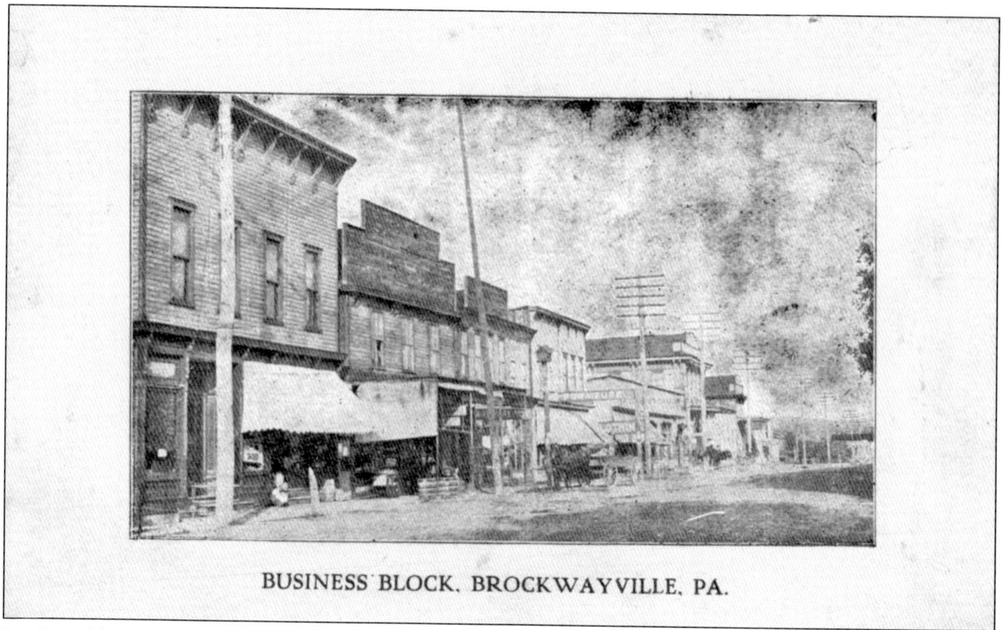

Lodges like the Independent Order of Odd Fellows (IOOF) provided contributions and aid to those suffering sickness, death, loss of job, and devastation. A two-hour fire in 1910 demolished the north side of Brockway's Main Street, including the IOOF lodge. The redbrick structure displaying "IOOF" (above, far left) replaced the original lodge. Humphrey's Furniture and presently Brockway Floral Boutique have occupied the former lodge building. Next to the Harrison Matson Building (below), the letters "IOOF" remain visible on the tall Parker B. Blood Building (1875), once home to the lodge, founded in 1847. Like Brockway's lodge, the first building in Brookville burned and was replaced. Other benevolent societies that existed in the county include the Masons, Knights of Columbus, Knights of Pythias, Patriotic Sons of America, and the Patrons of Husbandry. (Above, BAHS; below, JCHC.)

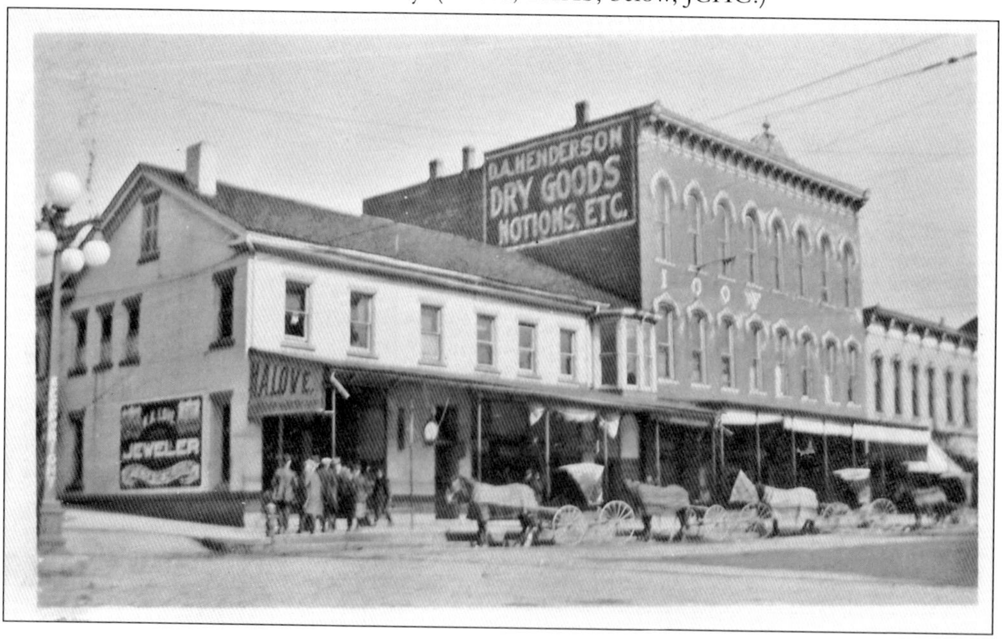

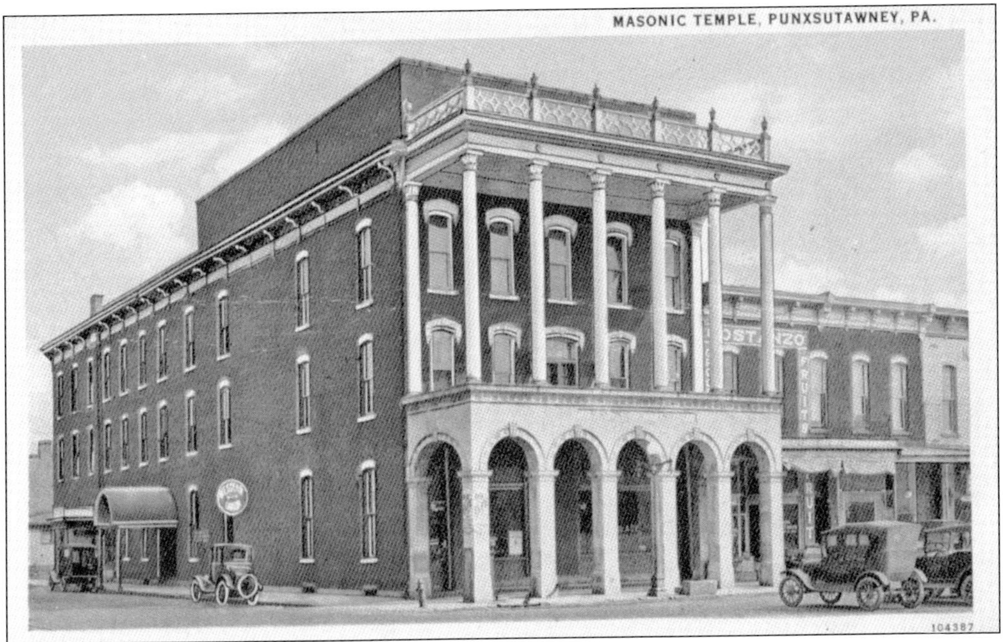

Punxsutawney once had nearly 50 fraternal, social, and benevolent societies. The temple of the John W. Jenks Lodge, Free and Accepted Masons (1875), formerly the Washington Hotel, faced the plaza at Mahoning and Jefferson Streets in the 1940s (above). An impressive facade was added to the hotel that served as the lodge's headquarters until the 1970s, when it was demolished during urban renewal. The lodge continues to meet in headquarters at 225 West Mahoning Street. The Fraternal Order of Eagles Aerie No. 1231, chartered in February 1906, met in the old opera house on East Mahoning Street until 1937, when it built a new facility (below) on the plaza that faced Barclay Square. The Eagles building was the only one saved from demolition during urban renewal. (Both, PAHGS.)

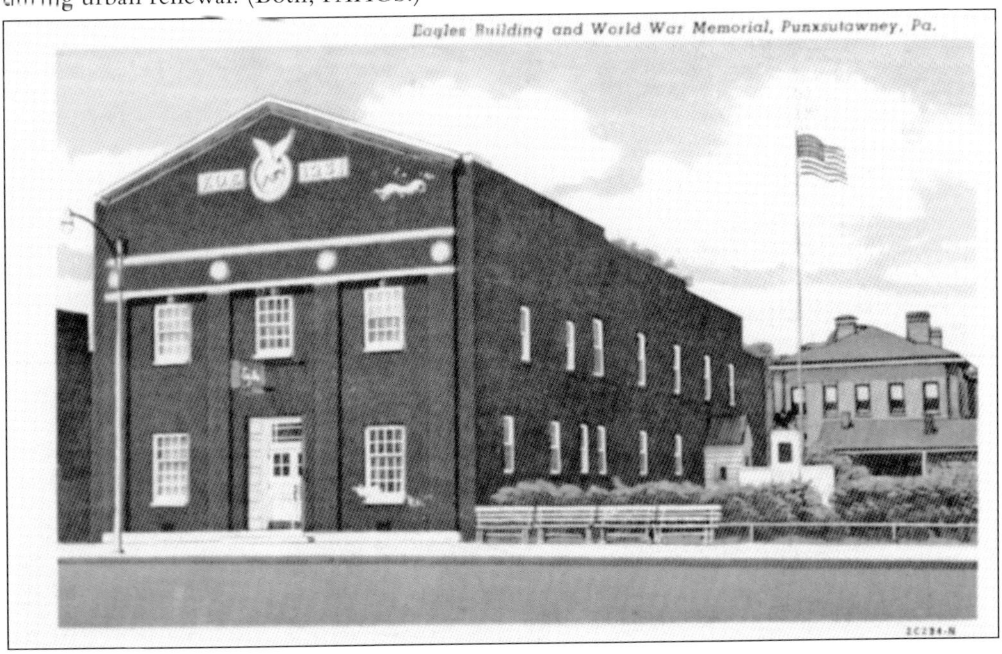

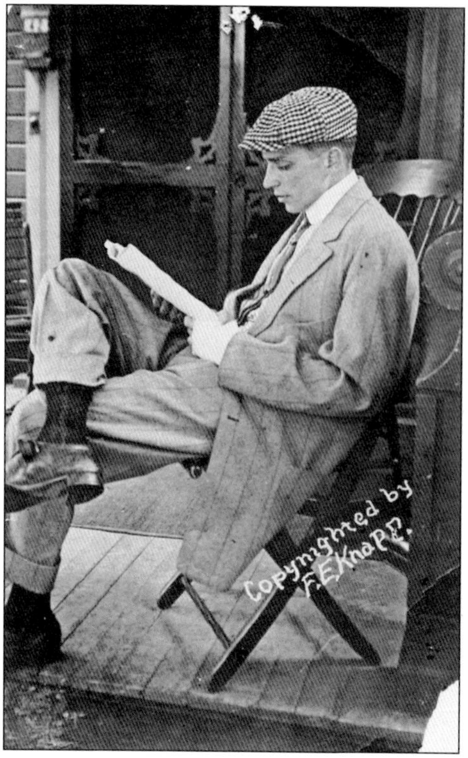

Brookville's Lewis Earle Sandt (left) had a passion for motorcycles, automobiles, and airplanes. In 1911, he made the first international flight by an American, flying from Erie to Canada, then he spent his summers as an exhibition flyer. Flying over Grove City in 1913, Sandt crashed and later died there of tetanus. Brookville mourned. A Pennsylvania State Historical Marker marks his birthplace. (JCHC.)

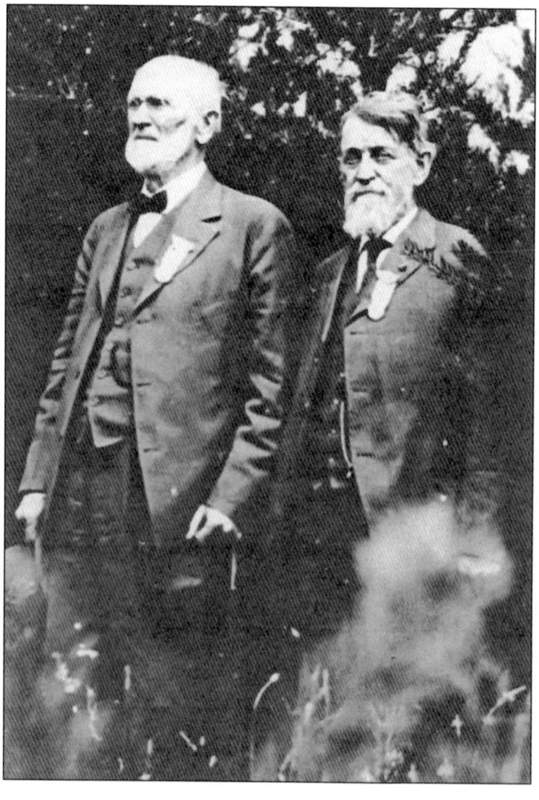

In addition to being general manager of the Bell, Lewis & Yates Mining Company, the Honorable Simon B. Elliott was a state representative, an accomplished architect, an engineer, a horticulturist, and an astronomer, but his true calling was forestry. While living in Reynoldsville, he wrote *Important Timber Trees of the United States*. Both Elliott (left) and another noted forester, Joseph T. Rothrock (right), have been honored with Pennsylvania state parks bearing their names. (RHS.)

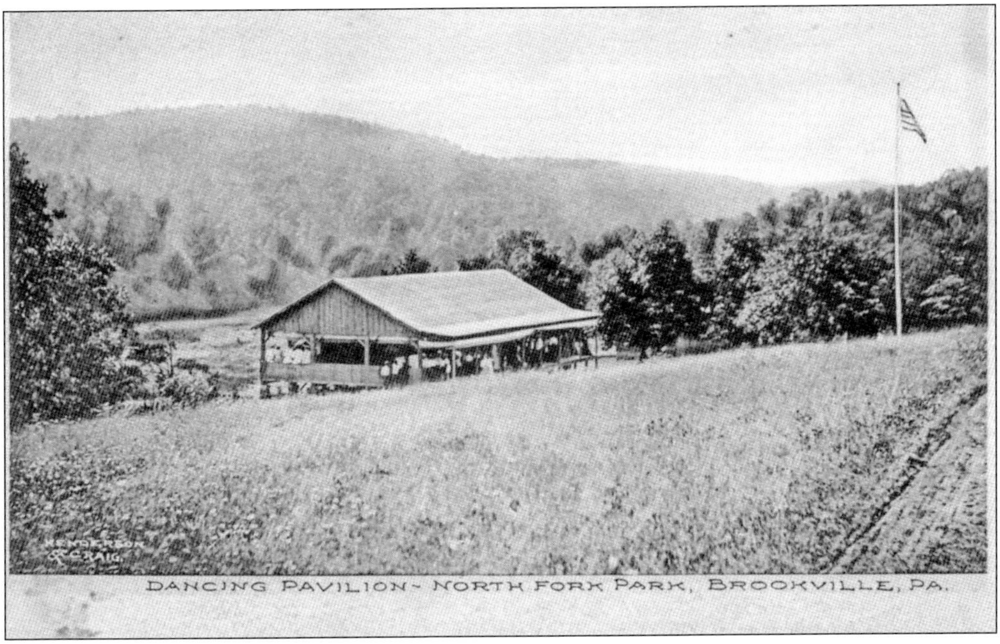

DANCING PAVILION – NORTH FORK PARK, BROOKVILLE, PA.

Many Brookville families did well during the timbering and mining days of the 19th century. They built large homes and often invested in several businesses at a time. About 1900, they developed an area along the North Fork referred to as the "Old Park." It included a dance pavilion (above). Some, like G.W. Stewart, built summer cottages (below) on the hillside near the water. The area also includes some of the rocks etched by Douglas Stahlman. Between 1911 and 1913, Stahlman, a devotee of faith healer John Alexander Dowie, lived in the woods and dedicated more than 500 rocks and engraved at least 160. Today, his rocks and his legacy are described at Scripture Rocks Heritage Park on State Route 28 north of Brookville. (Both, JCHC.)

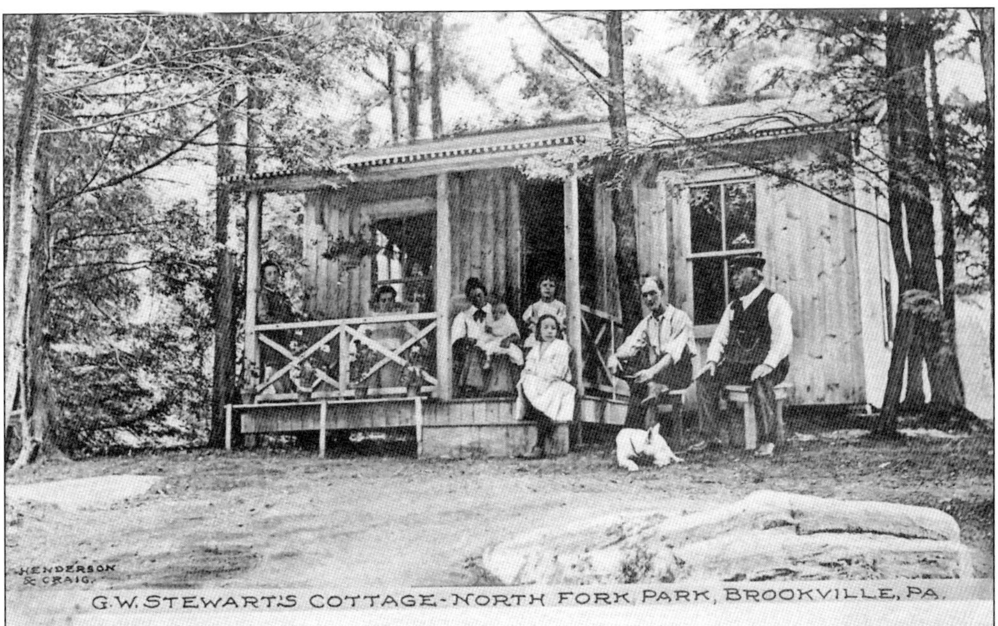

G.W. STEWART'S COTTAGE – NORTH FORK PARK, BROOKVILLE, PA.

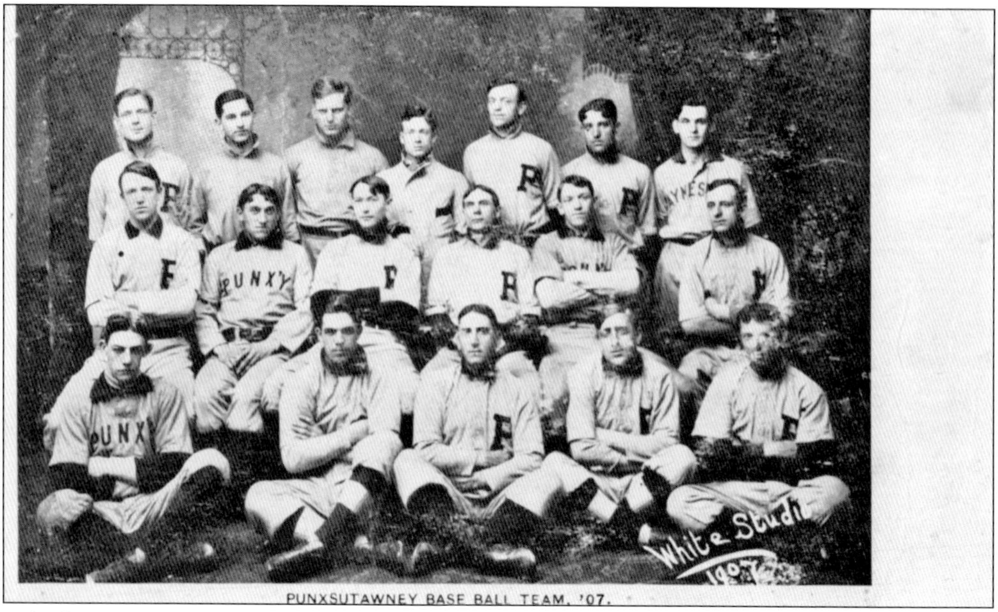

PUNXSUTAWNEY BASE BALL TEAM, '07.

Whether playing a sandlot game of baseball or watching an NFL game on television, sports remain an important pastime for many people in the county. The semiprofessional Punxsutawney baseball team above played its final season in the Interstate League in 1907. Competing against teams from Erie, Pittsburgh, Bradford, DuBois, and other western Pennsylvania towns, players received monthly salaries averaging $100 to $125 and traveled by train between cities. They played on an East End field near Mahoning Creek. Following the team's dissolution, a trolley league was formed among neighboring mining towns. Andy Hastings played basketball (below) for Brookville High School in 1912 before playing football at the University of Pittsburgh. In 1920, he played for the Cleveland Tigers in the NFL, and local reporters considered him "the greatest all-around athlete Brookville High ever produced." (Above, PAHGS; below, JCHC.)

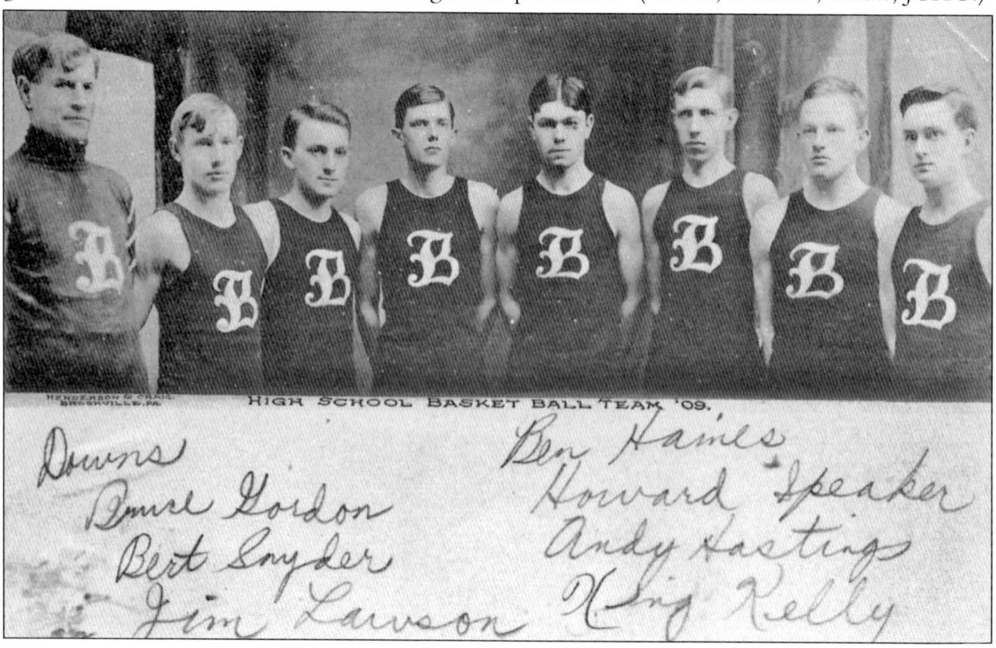

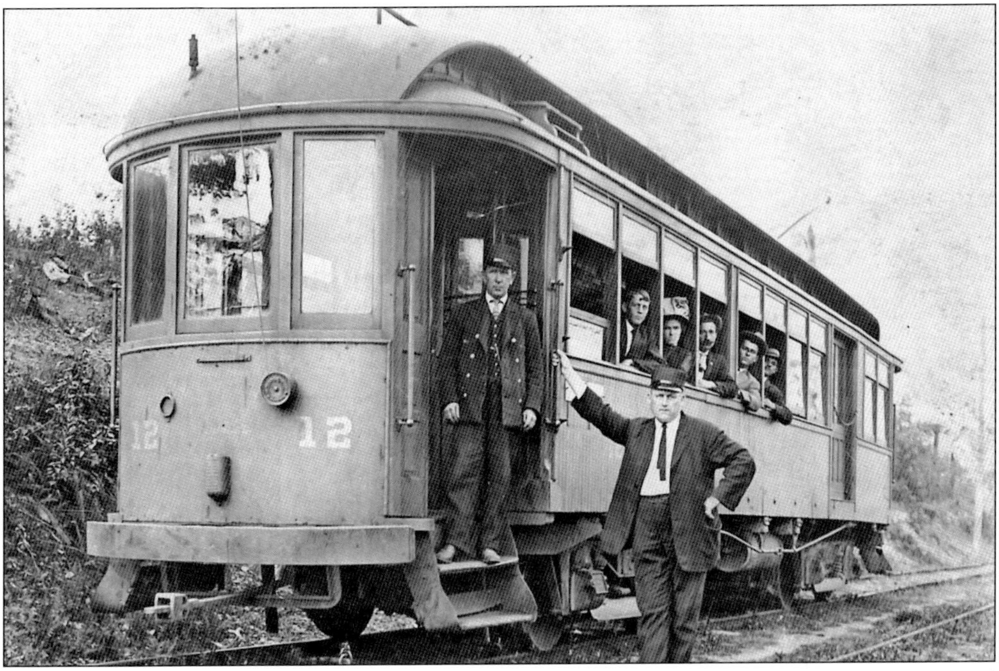

The Punxsutawney Street Passenger Railway Company (above) was organized in 1892 and provided transportation between Clayville and Punxsutawney. Reorganized as the Jefferson Traction Company in 1903, it provided interurban transportation connecting Punxsutawney with Big Run, Walston, Adrian, Anita, Reynoldsville, and Sykesville, where it interfaced with the United Traction Street Railway of DuBois. A spur line from Big Run connected with Eleanora. Rural residents found trolley transportation convenient, especially in the rain (below). The northern terminus of the line (below) was at the Iron Bridge in Reynoldsville. This line not only delivered passengers conveniently but also assisted in the delivery of the mail. Stops along the way included the mining communities of Soldier, Eleanora, Wishaw, Adrian, and Anita. (Above, PAHGS; below, RHS.)

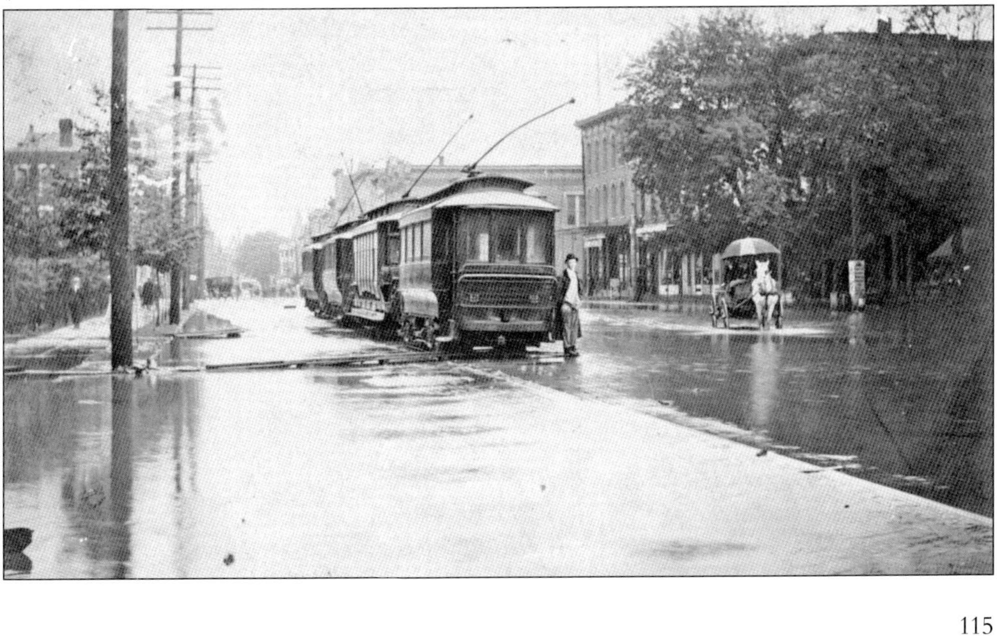

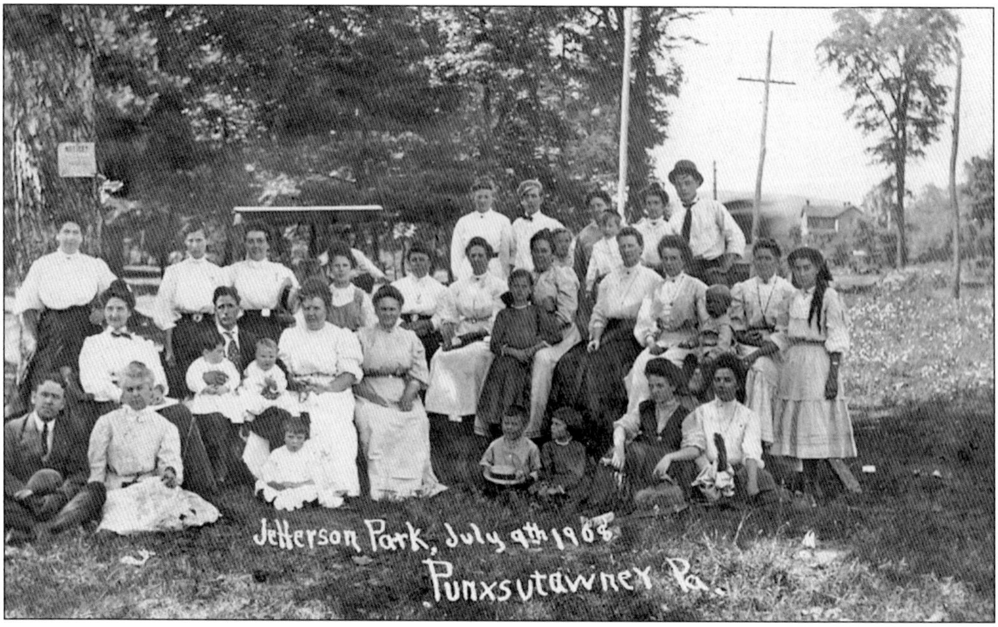

Recreational facilities created along the trolley line, like Jefferson Park near Punxsutawney, encouraged trolley use during weekends. Families like these pictured on a July day in 1908 (above) could enjoy picnics, reunions, or a summer afternoon at these sites. Highland and Mitchell Parks featured picnic pavilions, Wishaw Park had a dance pavilion, Aljoe Park had a lake with boating and swimming, and Jefferson Park was equipped with amusements, games, and rides. Automobiles, too, provided transportation for outings. In the summer of 1910, Alfred Truman arranged for more than 100 little girls to travel by car, many for the first time, to Truman's Grove in Sigel, north of Brookville. During the "automobile picnic party," they waded in a little lake, enjoyed the country, and had a sumptuous picnic before returning to Brookville in the evening. (Above, PAHGS; below, JCHC.)

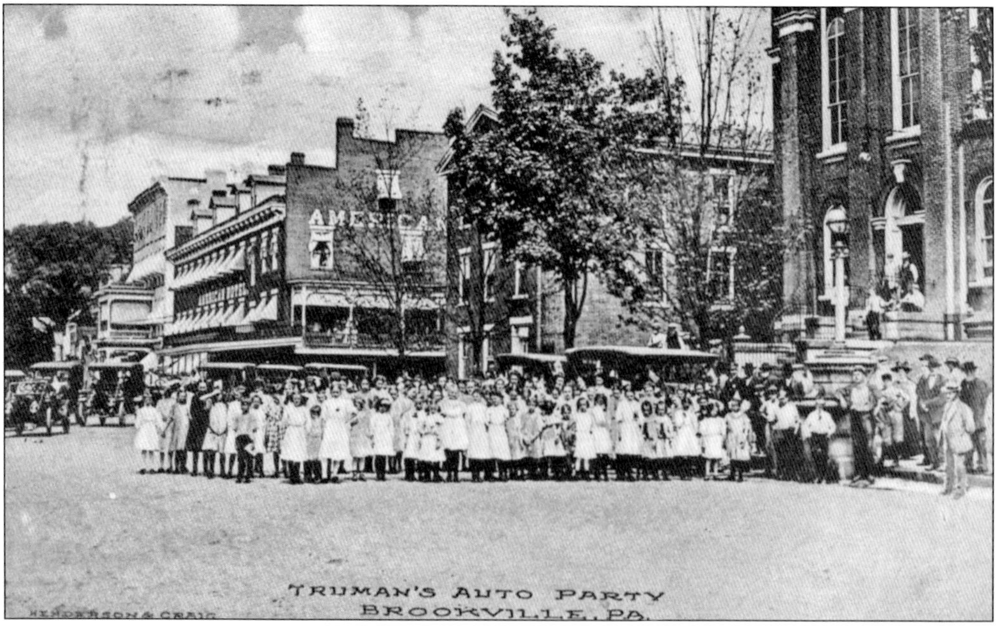

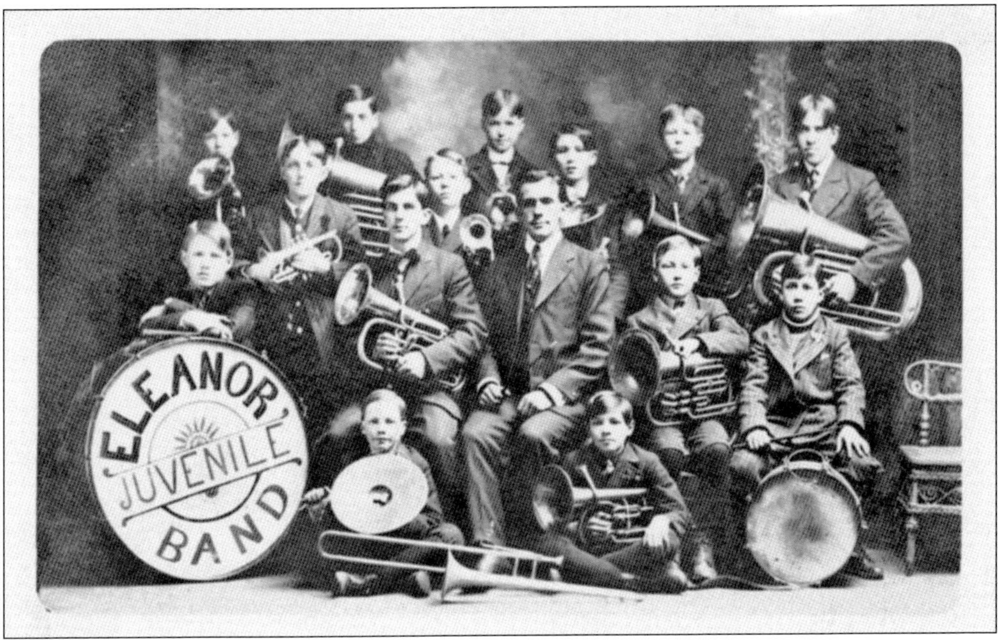

Music played a large part in the lives of the miners. The Juvenile Band (above), organized in the Buffalo and Rochester Coal and Iron Company mining community of Eleanora, provided an opportunity for youngsters to develop their musical abilities as well as to entertain local communities. Under the gifted direction of Richardson Ramsy, Reynoldsville's Keystone Band (below) quickly established itself as a premier ensemble. Newspapers from the 1880s on are filled with accounts of the members' playing abilities. The band's reputation spread, and an offer arrived to join a circus forming in Rochester, New York. The chance meeting of a band of backwoods Reynoldsville musicians and a newly formed circus is pure irony. Nine band members joined the Norris Brothers Circus, and they toured North America for many years. (Above, PAHGS, Samuel Mennetti Collection; below, RHS.)

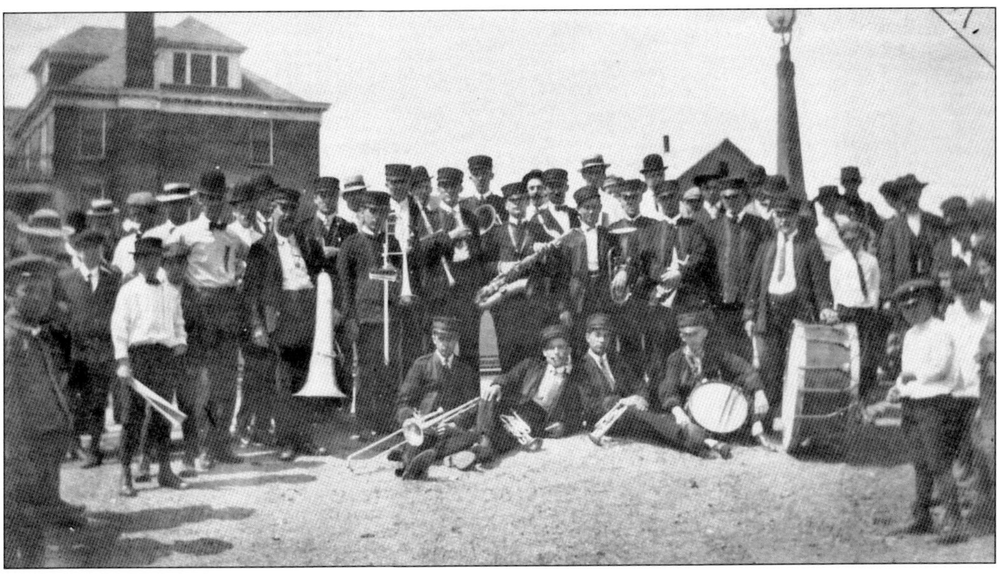

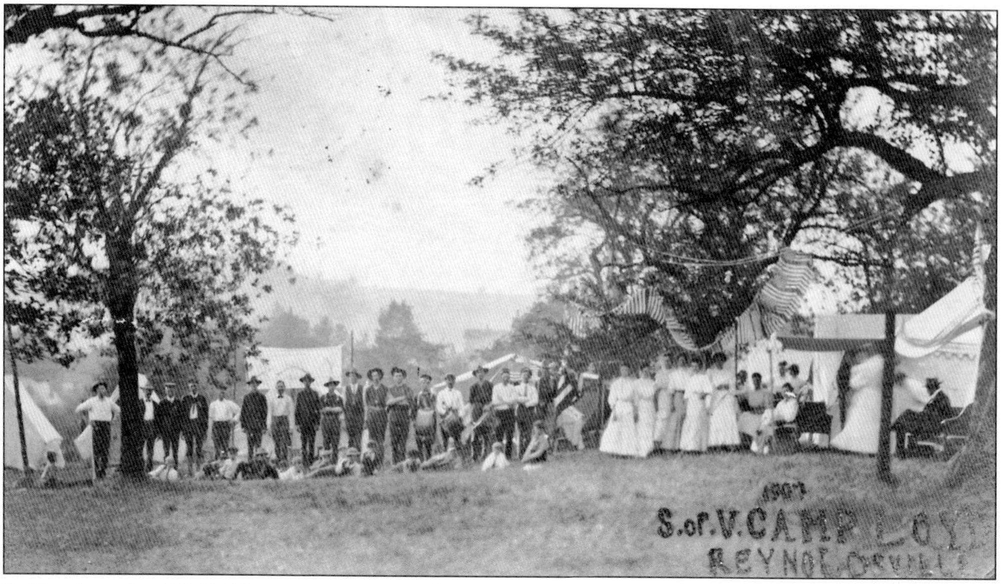

Following the Civil War, veterans met for encampments and reunions in places throughout the county. Several reunions of the 105th Pennsylvania Volunteers, or "Wildcats," were held in Reynoldsville, where they gathered to renew old friendships, reminisce about the war, and march in local parades. Over 300 veterans attended a reunion at Camp Loyd (above) during the first Old Home Week in 1907. Early social clubs and secret societies helped unite people with a common cause. The Patrons of Husbandry and the Grange brought together those who made a living from the soil. The Improved Order of Red Men traces its origin to patriotic societies founded before the American Revolution. The women's affiliate of the group is the Pocahontas (below), pictured standing in front of the Columbus Photography Studio in Reynoldsville. (Both, RHS.)

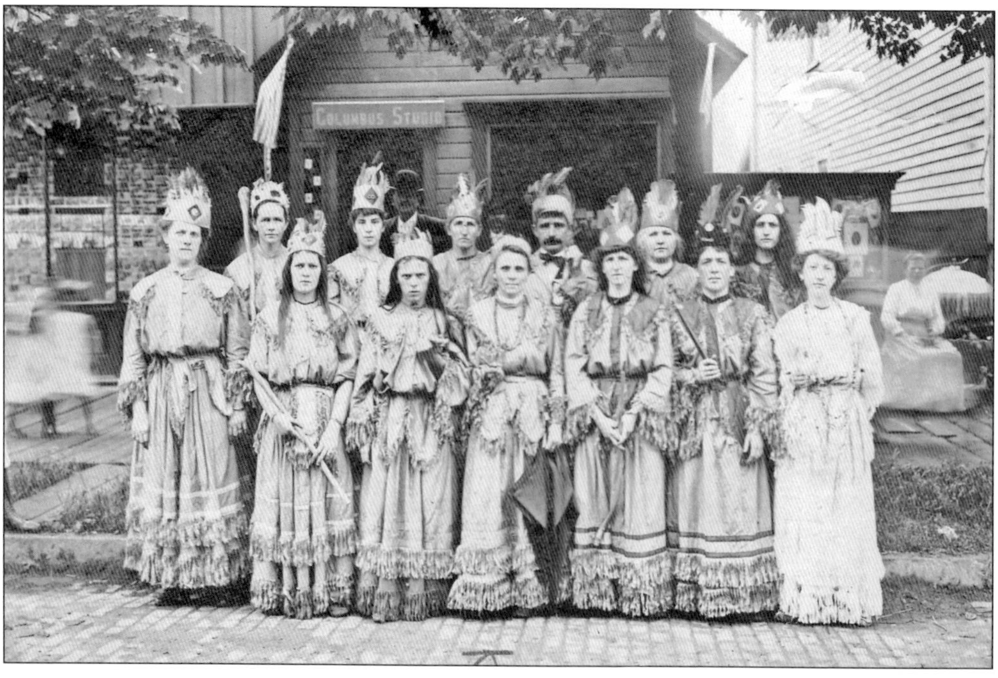

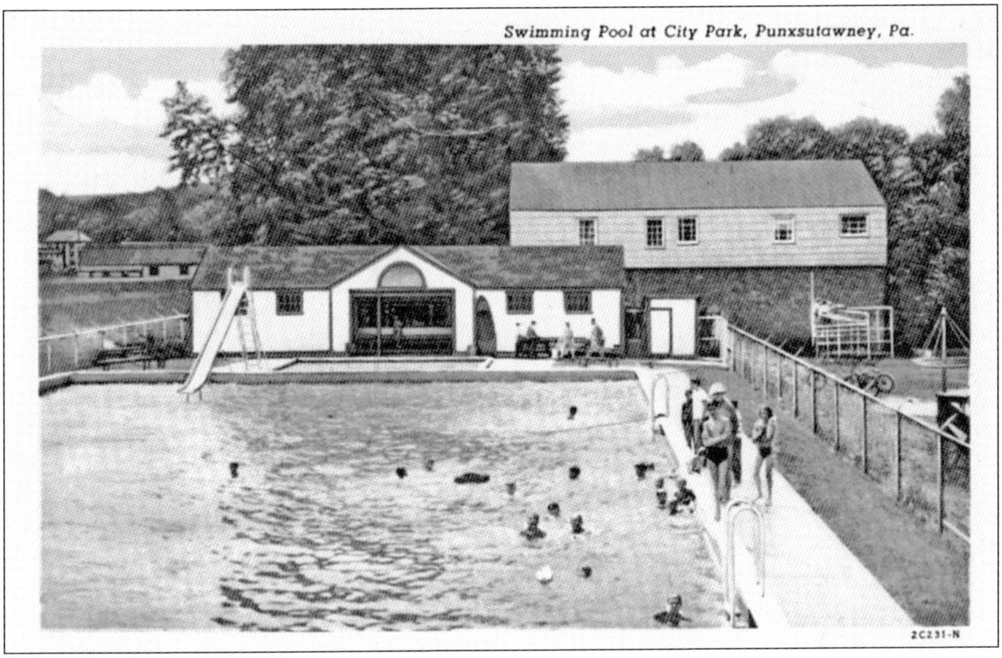

The George C. Brown Community Pool (above), named in honor of a local businessman who financed its construction during the Great Depression, is at Harmon Field, a recreational park with tennis courts that once served as Punxsutawney's sports stadium. This outdoor community pool continues to provide summer recreation for generations of Punxsutawney residents and visitors through the efforts of SPLASH, a nonprofit community organization. When Brookville's Litch Mill closed at the beginning of the 20th century, the location (below) became a popular swimming area. Prior to the construction of the YMCA in 1915, swimming classes for children took place at the dam. Swimming at Dr. Walter Dick Park, now developed by Brookville Borough and funded by a family trust, is always fun on a hot summer day. (Above, PAHGS; below, JCHC.)

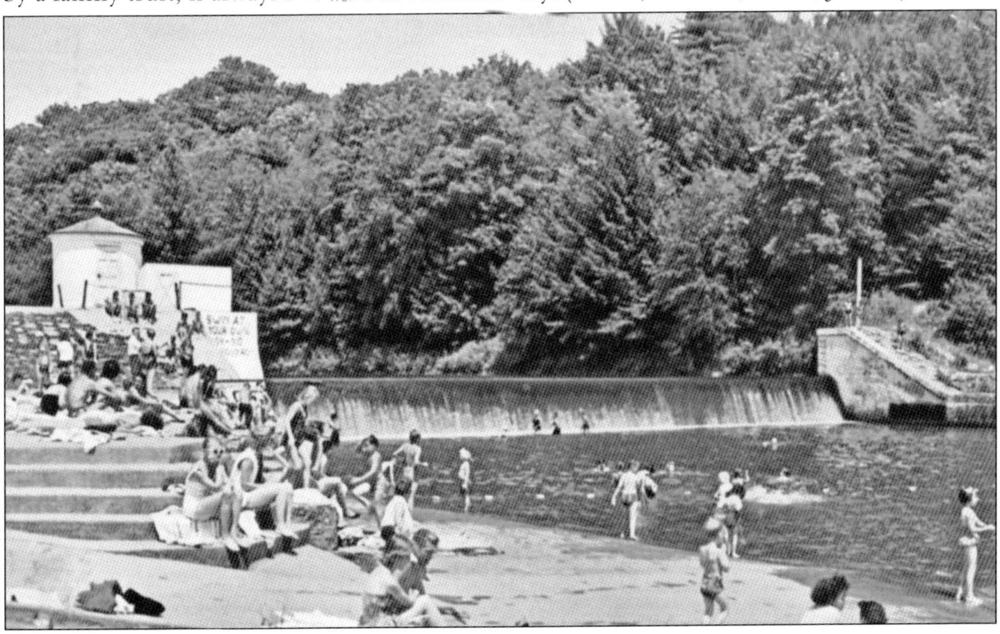

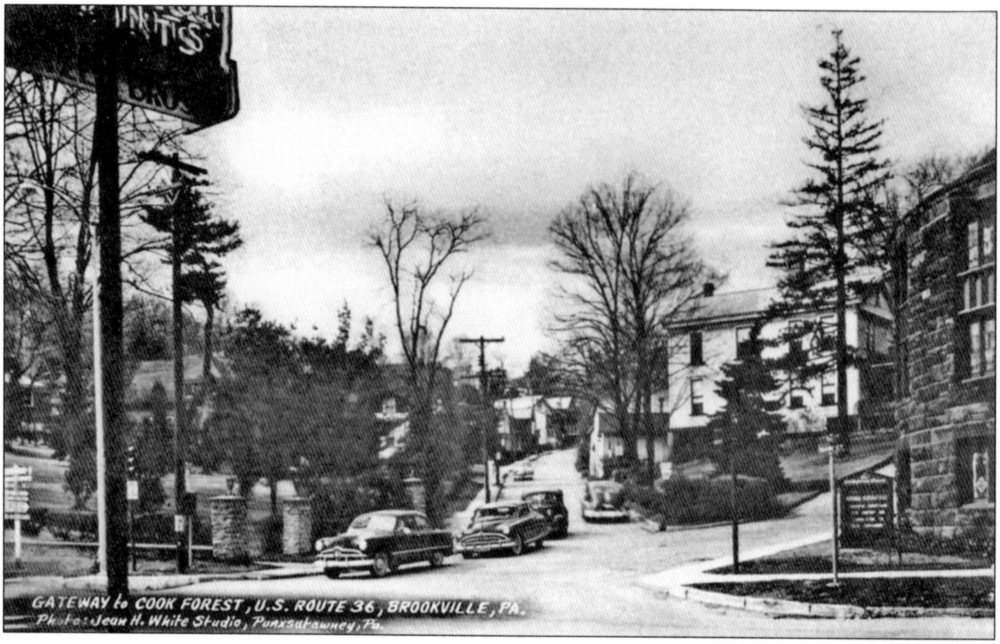

In the 1920s, timberman Anthony Cook looked for a way to leave a large stand of virgin pine for posterity. He worked with influential people in DuBois and Pittsburgh, and in 1927, legislators established Cook Forest State Park, an area of 8,500 acres. Due to Brookville's location on State Route 36, the town became known as the Gateway to Cook Forest (above), where today the Cook mansion (below), cabins, campsites, swimming, the Sawmill Center for the Arts, a theater, and more provide family-centered vacations. The Lumber Heritage Region, a 15-county area that preserves, relates, and enhances the history and heritage of the people and their relationship with Pennsylvania's forests, named Brookville a gateway to the region in the 1990s. (Both, JCHC.)

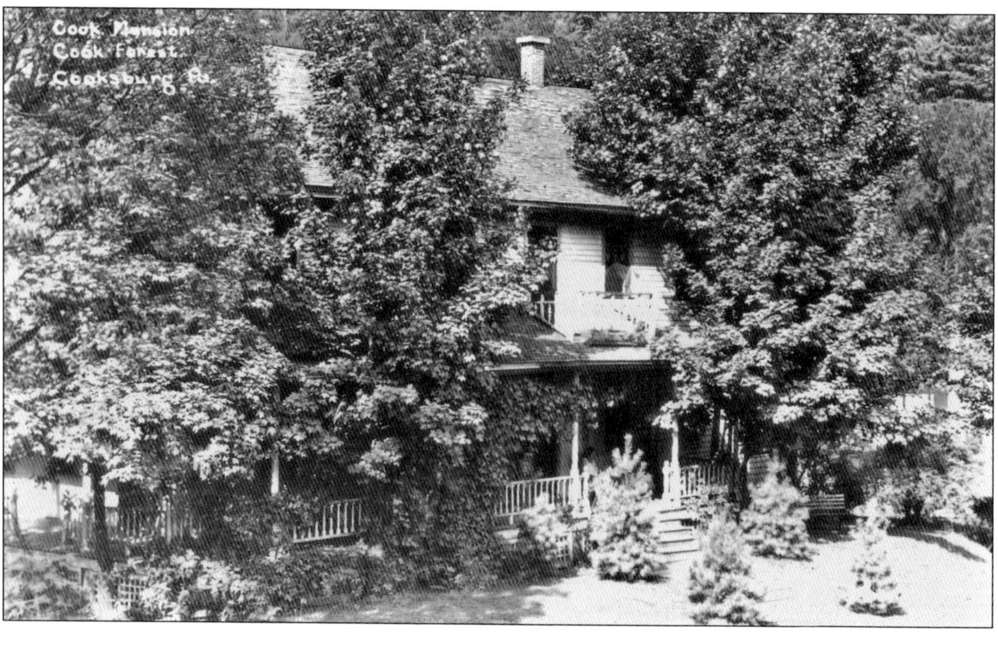

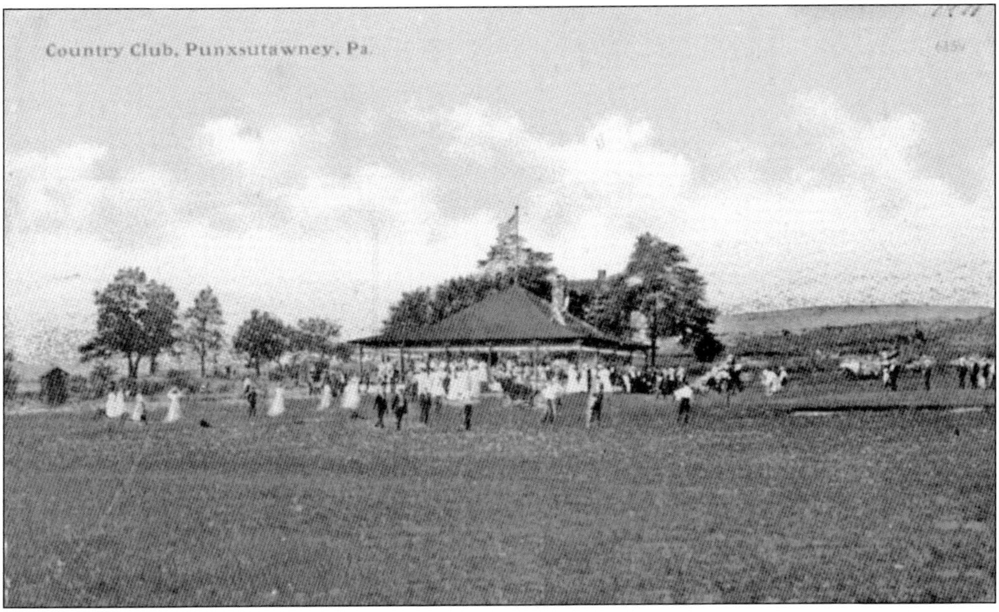

Businessmen organized the Punxsutawney Country Club on North Main Street in 1904, when they purchased the former Carmalt Farm, once a stop on the Underground Railroad, from the Rochester and Pittsburgh Coal and Iron Company. They added a clubhouse, a bungalow with a porch on three sides, a golf course, tennis courts, and other amenities. The clubhouse (above) was replaced in 1998, and today both the club and golf course remain active. Brookville's Sam Henderson learned the game when vacationing in the South and eventually bought 70 acres four miles west of Brookville. There, in 1921, he laid out the back nine, where he and his friends enjoyed playing, and built a clubhouse (below) and dining room. It was later named Pinecrest and expanded to 18 holes; people play and dine there today. (Above, PAHGS; below, JCHC.)

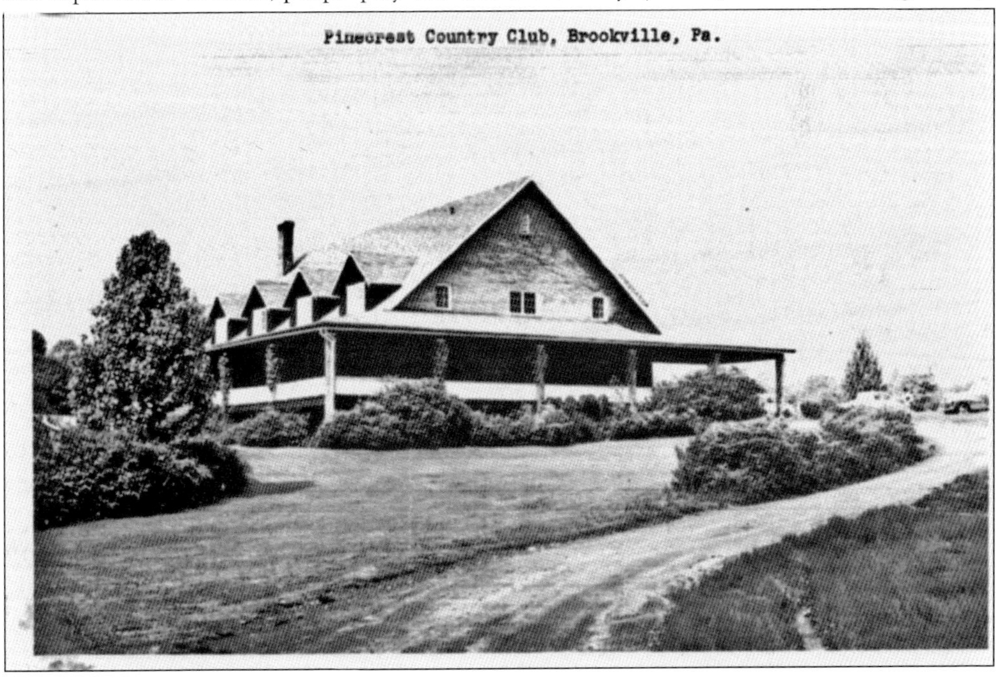

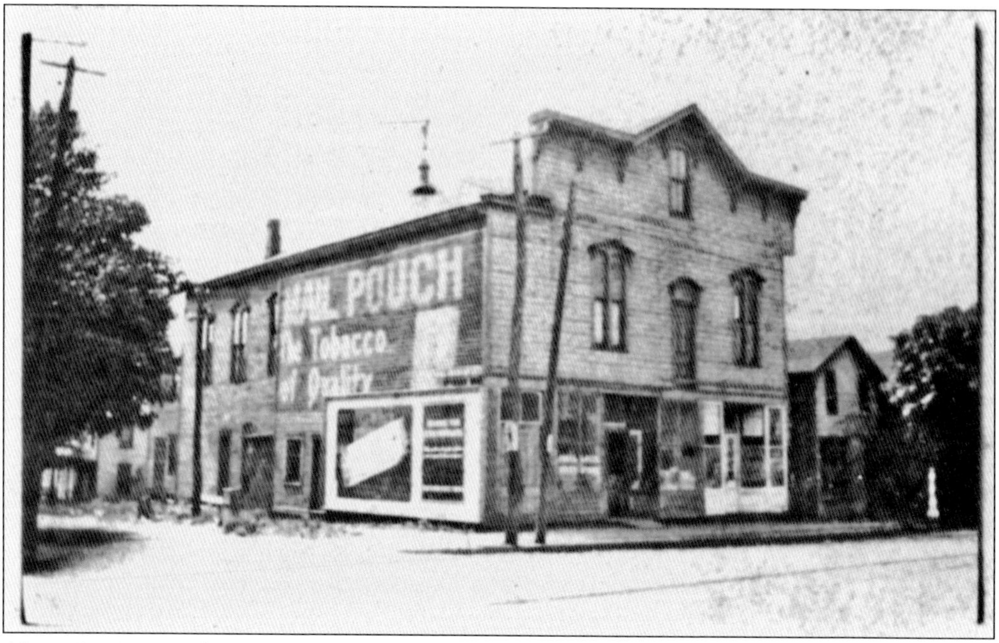

Above Joe Morrow's General Store was a heralded hall with a large stage known as the Reynolds Opera House (above). Built by Albert Reynolds in 1875, it served as the leading amusement resort of its era. In addition to the numerous plays presented by traveling troupes, the space provided a place for public meetings and dances. Fire destroyed the building in 1915. The first nickelodeon was established in Pittsburgh in 1905, and the concept quickly spread, even into rural Pennsylvania. When Charles K. Moorehead opened the Bijou Nickelodeon (below) in 1907, it was the first of its kind in Reynoldsville. Many vaudeville acts performed in this venue, and the moving picture show was made available to the masses. (Both, RHS.)

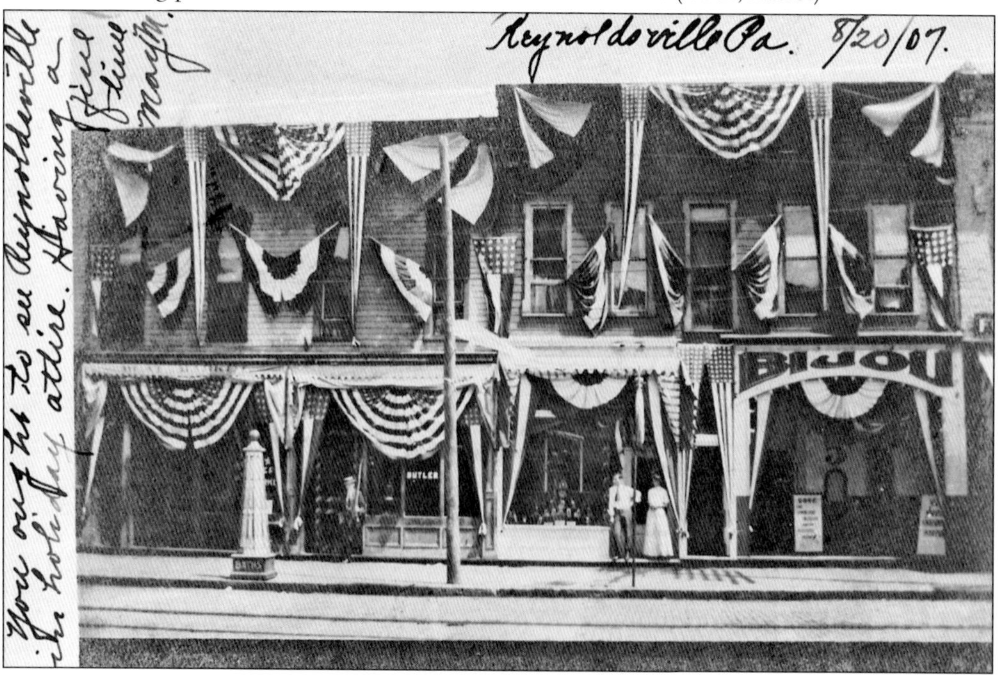

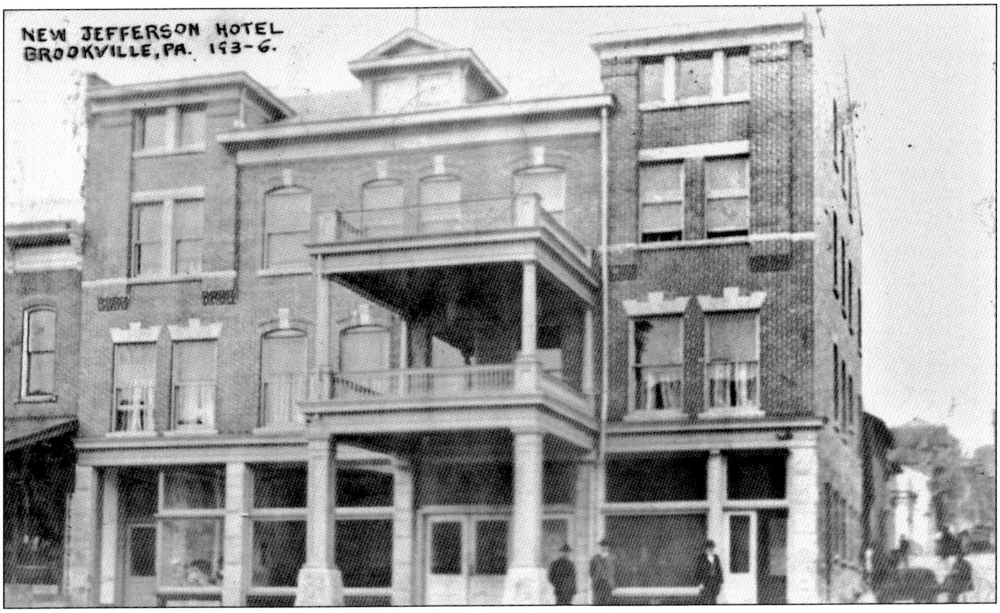

One of Brookville's first hotels, the Globe was situated at the corner of Main Street and Spring Alley. It was operated by a succession of men; one, C.R. Kretz, renamed it the Jefferson House. M. Allgier and L.L. Reitz kept the name when they purchased it in 1883. Allgier's son, Philip, kept the name but constructed the building above in 1904. It served as a hotel until 1918, when Frank Brown, of Mayburg, bought the hotel and turned it into the Columbia movie theater, which opened shortly after World War I ended. Moviegoing adults paid 20¢ and children 10¢, then entered through the hotel lobby with its fine arched ceiling, white wicker furniture, and fountain. Ruby Buffington accompanied the silent film *Tarzan the Ape Man* on the Seeburg-Smith organ. (Both, JCHC.)

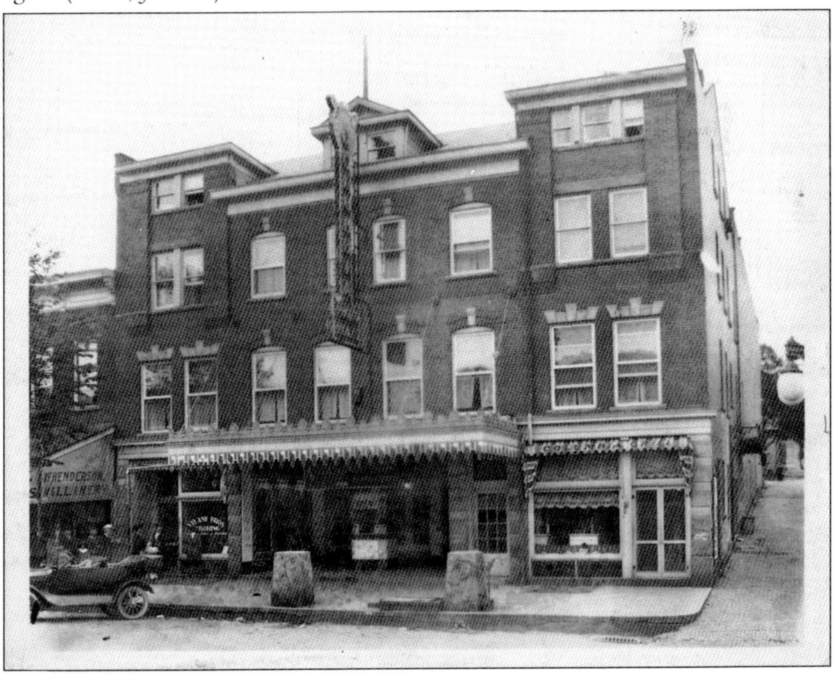

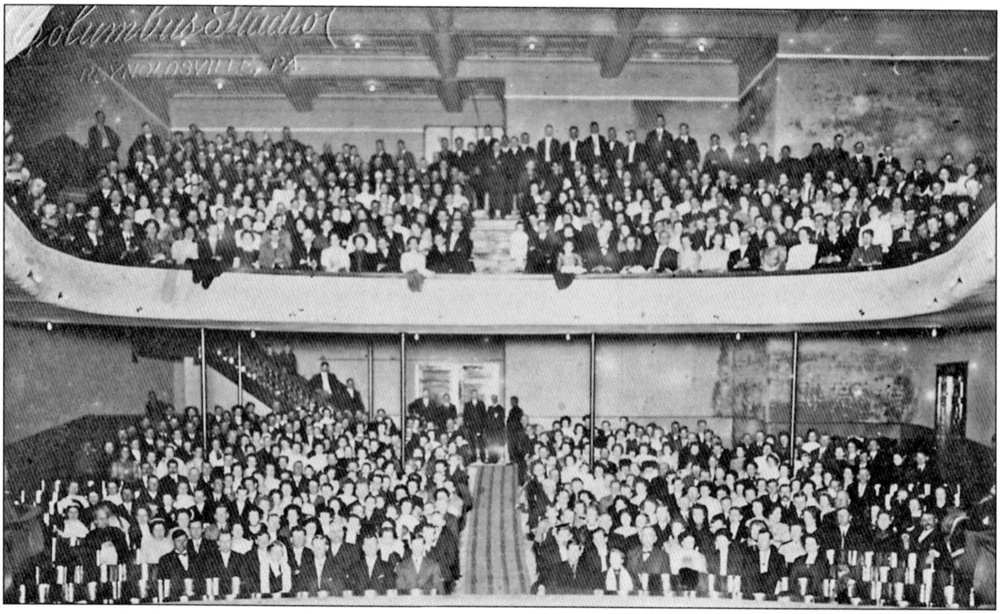

Movies were popular entertainment during the Great Depression, as indicated by this audience at the first show ever presented at Reynoldsville's Adelphi Theater (above). Harris Amusements owned and operated the theater until 1950, then Mid-States Theater, Inc., managed it until 1955, when the name was changed to the Regent. Fire destroyed the building in the winter of 1970. Movies were popular during wartime, too. On July 19, 1941, to ease the fear of war, Joe and Charlie Kosco opened the Kosco Theater (below) on Brockway's West Main Street. Adults paid 40¢ and children 10¢ for matinee tickets to the first show, *Tight Shoes*. The latest projection techniques, "Kool Komfort" air-conditioning, and highly rated films guaranteed moviegoers a good time. The theater was razed in 1972, and this is now the site of the S&T Bank. (Above, RHS; below, BAHS.)

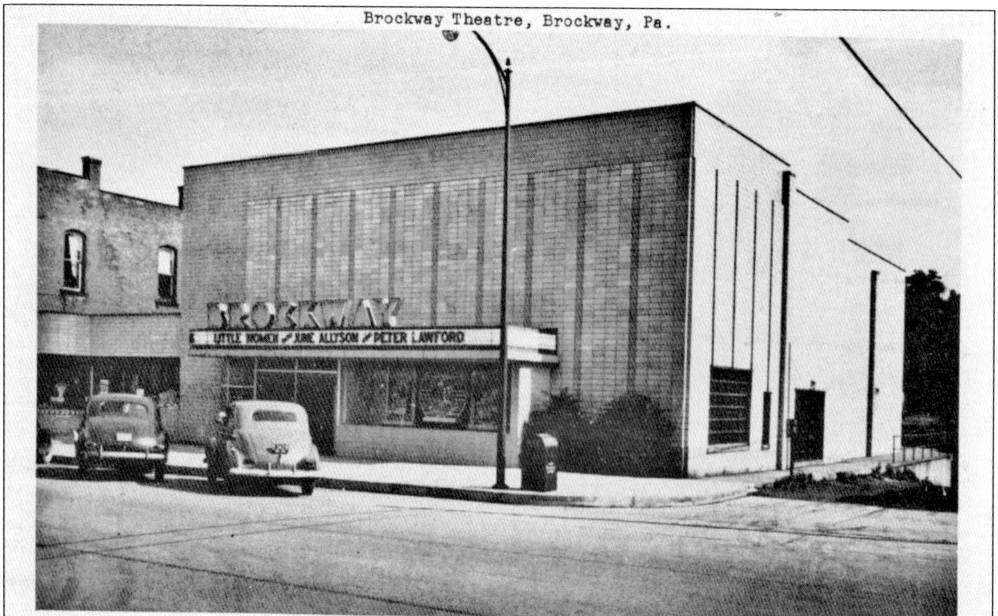

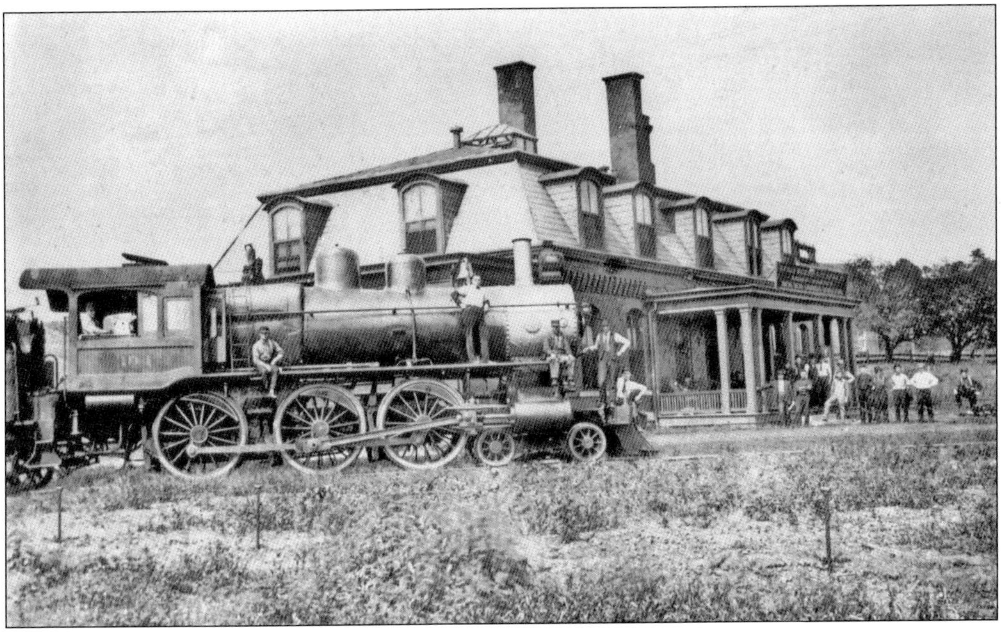

A YMCA organization began in Punxsutawney in the late 1880s. When the Buffalo, Rochester & Pittsburgh Coal Company constructed a new building in Punxsutawney in 1906, it converted its first building, located in Elk Run, for use as a railroad YMCA. The facility provided railroaders with sleeping, dining, study, and recreational facilities. When Mother's Day was first nationally celebrated in 1908, Punxsutawney celebrated it in this building. The Central YMCA opened in 1908. Brookville's Y had roots in the mid-19th century, shortly after the Civil War, but this building (below) was not completed until 1917, after a whirlwind campaign raised $40,000 in 1915. Considered to be the smallest full-service YMCA east of the Mississippi River, the building has undergone several renovations. (Above, PAHGS; below JCHC.)

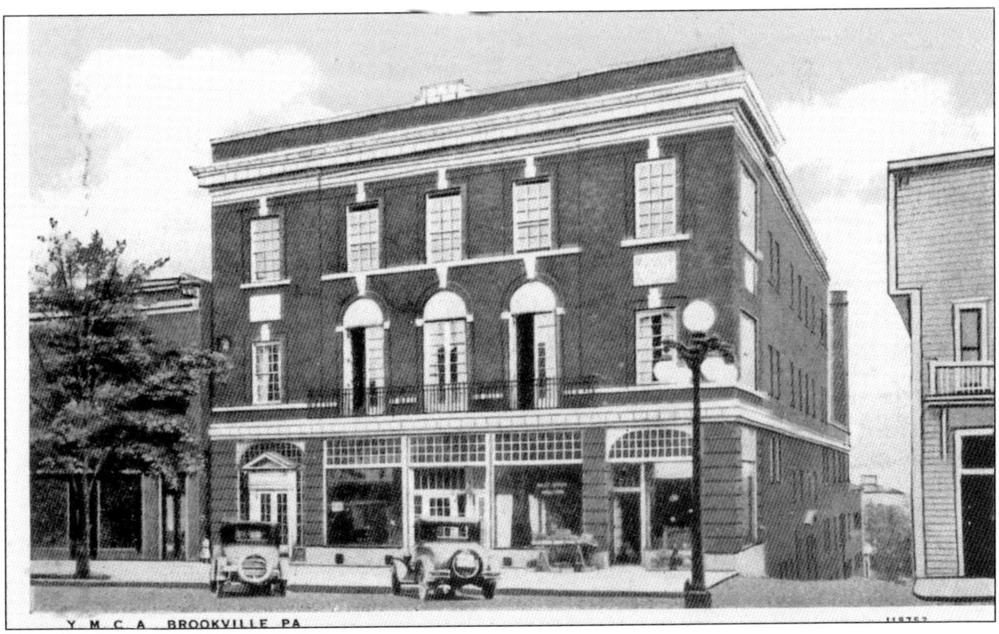

Bibliography

Briggs, Carole, Thomas Curry, Eugene Deible III, and James Sterrett. *Jefferson County, Pennsylvania: An Illustrated History.* Norfolk: Donning Company, 2004.

Caldwell, J.A. *Caldwell's Illustrated Historical Combination Atlas of Jefferson County, Pennsylvania.* Condi, OH: J.A. Caldwell, 1878.

Casler, Walter, Benjamin F.G. Kline, and Thomas T. Taber III. *A History of the Lumbering, Chemical, Wood, and Tanning Companies Which Used Railroads in Pennsylvania.* Williamsport, PA: Lycoming Printing Company, Inc., 1970–1978.

Cooper, Eileen Mountjoy. *Rochester & Pittsburg Coal Company: The First One Hundred Years.* Indiana, PA: Shick Printing Co., 1982.

Cory, Lee. *Pittsburgh, Shawmut & Northern R.R.* Canaseraga, NY: Pittsburg, Shawmut & Northern R.R. Company Historical Society, 1993.

Imhof, John D. *Elk County: A Journey through Time.* St. Marys, PA: Clarion River Publishing, 2003.

Keith, John. *Brockway and Little Toby Valley.* Charleston, SC: Arcadia Publishing, 2010.

Kilmer, Lawrence W. *Erie Railroad 1863–1976: Bradford Branch.* New Port Richey, FL: William J. Fries, 1990.

McKnight, William J. *The Pioneers and People of Jefferson County, Pennsylvania.* Chicago: J.H. Beers & Company, 1917.

Pietrak, Paul. *Buffalo, Rochester and Pittsburg Railway.* North Boston, NY: Paul Pietrak, 1979.

———. *Pittsburg, Shawmut & Northern.* North Boston, NY: Paul Pietrak, 1969.

Punxsutawney Centennial, 1849–1949: One Hundred Years of Progress. Punxsutawney, PA: Centennial Committee, 1949.

Reddinger, Lewis D. *The Brockway Story, 1822–1986.* Brockway, PA: Brockway Historical Society, 1986.

Scott, Kate M. *The History of Jefferson County, Pennsylvania.* Syracuse: N.& D. Mason & Co., Publishers, 1888.

Sterrett, James H. *A History of Beechwoods, a Farming and Mining Community in Western Pennsylvania.* Kent, OH: Kent State University, 1970.

About the Jefferson County Historical Society

In 1927, George Washington Heber, a Brookville resident and history-minded man, incorporated a historical society for Jefferson County in time for the 1930 centennial of the county seat. During the county fair that year, the county's history was celebrated with special editions of local papers, exhibits in shop windows, and a special exhibit at the fairgrounds created by noted miniaturist Charles Albert Bowdish called Brookville as It Was in 1830. Unfortunately, after Heber's death in 1936, the organization faded and the objects he had collected disappeared.

In 1967, with a push from the local tourist promotion agency, community leaders came together and once again formed a countywide historical society. Members of the Jefferson County Historical & Genealogical Society (JCHGS) met in various locations around the county, attended lectures, and took trips to historic locations. In 1971, the JCHGS purchased Brady Craig House in Brookville and began to hold meetings there, to provide research materials, and to produce small exhibits. The sale of reprinted histories underwrote operating expenses. In 2000, the society purchased the Nathan Greene Edelblute building and preserved and adapted it as the Jefferson County History Center. The new facility opened on historic Brookville's Main Street on the 200th anniversary of the establishment of the county.

Renamed the Jefferson County Historical Society, Inc., the society cooperates with other 501(c)(3) history organizations in Jefferson County: the Brockway Area Historical Society, the Coolspring Power Museum, the Punxsutawney Area Historical & Genealogical Society, the Punxsutawney Weather Discovery Center, and the Reynoldsville Historical Society. Collections, smaller exhibits, and speakers are shared. In 2004, historians from Brockway, Brookville, Punxsutawney, and Reynoldsville wrote and published *Jefferson County, Pennsylvania: An Illustrated History*. Once again, in 2017, these organizations have come together to write and publish this book.